SHARING HER WORD

SHARING

Feminist Biblical Interpretation in Context

HER

Elisabeth Schüssler Fiorenza

WORD

Beacon Press / Boston

Beacon Press
25 Beacon Street
Boston, Massachusetts 02108-2892
www.beacon.org

Beacon Press books are published under the auspices of
the Unitarian Universalist Association of Congregations

02   01   00   99   8   7   6   5   4   3   2

Text design by Christopher Kuntze

Composition by David G. Budmen, Willow Graphics, Woodstown, NJ

Library of Congress Cataloging-in-Publication Data

Schüssler Fiorenza, Elisabeth, 1938–
    Sharing her word : feminist biblical interpretation in context / Elisabeth Schüssler Fiorenza.
        p.   cm.
    Includes bibliographical references and index.
    ISBN 0-8070-1230-0
    ISBN 0-8070-1233-5 (pbk)
    1. Bible—Feminist criticism.   I. Title.
    BS521.4.S38   1998
    220.6'082—DC21   97-33570

In kinship with Wisdom[-Sophia]
there is immortality,
and in friendship with Her,
pure delight,
and in the labors of Her hands,
unfailing wealth,
and in the experience of Her company,
understanding,
and renown in sharing Her words.

WISDOM 8:17–18 (NRSV)

In Celebration

of the

Twenty-Fifth Anniversary

of the

Women Doing Theology Conference

at Grailville, Summer 1972

and the

AAR Women in Religion Section

Los Angeles, September 1972

inaugurating events

of

Feminist Studies in Religion

CONTENTS

PREFACE

The conceptualization and chapters of this book seek to root feminist biblical interpretation in a feminist history of emancipatory struggles. These chapters do not owe their existence to postmodern academic debates, although they can be read as an intervention in these debates. Rather they examine the relationships between feminist biblical interpretation and the feminist study of religion, between feminist studies and the women's movement, between contemporary biblical interpreters and our foremothers, between biblical interpretation and the religious goals of justice, community, and peace. In structuring the book in this way, they attempt to instantiate the *ekklēsia* of wo/men as a hermeneutical space for debate and deliberation. By seeking to create such an alternative intellectual space, they intend to create an opportunity for feminist biblical students to free themselves from malestream theoretical frameworks and disciplinary measures.

The title of this book is derived from Wisdom literature, and I have placed the book under the patronage of Divine Wisdom-Sophia; therefore I have introduced the chapters accordingly, using Wisdom sayings as epigrams to provide a hermeneutical key to each chapter's theoretical explorations. These epigrams invite us to the table of Wisdom, which provides a rich array of knowledge, insight, and vision as *Lebensmittel*,[1] the "daily bread" that nourishes not only liberating biblical interpretations but also a new understanding of our wo/men selves. "No one, after lighting a lamp, puts it under the bushel basket, but on the lampstand, and it gives light to all in the house" (Mt 5:15).

The chapters of this book were first conceptualized and presented as lectures to very different popular and academic audiences not only in the United States and Europe, but also in South

Africa, New Zealand, Australia, India, the Philippines, Argentina, Brazil, Chile, and Korea. I want to thank all of the wo/men who have fashioned such a global *ekklēsia*, engaged in critical feminist theology and the biblical hermeneutics of liberation. I have learned much from all of those who came to my lectures, who carefully listened, debated, questioned, disagreed, or made suggestions to improve my argument; and I am grateful to all of them. All over the world I had the same experience. Everywhere I was surprised and deeply moved by the great number of people who came (and sometimes paid) to hear an academic lecture pronounced in German-accented English. Yet even though (or because?) we spoke in a differently accented English, we all could hear and understand each other.

My grateful appreciation for making these conversations possible goes especially to Rev. Dr. Susan Adams, Dr. Patricia Brennan, Dr. Musimbi Kanyoro, Professors Wanda Deifelt, Elaine Wainwright, Johannes Vorster, Renate Rose, Chung Hyun Kyung, Hyun Sook Lee, Gabriele Dietrich, and to Judy Ress and all those whose gracious hospitality I enjoyed. I am grateful to have had the opportunity to present and discuss feminist biblical hermeneutics at various lectures and workshops. My thanks go to the institutions and organizations for inviting me to the following distinguished lectureships: the Kresge Lectures, Waterloo Lutheran Seminary, Waterloo, Ontario, Canada, 1991; Morgan Lectures, Lutheran Theological Southern Seminary, Columbia, South Carolina, 1993; Hanley Lectures, St. Paul's College, University of Manitoba, Canada, 1994; Mullen Lectures, St. Mary Seminary, Wickliffe, Ohio, 1995; Selwyn Lectures, the College of the Southern Cross, Aukland, Aotearoa/New Zealand, 1995; the Carnahan Lectures, Instituto Superior Evangelico de Estudios Teologicos (ISEDET), Buenos Aires, Argentina, 1996; Pinecrest Lecture, South Florida Center for Theological Studies, Miami, Florida, 1997, as well as to lecture at the universities of Pretoria, Stellenbosch, Natal, Zululand, and Johannesburg, South Africa, 1994; Tamilnadu Theological Seminary, Madurai, India, 1995; Trivandrum, Ecumenical Women's Association, Kerala, India, 1995; Villanova University, Spring Lecture Series, 1995; Österreichisches Frauenforum, 100 Jahre Frauenbibel, Wien, 1995; lectures at

Pharmacy College, Melbourne, Sophia Center, Adelaide, Santa Sabina College, Sydney, and Griuffith University, Brisbane, all of which were sponsored by the Autralian Feminist Theological Foundation, 1995; Women's Center, Aukland, University of Otago, and Christchurch, Aotearoa/New Zealand, 1995; Lutheran World Federation's International Consultation on the Status of Women, Geneva, Switzerland, 1995; the Colorado College, Colorado Springs, 1995; Union Theological Seminary, Dasmarinias, Cavite, and the Center for Women's Studies, St. Scholastica, Manila, Phillipines, 1996; Women's Ministry Lecture, Princeton Theological Seminary, 1996; Instituto Ecumenico de Post-Graduacao, Sao Leopoldo, Brazil, 1996; Conspirando Collective, Santiago, Chile, 1996; EWHA Women's Institute and Yonsei University, Seoul, Korea, 1996; Twenty-fifth Annual Meeting of the Korean Association of Christian Studies, Yunsug, Korea, 1996; Mile High Conversations Conference, Denver, Colorado, 1997; Stetson University, Winter Pastor's School, DeLand, Florida, 1997, and Humboldt Universität, Berlin, 1997.

Every book depends on the work of many people. My former faculty assistant, Deborah Hecht, deserves special thanks for her tireless work during the last year and her cheerful support in many ways and on numerous projects. Her successor, Paula Shreve, has also provided much organizational assistance and expert support. I also want to thank Anne Custer, who has compiled the index and proofread the manuscript. I am again grateful to my research assistant, Julie Miller, for polishing my text, as well as for proofreading and library assistance. For her expert feedback and prudent advice I owe special thanks to my editor at Beacon Press, Susan Worst, whose critical work saw this book from manuscript to the first editing stages, to Chris Kochansky for her expert copyediting, and to Margaret Park Bridges, managing editor at Beacon Press, who cared for the book after Susan's departure.

As always, I am deeply in debt to Francis for his everyday support and critical solidarity. Last but not least, I want to thank Chris for sharing with me a wonderful time in Philadelphia and numerous rich conversations.

[Sophia-]Wisdom has built Her house,
She has set up Her seven pillars.
She has slaughtered Her beasts,
She has mixed Her wine,
She has also set Her table.
She has sent out Her women servants
to call from the highest places in the town, . . .
"Come eat of my bread
and drink of the wine I have mixed.
Leave immaturity, and live,
and walk in the way of Wisdom-Sophia."

PROVERBS 9:1–3, 5–6

The Invitation of Wisdom-Sophia: Introduction

CHAPTER I

TWENTY-FIVE YEARS ago, in the summer of 1972, a historic meeting took place in Grailville, Ohio.[1] Approximately seventy-five women—Jews and Christians, Protestants and Catholics, ordained ministers and academic theologians—were brought together by the National Council of Churches, under the leadership of Clare Randall and Janet Kalven of the Grail,[2] for a workshop called "Women Doing Theology." This workshop proved to be one of the birthplaces of feminist theology—a movement that has since profoundly changed both theology and church.

I was privileged to be invited to this gathering. In the previous year, at the annual meeting of the American Academy of Religion and the Society of Biblical Literature in Atlanta, the Women's Caucus in Religious Studies was called together by Carol Christ.[3] Since I was the only SBL member willing to serve, I was elected as first co-chair of the caucus, although I had just immigrated to the United States, in 1971.

These two events turned out to be decisive, not only for me personally but most importantly for the development of the fields of feminist studies in religion[4] and feminist theology, which provided the twin roots of feminist theological and cultural-religious studies during the second wave of the wo/men's[5] movement. Both of these approaches to feminist religious studies are important, and they are distinct but not exclusive of each other; in fact, many of us were involved in both the theological and the cultural study of religion.

After lectures, I am often asked by students, "With whom did you study feminist theology?" My general response is that feminist studies in religion was not yet born when I was a student—that is why we had to invent the field! However, this question does not just bespeak historical innocence and forgetfulness, it also reveals how far we have come in the past twenty-five years. The paradigm shift that has taken place in theology and religious studies has been so successful that students today no longer remember a time when feminist studies in religion and theology did not exist. At the same time, it must be pointed out that neither the workshop at Grailville nor the AAR/SBL Women's Caucus chose to call their theoretical and practical work feminist. We do not know when or by whom the expression "feminist theology" was introduced; whereas Gustavo Guitierrez is rightly being credited for being the "father" of liberation theology, research needs to be done as to who coined the expressions "feminist theology" and "feminist studies in religion."[6]

Feminism has found diverse theoretical articulations, and both "feminism" and "feminist theology" still (or again) are considered by many to be "dirty words," associated with ideological bias and heresy. Hence it is necessary to explain how I use and understand the f-word, "feminism". Since Rush Limbaugh and

others have made "femi-nazi" a popular label, one needs to explicate the notion of feminism in order to address the emotional
constraints which this term imposes on the intellectual understanding of academic and popular audiences. Polls have shown
that in this country the vast majority of wo/men refuse to identify
as feminists because in their minds this label characterizes a person as a fanatic—biased, man-hating, and crazy. No wonder
wo/men do not want to be tarred with this brush! Yet studies
have also shown that the majority of wo/men subscribe to feminist
political goals such as the following: efforts to change discrimination against wo/men; equal pay for equal work; that married part-
ners should share both homemaking and child-rearing; that ter-
mination of pregnancy should not be criminalized; that violence
against wo/men and sexual harassment are wrong; and that wo/men
should be ordained.[7]

In a time when affirmative action is maligned, mothers and
children on welfare are scapegoated, and backlash feminism rules
in the media and the academy, the struggle over the meaning of
feminist discourse intensifies.[8] It has again become a liability for
scholars and theologians to be called feminists or to identify
themselves as advocating feminism, because the term continues to
be both contested and shunned as either too political or too ideological by those scholars who profess value neutrality and a positivist ethos of inquiry.[9]

Although there are so many divergent forms and even contradictory articulations of feminism today that it is appropriate to
speak of "feminisms," in the plural, most agree that contemporary feminism is not only a political movement akin to other
emancipatory movements but also an intellectual methodology
for investigating and theorizing the experience and structures of
wo/men's oppression. The diverse theoretical articulations of feminism, I suggest, come together in their critique of elite male supremacy and hold that gender is socially constructed rather than
innate or ordained by G*d.[10]

My preferred definition of feminism is expressed by a well-
known bumper sticker from the wo/men's movement: "Feminism
is the radical notion that women are people." This popular
tongue-in-cheek definition accentuates the irony that feminism in

the twentieth century is both a radical concept and at the same time a "commonsense" notion. Wo/men are not ladies, wives, handmaids, seductresses, or beasts of burden but people, full citizens. This definition also alludes to the democratic assertion "We, the people" and positions feminism within radical democratic discourses that argue for the rights and well-being of all the people without exception, evoking memories of struggles for equal citizenship and decision-making powers in society and religion.

Theologically, feminism understands wo/men as people of G*d and indicts the death-dealing powers of oppression as structural sin and life-destroying evil. Hence feminist theologies and studies in religion have the dual goal of not only fundamentally altering the nature of malestream[11] knowledge about the Divine and the world but also of changing institutional religions, which have tended to exclude wo/men from religious authority and leadership positions. Feminism is thus best understood as a theoretical perspective and a historical movement for changing sociocultural and religious institutions and structures of domination and exploitation. Christian feminism attempts to do so both by seeking full citizenship for wo/men in church and society, and by reformulating the study of scripture, tradition, theology, and community in feminist terms.

In discussing the critical social theory of Jürgen Habermas, Jean L. Cohen has argued that because of the dualistic character of the public and private spheres of modern capitalist-democratic societies, emancipatory social movements have to engage in a two-pronged strategy if they are to bring about change. She also points out that almost all studies of the feminist movement in the United States have documented that the movement has indeed adopted such a dual politics, one which targets not only the state, the law, and the economy but also the institutions and normative presuppositions of civil society. Such a two-pronged strategy can be shown to have engendered the second wave of the wo/men's movement, in Cohen's view, because preconditions for any emancipatory collective action are the presence of critical group consciousness, solidarity, and a sense of injustice and of discrimination: "In the case of women, attaining group consciousness involved an explicit challenge to traditional norms that identified women primarily in terms of the roles of mother and wife and justified inequality, exclusion, and discrimination."[12]

In other words, it was in the context of the free speech, civil rights, Third World liberation, and antiwar movements that the feminist movement could be articulated because of the emerging consciousness that wo/men as a group were discriminated against and oppressed.

> Indeed it quickly became evident to key sectors of the women's movement that there was a deeper problem underlying the otherwise inexplicable resistance to equal rights. . . . Thus, before any standard offensive politics of reform and inclusion could be fruitful, a feminist consciousness and ideology had to be developed on the part of movement women and then communicated to others through a different politics of identity, one aimed at the public and private spheres of civil society. Hence the focus on precisely those institutional arrangements and processes involved in the construction of gender identity and the slogan that "the personal is political."[13]

In short, a change in consciousness must occur. At the same time, the strategy of the wo/men's movement must always remain two-pronged.

In my own experience, the existence of a movement was as important as—if not more important than—the change of consciousness. I had come to the Women's Caucus meeting in 1971 and to the Grailville conference in 1972 with a "raised consciousness" and a critical understanding of wo/men's role and identity. For my first dissertation, published in 1964,[14] I had investigated the theological essentialism and practical issues that stood in the way of wo/men's leadership and ministry in the church. When writing this thesis, I had desperately searched for scholarly "authorities" who would validate my critical rejection of the liberal-romantic "theology of womanhood" and constructions of "the eternal feminine."[15]

As far as I can remember, I have always questioned the Catholic definition of women as mothers or virgins and resisted all anti-intellectual "feminine socialization" attempts. Hence, in my research I looked for a theoretical articulation that would validate my own experience and anti-essentialist perspective. Yet such a theory was not forthcoming in the early 1960s because academic discourse in political science, sociology, psychology, history, and literature worked with the same theoretical essentialized understanding of "woman" that determined theological thinking.

Because I had done work on "wo/men in the church," the Grailville discussions proved to be sometimes difficult for me since they seemed to presuppose an essentialist understanding of "woman." Hence I did not quite share the experience of most of the wo/men there, who were discovering a new and different consciousness as wo/men. Some of the new insights presupposed an essentialist-romantic understanding of "woman," which was often combined with an anti-intellectual stance: scholarship and footnotes were considered to be male, whereas relationality and emotion were thought to be female qualities. Men supposedly lived in their heads, whereas wo/men lived in their bodies; theology was masculine-typed while ministry was considered to be more congenial for wo/men. Whereas I had experienced the study of theology during the Second Vatican Council as liberating and "opening windows and doors" that were previously shut, many of the Grailville participants came from Protestant seminaries where they had experienced theological education as negative and destructive of wo/men's self-confidence.

What was, however, a new and exciting experience for me was encountering for the first time a group of wo/men who claimed "doing theology" as their birthright, reflected on their negative experiences of feminine socialization and role determination, and set out to change the situation. It was the experience of a wo/men's liberation movement that validated my own personal experience and perspective and enabled me to understand myself as an intellectual "doing theology" with a focus on and in the interests of wo/men as my very own people. The criterion for evaluating such a different theology was not whether it was orthodox or doctrinally acceptable, but whether it was able to change religious structures of wo/men's second-class citizenship in the academy and the church as well as transform theological and religious mind-sets of self-alienation and indoctrination. In short, it was the wo/men's movement in society and church that enabled me to define myself as a critical feminist theologian.

Also decisive for my feminist theological work were team-teaching a course on "Images of Women" with Dr. Marilyn Broe, a professor of modern English literature, at the University of Notre Dame in 1973,[16] and my enthusiastic participation in the New York Area Feminist Scholars in Religion group, which was also called into being by Carol Christ, in 1974–75. These endeavors helped me to begin to articulate my own theoretical feminist framework. In the period between 1972 and 1975 I wrote four articles that presaged my future work and which had a significant impact on feminist theology of biblical studies.

The most important of these was "Feminist Theology as a Critical Theology of Liberation,"[17] in which I sought to develop a theoretical understanding of feminist analysis not in terms of gender/femininity but in terms of the oppression of wo/men, and I did so in conversation with the critical theory of J. Habermas and with liberation theology.[18] The second essay, "Women in the Early Christian Movement,"[19] has never been published in English (although it has appeared in the six other languages of *Concilium*). It was the first step toward my later book *In Memory of Her*, because in it I began to reconceptualize the study of wo/men in early Christianity in light of the newly emerging "Social World Studies" section of the Society of Biblical Literature. In the third article,[20] which appeared in *The Liberating Word*, edited by Letty Russell, I argued over and against an apologetic approach—one which focused on "positive" texts about wo/men in the bible—that feminist interpretation must pay attention to the patriarchal texts inscribed in Christian scriptures and not seek to explain them away. Finally, in "Feminist Spirituality, Christian Identity, and the Catholic Vision,"[21] I articulated my religious location and positionality as a Christian Catholic theologian.

Although from the very beginning I was critical of the dominant cultural and theological notions of femininity and conceptualizations of gender, I nevertheless continued to work with the then prevalent dualistic theoretical framework of "sexism" and "patriarchy," which was understood as the domination of all men over all wo/men in the same way. Two challenges that came from the wo/men's movement in the mid-seventies stand out in my memory as having moved my thinking away from such a dualistic conceptualization of gender oppression.

The first confrontation came in the mid-seventies, at a public lecture, when an African-American wo/man in the audience challenged me to develop a notion of patriarchy that would include her experience as a black wo/man. She pointed out that she did not understand herself as oppressed primarily by black men but by the racism of white men and white wo/men. Her challenge made immediate sense to me because I myself had argued with my feminist colleagues for quite some time that my own experience *as a wo/man scholar* was determined not only by my gender but also by the facts that I was a professor, a Catholic, and a "resident alien" immigrant who spoke with a German accent. While immigrant wo/men from Europe do not face the same or even similar oppressions as immigrant wo/men of color do, I argued, we nevertheless experience some discrimination as foreigners. Hence the need for a category of analysis that could conceptualize such complex and shifting experiences of identity.

The second challenge materialized in a telephone call from a feminist journalist asking what feminist scholars had to say about the biblical texts preaching the subordination of wo/men, texts which fueled the rhetoric of the Moral Majority. I remember answering quite smugly that scholarship had long recognized that these so-called household code texts were "time conditioned" and therefore not normative for Christians. Nevertheless, after her phone call I began to work again on these texts, only to discover that scholarship had begun to see them in a new light—as texts espousing neo-Aristotelian, antidemocratic political philosophy[22]—without, however, reflecting on the theological and cultural implications of this shift in interpretation. Again, in my theoretical work I set out to respond to the need of the wo/men's movement for clarification of these texts.

This work led me to recognize the structural and political significance of these texts not only for society and church but also for articulating a theoretical framework that could explore wo/men's oppression in antiquity and today as multiform and interstructured. Susan Moller Okin's book *Women in Western Political Thought*, which appeared in 1979, provided the political-philosophical framework for such a reconceptualization of the notion of patriarchy.[23] This theoretical development brought with it the recognition that androcentric dualism—which at the time was almost universally understood as the root of oppression—was an ideology that was developed in critical opposition to the ideal of democracy.

I have focused here on my own experience and spoken of my early work in such detail because I want to contradict the new vogue of periodizing and conceptualizing feminist history in liberal progressivist terms. In my view, important theoretical and practical issues are at stake in how we write our own history and tell the story of feminist studies in religion and theology. In the following, I single out three such instances for debate because, in my view, their authors seem not to have taken the wo/men's movement sufficiently into account when telling the story of feminist biblical interpretation or classifying its approaches. I do so not in order to silence the debate but in order to focus it.[24]

First: In an article on the interpretation of the Book of Judith, Pamela Milne follows the by now familiar pattern of telling the story of feminist theory by roughly dividing it into three decades.[25] According to Milne, during the 1970s, studies appeared which argued "that, for the most part, the patriarchal or misogynist bias of readers/interpreters had produced anti-woman interpretations not well rooted in the biblical text."[26] As is typical of this approach, she points to the early work of Phyllis Trible.[27] In Milne's view, the approach of the 1980s is represented by Trible's second book, *Texts of Terror*,[28] and especially by the work of the Israeli-American scholar Esther Fuchs.[29] This approach, Milne asserts, "began to explore the subtle literary devices and strategies through which biblical texts gave expression to the patriarchy of Israelite and/or Christian societies."[30]

Finally, in Milne's view, the feminist work of the 1990s, in conjunction with other biblical scholarship, has shifted attention from historical and theological scholarship, which asked questions about authors and their intentions, to more literary questions about readers and texts. Milne cites the work of Mieke Bal, a literary theorist, as paradigmatic for this new, more sophisticated hermeneutical approach.[31] What is important in Bal's work, according to Milne, is "the ethical responsibility for, and the political consequences of, reading. The central issue is one of power."[32]

Although Milne discusses only literary scholarship in all three periods, she nevertheless asserts that the shift to more sophisticated work in the 1990s was a shift away from historical-theological work. Moreover, her discussion of recent feminist interpretation combines this periodization of biblical scholarship with a method pioneered by Leonard Swidler,[33] which has been justly criticized. This method classifies biblical texts into positive, negative, or neutral ones.

According to Milne, of the scholars who wrote in the early and mid-1980s, I and two male scholars, George Nickelsburg and Carey Moore, allegedly understand Judith as a positive heroine in feminist terms; three scholars—Toni Craven, John Craghan, and Amy-Jill Levine (1992!)—do not see Judith as a feminist heroine but argue that certain elements in the story allow her to be understood by feminists in positive terms.[34] Milne herself, however, concurs with the negative judgment and universalizing reading of Betsy Merideth, who maintains that we cannot assume that the story of Judith is positive for wo/men because in "Judith beauty and deceit go together so that, at one level, the story inevitably carries the clear message that a 'woman's beauty and sexuality are dangerous to men because women use their attractiveness to deceive, harm, and kill men.'"[35]

A genre analysis, according to Milne, confirms this interpretation because while Judith has no role in the romantic epic genre, "in the epic-struggle genre her actions" are "related closely to the functions performed by the helper-seducer role."[36] However, such an interpretation ascribes too much of an "objectivist" character to the constraints genre places on readers. As Burke O'Long has pointed out in his response to her article, Milne assumes that genre has a "rather stable constraint on her reading, so stable" that she must conclude that "the text offers no possibility of fostering the kind of social change she seeks. Translating this result in terms of the underlying hermeneutical model it seems that a text, or at least its generic features, imposes itself forcefully, if subtly on a reader."[37]

If, however, genre had the power to place such deterministic constraints on readers, Milne's reading would have been equally constrained in its interpretation, for example, by the historiographical genre in which my book *In Memory of Her* (1983) was written. If genre could exercise such a determining and restraining power, Milne could not have misread my interpretation in the way she does because I did not attempt to evaluate the Book of Judith as to whether it is "feminist," but instead sought to make a literary-historical argument suggesting that Judith, as a strong fictional wo/man character, "must have appealed to the theological imagination of various Jewish groups of the time."[38] My point was not that Judith was a feminist, or that her portrayal was liberating for modern wo/men, or that her story was not androcentric. Rather my point was that contrary to the then widespread negative view of Jewish wo/men in biblical scholarship, such a story about a strong wo/man was told, and therefore must have appealed to the Jewish imagination of the time. Thus my argument was a reconstructive literary-historical one that underscored the liberative elements in the narrative, elements which cannot be appreciated by an approach that utilizes only the lens of genre in a deconstructive mode.

I do not want to argue here for a positive feminist rereading of the story of Judith or that such a reading is possible. Rather I want to point out that there is a tendency in feminist scholarly discourses to reinscribe the antagonism between historical and literary methods, and between "value-neutral" and "theological" approaches, in malestream biblical scholarship. I also want to critique the trend to construe feminist intellectual history in terms of linear progress, as in Milne's case, from an apologetic historical-theological reading to a theoretically sophisticated ideology-critical one. Such a periodization of feminist interpretation can only be sustained if one engages in a blatant misreading of earlier feminist work. I do not want to be misunderstood. I am not arguing that we should not employ methods of periodization and categorization. Rather, I want to argue that these methods import assump-

tions which need to be articulated in feminist terms for critical reflection and discussion.[39]

Second: The hidden interests of such a periodization of feminist
interpretation and scholarship in terms of "progress" comes also to
the fore in a recent article by Sarah Blustain[40] in *Lilith*, a popular
Jewish feminist magazine. However, here it has become an argument *ad hominem*, or, more accurately, *ad feminam*.[41] The article is
entitled "Constructing (Not Deconstructing) the Jewish Feminist
Pantheon: What's Going on Behind the Pillars of Academia?" and
explicitly contrasts "older" scholars with theoretically more sophisticated younger ones.[42] Since the same modernist periodization
in terms of progress could be—and has been—applied to Christian
feminist theology, I feel justified to intervene in this discussion.

The article asserts that in the twenty years "since feminist ac-
tivism inspired women to take a stance in the hallowed halls of
academe, feminist theory has become a reigning discourse."[43] A
"quantum leap" has allegedly taken place as is evidenced by the
number of feminist scholars in the academy, the publication of
numerous articles and books, and the establishment of Jewish
wo/men's studies programs at the masters level. It also is evident
in off-campus wo/men's groups who celebrate their own rituals,
and in the general expansion of wo/men's participation in all
areas of Jewish life.

The article provides contradictory information on the issue of
whether Jewish feminist scholars and their work are still marginalized and in such jeopardy that students are still advised (but
now by leading feminist scholars) to hide their feminist interests
until they get tenure, or whether they have found a respected
place in the academy. The article is, however, clear on one point:
the intellectual work of "first generation" scholars insisted—in
the words of Judith Plaskow—that "the connection between politics and spirituality requires the transformation of Judaism
itself,"[44] whereas a younger generation of Jewish feminist scholars, participating fully in academia, argues for drawing a rigid
boundary line between the community and the academy.[45]

This construal of a conflict between "older" and "younger"
scholars is interpreted as a generational conflict,[46] although not

so much in terms "of a sort of Electra complex," that is, the killing off of the mothers. Instead it is seen as rooted in two "very different eras in which these two generations of scholars developed their work: one, in an era of political struggle and the other in one of 'theoretical sophistication.'"

Whereas Judith Hauptmann, a scholar of the first generation, is said to continue "to give non-academic women the tools they need to create a more participatory Judaism," Laura Levitt, a member of the so-called sophisticated generation is quoted as "hoping to give academics a Jewish tool with which to hone their theory."[47] The following assertion, which drives home the point, is attributed to Naomi Seidman, who is characterized as a recent Ph.D.: "We are standing on their shoulders but—they may hate me for saying this—the scholarship is a lot better. The ignorance that scholars were working on even ten years ago is astonishing. . . . The work that they did is basically obsolete."[48] In this debate among Jewish feminists, the progressive periodization scheme advocated by Milne is translated not only into a generational conflict but also into one of either loyalty to the wo/men's movement or loyalty to academic theory and scholarship.[49]

In my view, this conflict is not so much a symptom of the Electra complex as one of what I have called the Athena complex.[50] This expression must not be understood as diagnosing individual psychological or "pathological" problems. Rather I understand this expression in terms of a systemic analysis of domination. This calls for a type of "symptomatic reading" which Rosemary Henessy defines as follows:

> To read a text [or situation] symptomatically is to make visible that which hegemonic ideology does not mention, those things which must not be spoken, discursive contestations which are naturalized in the intercourse but which still shape the text's diseased relation to itself. To read symptomatically is to reveal the historicity in the texts of culture and in so doing put on display the exploitative social arrangements that they so often manage.[51]

The notion of an Athena complex introduces a heuristic-feminist concept that not only refers to the myth of the Goddess

Athena but also seeks to read it in such a way that "what is not spoken of" in feminist discourse comes to the fore. Athena, the patron Goddess of the Athenian city-state in antiquity, was not only the patron of art and technological and scientific knowledge but also a war Goddess. According to Hesiod, she came fully grown and armored from the head of her father, Zeus. However, she only appears to be motherless. Her real mother is the Goddess Metis, the "most wise woman among Gods and humans." According to the myth, Metis was duped when she was pregnant with Athena. Since Zeus, the father of all Gods and peoples, feared that Metis would bear a child who would surpass him in wisdom and power, he changed her into a fly. But this was not enough! In addition, Zeus swallowed Metis whole in order to have her always with him and to benefit from her wise counsel.

When the time of Athena's birth came, Hephaestos (or another of the Gods) split the head of Zeus with an ax and Athena emerged from the patriarchal godhead in full warrior gear and with a battle cry on her lips. The mythological story of Athena's birth not only reveals the Father of the Gods' fear that the child of Wisdom (Metis) could surpass him in knowledge, it also lays open the conditions under which wo/men in *kyriarchal* cultures[52] are able to claim knowledge and wisdom. Feminist scholars do not have the same power and standing in the academy as "doctor-fathers" do. Hence young wo/men scholars must prove themselves to be the "daughters" of their intellectual academic father-mentors and must learn to understand themselves as the "motherless" offspring engendered from the brains of powerful "fathers."[53] They have to prove their loyalty by denying or belittling their intellectual "mothers" in order to compete with them for the respect and confirmation of their intellectual "fathers."

However, read with a hermeneutics of suspicion, the myth of Athena also documents that kyriarchal power and knowledge systems can bring forth warring father-daughters and mediating father-mothers *only* if they manage to commit the "wise wo/men" to historical oblivion and forgetfulness.[54] Such forgetfulness is the enabling ground on which science turns wo/men—like insects—into "objects" for dissection. Since they continue to incorporate and to co-opt wo/men's wisdom and knowledge in the interest of societal-religious domination, hegemonic science and theology cannot recognize wo/men as either intellectual, scholarly, and theological subjects or figures of authority and legitimization.

Third: A rhetoric similar to that of Blustain's article in *Lilith* can be found in a more sophisticated form in *The Postmodern Bible*,[55] authored by a collective of ten male and female, young and established, feminist and not-so-feminist scholars.[56] Just as the discussion in *Lilith* does with respect to Jewish feminist theology, so too *The Postmodern Bible* tells the story of feminist biblical interpretation in rather modern terms as a story of steady progress from naive intellectual beginnings to the sophisticated heights of postmodernism.

Lest I be accused of "projecting" onto the text my alleged bias against postmodernism, I will quote this argument extensively: "The first attempts to understand women in the Bible were *naively* [emphasis added] focused on the image, perceived to be in some measure a distortion of reality, and one obvious corrective lay in the attempt to reconstruct that reality historically."[57]

A similar condescending tone, here coupled with a strangely apolitical definition of the political roots of feminism, is found in the following statement:

> The political impulse of feminist critique grows out of some women's encounters [*sic*] with institutions (be they religious, social or academic) and their interpretations of those encounters [*sic*]. When the intellectual categories of received traditions were found to be inadequate for thinking about the meanings of such encounters [*sic*], feminism provided some new conceptual vocabulary organized around such notions as "women's experience," "androcentrism," "patriarchy," and so on. Many of these notions now seem *naïve, quaint, or imprecise* [emphasis added] and are used now only hesitantly, framed by quotation marks to signal the difficulty; still they functioned (for a time and for some) as helpful ideas [*sic*] for refocusing some aspects of discussion of culture.[58]

Here experiences of oppression and marginalization become "encounters" and key feminist categories of analysis are seen as "helpful ideas" presumably now replaced by postmodern categories of analysis. Yet nowhere does the Collective provide an extended argument as to why the functionalist category of gender, which does not articulate power imbalances in gender relations, is preferable to the feminist analytic category of "androcentrism," which conceptualizes gender dualism as asymmetric power relation.[59] My point here is not to defend the analytic categories of "woman's experience," "patriarchy," and "androcentrism," which I myself have criticized; rather, I want to point out the dismissive and condescending attitude of *The Postmodern Bible* toward previous feminist work.

Since my critical intervention in *But She Said* and in *Jesus: Miriam's Child, Sophia's Prophet* interrupts this modernist tale of feminist progress from an engaged naiveté to a theoretically sophisticated state, the Collective singles my work out for criticism. Yet such a disciplining criticism can only be justified if one severely misreads my work. Since in the time of "the death of the author" it is impossible to correct such (willful?) misrepresentation, I will focus here on two points of the argument which in my view display the symptoms of the Athena complex.

The Collective claims not only that I construct an opposition between feminist practices grounded in the academy and those grounded in the women's movement, but also that I so construe this opposition in order to claim that theological interpretation is a sign of "good feminism" whereas cultural academic gender studies are "bad feminism."[60] Hence they allege that I judge the excellent collection *Gender and Difference*, edited by Peggy Day, "as an example of feminist work that embodies 'objectivist and depoliticized academic practices of biblical interpretation.'(40)"[61] Yet, as any close rereading of my text could show, I did not refer to the whole work of Peggy Day but only to a statement in her introduction in which she seems to introduce a dualistic opposition between theological (biased) biblical studies dependent on the dogmatism of religious institutions, and scientific (theoretical) studies located in the academy—a prejudice which is widespread in university circles.[62]

Over and against this malestream construction of a dualistic opposition between religious and academic institutions, I have argued that *both* kinds of institutions are kyriarchal. Far from seeking to drive a wedge between activist and academic feminisms, I have consistently maintained that feminist academic studies must derive their research questions from and must remain accountable to wo/men's movements in society and religion. When formulating this argument in *But She Said*, I pointed to the distinction between *feminist* and *gender* studies in both academic and religious institutions:

> Since feminist studies, in distinction to gender studies, are explicitly committed to the struggle to change patriarchal structures of oppression *in religious and cultural institutions* [emphasis added], they must disentangle the religious-theological ["cultural" in the discourse of *The Postmodern Bible*] functions of biblical texts for inculcating and legitimating the patriarchal order.[63]

If one agrees with this articulation of the goal and task of feminist biblical studies, then one cannot escape the conclusion that in formulating their theoretical analytic methodologies feminists must remain rooted in a wo/men's movement for change. This argument has been made by Evelyn Fox-Keller, Helen Longino, and many other feminist theorists, who have pointed out that experiences, visions, and social locations are fundamental to one's practices of inquiry and knowledge. To quote the feminist political philosopher Jane Braaten, "Visions of community and solidarity, of friendship, of self located by solidarity, serve to affirm and cultivate the ways in which we are learning how to communicate, to analyze, to self-critically reflect; in other words to reason or know."[64]

My insistence that feminist scholarship must remain rooted in and accountable to feminist movements for change is reduced by the Collective to a position that stresses politics versus theory. I allegedly embrace "the opposition between theory and politics" as a part of my anti-postmodern rhetoric, an "opposition constructed by opponents of postmodernism in feminist studies and frequently quoted by them."[65] Worse yet, the Collective reads my understanding of academic biblical scholarship and theological education "as a site of ongoing feminist struggle" as arguing "that the institution of the academy with its processes of socialization, professionalization, and dedication to scientific description is inimical" to the feminist project.[66] Being politically sophisticated, the Collective must have realized that at least in the eyes of a malestream academic audience their rhetorical apology for the academy and wholesale accusation of antiprofessionalism on my part would be a welcome means for undermining my feminist work—work which has been and still is widely used because of its responsible scholarship, not only in theological schools and religious education but also by wo/men around the world.

This totalizing indictment of my work as being against theory seems to be triggered by the fact that I critically reject certain forms of postmodernism which Teresa Ebert—whom the Collective quotes approvingly—has called "ludic" (playful) feminism.[67] However, as evidence for my alleged wholesale rejection of theory, the Collective does not refer to this substantive critique but rather to my use of the expression "malestream" and to my frequent argument that feminist theology and biblical studies should not claim male intellectual figures as their "Godfathers": "Neither Jerome nor Thomas, Bultmann nor Albright, Troeltsch nor Geertz, Derrida nor Foucault are their [liberationist scholars of all colors] exegetical or theoretical 'Godfathers' (38; the capitalization of the term here suggests the criminal rather than the spiritual kind)."[68]

My statement, which is clearly suspicious of the *paternity claims* of established malestream theories and theologies, and rejects their wholesale adoption, is misread as being "suspicious of some feminist critics who make use of male theorists' work and insight" and as alleging that the "goddaughters of such godfathers possess no autonomy." Yet anyone familiar with my own work can easily see that it is full of references to both feminist and male theologians and theorists. Why would I then indict others for doing the same? The Collective recognizes that *But She Said* utilizes postmodern theories and finds many resonances with postmodernism, but they choose to interpret this as inconsistency on my part. They do not or will not recognize that what I advocate is that feminists must filter all formulations through a feminist critical lens before using them—including postmodernism and other malestream theories—as frameworks for their own work. Why then is this insistence read as rejection of theory altogether?

Such a tendency to misread my work, I suggest, is engendered by the fact that the Collective seems to have a quite modern stake in telling the story of feminist biblical interpretation as one of progress from naive beginnings to the theoretical heights of postmodern feminism. To that end, the Collective establishes, under the heading "History and Practice of Feminist and Womanist Reading," a new classification scheme which, by their own account, does not quite work. Without discussing other such attempts,[69] they divide feminist biblical interpretation into four approaches and classify them as "hermeneutics of recuperation," "hermeneutics of suspicion," "hermeneutics of survival," and "postmodern feminist critique." Whereas the first three are categories of interpretation that "share, to a degree at least, a location within religious traditions," the last one, "the work of postmodern feminist critique has, by contrast, been shaped less by theological constraint than by legitimizations imposed from within academic and intellectual disciplines. Postmodern critique focuses its resistance, then, on disciplinary constraints and the theoretical foundations of those disciplines."[70]

The Collective seems to have come full circle. They appear to agree with me that one must critically interrogate and interrupt the intellectual frameworks of "the Fathers." Yet they cannot acknowledge this because such a concession would throw into question their modernist typology of feminist biblical studies as a progress from recuperation to postmodern critique. In order to establish this conceptualization of the development of the discipline that climaxes in postmodern critical theory, they not only have to misconstrue my own work (which for quite some time has claimed critical theory and liberation theology as its lineage), they must also erase the direction in feminist biblical studies that has named itself as "systemic-analytic feminism" and has as its object liberation and emancipation.

What is at stake in such a developmental typology of feminist biblical studies is the theoretical status of such studies. Whereas I utilize feminist critical theory as the matrix and methodological frame that can employ various modes of analysis and interpretation—including postmodern critical theory—*The Postmodern Bible* advocates the postmodern as such a matrix, although by their own account "postmodern" is a "fashionably ambiguous term," "unruly, nebulous, elusive, decentered and decentering."[71] True, the Collective claims that "what has come to be called 'feminist biblical interpretation of the Bible' is not parallel to the other interpretive strategies explored in this volume insofar as feminism is in itself not a method of reading, but rather both a set of political positions and strategies and a contested intellectual terrain."[72] But the structure of their book nevertheless positions feminism as one among the seven approaches—reader response criticism, structural and narratological criticism, poststructuralist criticism, rhetorical criticism, psychological criticism, feminist and womanist criticism, and ideological criticism—that they discuss under the umbrella of postmodernism. Thus, de facto, the Collective deploys the "add and stir" approach despite its explicit claim not to do so. Feminist biblical interpretation becomes one more player in the pluralism of methods that reigns in the postmodern academy.

Although for some readers this feminist debate about how to write the history of feminist biblical interpretation may look like a tempest in a teapot, I have elaborated upon it in and through a symptomatic reading because in my view a very real danger exists today that feminist critical work may again be swallowed up by forgetfulness, just as the pregnant Metis was incorporated by Zeus, the almighty Father of the Gods.

In this fear I am not alone. Referring to the work of Carroll Smith-Rosenberg, the historian Joan Hoff has pointed to a similar crisis which occurred at the beginning of this century.[73] During the 1920s and 1930s, a younger generation of wo/men began to adopt male scientific and literary language, especially medical terminology, and to turn to Marx and Freud as wo/men-friendly theorists. However, in their attempt to give a feminist or female interpretation to male theories, these elite, well-educated women were coopted (in Hoff's view) and silenced by these malestream theories in the long run. This resulted in a communication gap between academic wo/men and other wo/men, especially those with less education. It was this communication gap that the wo/men's movement was beginning to bridge by the late 1970s and early 1980s, by fashioning a shared language of analysis and interpretation.

In discussing the task of feminist theory, Laura Donaldson argues that it must "discern the experiential connections that surely exist among women and simultaneously refuse to privilege any particular connection which subsumes the rest." She exemplifies this task by citing and quoting a story by Olive Schreiner:

> Surrounded by her racially mixed children in the country of apartheid, Rebekah dreams of a new material space of women: "Out there in the garden," she said softly, "there are flowers of all kinds growing—tall queen-lilies, and roses and pinks and violets and little brown ranunculuses—and I love them all. But if the tall queen-lilies were to say, 'We must reign here alone, all the others must die to give place to us,' I do not know, but I think I may say, 'Is it not perhaps then best you should go?'"[74]

When I wrote *But She Said* I was concerned that the debilitating theoretical moves which give all power to the androcentric script and reduce historical wo/men to textuality or use "woman" just as a figure of speech may also gain ground in feminist biblical studies. In order to forestall such a development, I polemically addressed certain forms of "ludic postmodernism." As the preceding discussion indicates, my apprehension was justified. Hence in the remaining chapters of this book I seek to place at the center of attention the interpretations and interactions between wo/men of all walks of life as the specific audience and focus of feminist scholarship. And I argue, with Laura Donaldson, that feminist studies in religion must "construct an elsewhere of vision that will lead us into a truly liberating future."[75] By focusing on the image of the rich table prepared by Divine Wisdom, the biblical name for Metis and Athena, I invite feminist biblical scholars to understand themselves as the "wo/men workers" of Divine Wisdom who fashion biblical studies as public-political interpretation.

The Call of Wisdom-Sophia:
Feminist Biblical Studies

CHAPTER 2

IN THE PREVIOUS CHAPTER I argued that we should not construe the history of feminist theories and approaches in terms
of generational conflicts or by utilizing a typology of progressive development. Instead, we must develop an interpretive lens
and methodological[1] approach that does not pour the "new
wine" of feminist thought into the "old wineskins" of malestream
theories and disciplines. In this chapter I want to continue this
discussion by contextualizing feminist biblical studies within the
field of feminist studies in religion and theology.

Introducing the Problem

I have chosen to approach this task by introducing the most recent conceptual definitions and contextual delineations of feminist studies in religion and theology as put forth by two leading feminist scholars. My aim in doing so is to show how the story of the field is named and told differently depending on the audience to whom it is told, and to highlight how different theoretical frameworks and social locations shape this story in different ways. I also present these two discussions in contrast to my own mode of structuring the story of the field in a different way.

Speaking to a wo/men's studies audience in the United States, the Jewish feminist scholar Judith Plaskow has pointed to the widespread suspicion in so-called secular wo/men's studies that anyone interested in religion must be either co-opted or reactionary. Plaskow argues that this widespread notion is not justified. The assumption that feminists in all fields must—and do—critically study patriarchal ideologies, she argues, has not been extended by secular theorists to the serious work done by feminists in religion. This attitude of suspicion toward feminist studies in religion is regrettable for three major reasons.

First, *all* feminists need to study religion because it has played and still plays a key role in both wo/men's oppression and their liberation. Hence an understanding of how religion is implicated in the continuing political exploitation of wo/men, as well as how it actively participates in social movements for change, must be a central task of feminist studies. Plaskow asserts that an explicit connection between feminist critiques and social change movements has been made in feminist studies in religion from its very beginnings.

Second, wo/men's studies in religion is a variegated and vibrant field that has moved from analysis and critique of male texts toward reconstructing wo/men's heritage in and outside of kyriarchal religious traditions; most recently it has focused on the deconstruction of kyriarchal traditions and the construction of new transformative ones.

Finally, Plaskow maintains that to a much greater extent than feminist scholars in other areas, feminists in religion have sustained strong connections to wo/men's communities outside the academy. Much of the work of scholars in feminist studies in religion has been generated and challenged by wo/men in and outside of organized religions who search for a feminist spirituality and politics of meaning for their lives. Conversely, many feminist scholars are also involved either in traditional religious feminist groups or in the Goddess and spirituality movements that have critically challenged and enriched biblical articulations and religious formations.[2]

The well-known South African theologian Denise Ackermann does not speak about womanist, gender, or feminist studies in religion, but she entitles her exploration of the field "Faith and Feminism: Women Doing Theology."[3] Although Ackermannn does not use the term "feminist theology" in the title of her article, she clearly speaks to a feminist theological audience. She begins by characterizing her own perspective as indebted to the Christian tradition and then goes on to define and delineate feminism, feminist theology, and the diversity of feminist theologies by briefly characterizing the different approaches taken in the United States, Europe, South Africa, and by other wo/men in the Third World.

In a second step, Ackermann attempts to articulate a feminist theological agenda for wo/men in South Africa and argues that context and experience must be points of departure for liberating praxis and for defining a more inclusive view of all of humanity. Other issues discussed by her are "women and the church," the use of sexist and racist language, "women and sexual violence," and the creation of a contextual spirituality that is relevant for the people of South Africa. Following Sharon Welch, she recommends a spirituality of risk, which entails, in her view, "making oneself vulnerable in every aspect of one's life."[4] Although she is aware that an ethics of vulnerability has been part and parcel of the kyriarchal oppression of wo/men, Ackermannn nevertheless advocates such a contextual spirituality of vulnerability for white wo/men. Yet, in my view, she overlooks the fact that structurally this notion has been determined by the cultural and theological ideology of femininity.

My own story of the field will follow the lead of Plaskow in order to expand the theological frame proposed by Ackermann. I will begin with a sketch of the wo/men's liberation movement and its key analytic category of oppression. I will then sketch the theoretical frameworks generated by this movement and discuss the social and institutional location of feminist studies in religion.

Wo/men's Movements for Changing Systemic Oppressions

More than one hundred years ago, the educator Anna Julia Cooper, a womanist foresister, spelled out a vision of solidarity as the rationale and argument for a wo/men's movement for change and transformation:

> It is not the intelligent woman vs. the ignorant woman; nor the white woman vs. the black, the brown, and the red,—it is not even the cause of woman vs. man. Nay, it is woman's strongest vindication for speaking that *the world needs to hear her voice.* It would be subversive of every human interest that the cry of one half of the human family be stifled. Woman . . . daring to think and move and speak,—to undertake to help shape, mold and direct the thought of her age, is merely completing the circle of the world's vision. Hers is every interest that has lacked an interpreter and a defender. Her cause is linked with that of every agony that has been dumb—every wrong that needs a voice. . . . The world has had to limp along with the wobbling gait and one-sided hesitancy of a man with one eye. Suddenly the bandage is removed from the other eye and the whole body is filled with light. It sees a circle where before it saw a segment. The darkened eye restored, every member rejoices with it.[5]

A critical feminist hermeneutic of liberation, I submit, must follow the lead of Cooper in articulating such a different theo-ethical vision and a religious imagination which can inspire a new wo/men's movement for liberation. It seeks to reform religious institutions and malestream knowledges about the world and G*d[6] in order to correct and complete the world's and the church's one-sided vision. It seeks to rectify our gendered knowledge and spiritual perceptions of the world, which are still very limited to the extent that they continue to be articulated in the interest of elite white educated men. Such a critical feminist theology, I suggest, in the interest of wo/men suffering from multiple oppressions, seeks to restore the world's full spiritual vision, correct the fragmentary circle of Christian vision, and change the narrow and biased perception of the world and of G*d.

In the past, as in the present, feminist movements and thought have emerged from the participation of wo/men in emancipatory struggles for full democratic citizenship, religious freedom, the abolition of slavery, civil rights, and national and cultural independence, as well as the struggles of indigenous peoples and the ecological, labor, peace, and gay movements. In these struggles for religious, civil, and human rights, feminists have learned that words and phrases such as "human," "worker," "the poor," and "civil society" are all too often gender-typed and do not always mean nor include the rights and interests of wo/men. Therefore it becomes necessary to focus specifically on the struggles of wo/men for their rights and self-determination in society and church, and against institutionalized violence and cultural-religious self-alienation. In short, feminist movements are engendered and renewed by wo/men's participation in emancipatory radical democratic struggles, a participation which leads to a different self-understanding and a more complete vision of the world.

Such a critical feminist hermeneutic of liberation seeks to transform traditional theological discourses by interfacing the particular struggles of wo/men in diverse societies with those in the Christian churches and other world religions. Just as other religious feminists want to transform their own religious "home bases," so Christian feminists attempt to do so by introducing wo/men into theological discourse as new thinking and speaking subjects. By critically reflecting on their own location within institutionalized biblical religions, feminist theologians are able to claim their own religious voice, heritage, and community in the struggle for liberation.

Christian feminist theologies speak in their own particular voices to their own communities and traditions in order to change them, just as Jewish, Moslem, or Buddhist ones do. Therefore the critical insights and constructive visions that are articulated by feminists in diverse religions and denominations do not seek to revive malestream confessional controversies but must be seen as strengthening each other in global feminist struggles for liberation. For feminist debates on difference and commonality show that particular feminist discourses are not only shaped by their cultural-religious locations but are also defined through their interface and interaction with feminist movements and theoretical articulations. Such an appreciation of religious differences in turn leads to an articulation of a feminist politics and spirituality that can empower wo/men to bring about further change in society and religion. Religion has played and still plays an important role in these emancipatory struggles, although all too many feminists have tended to see it more as a part of the problem than as part of the solution.

Today millions of wo/men around the world actively participate in religious practices and institutions. They derive their self-identity, self-respect, sense of worth, dignity, courage, and vision from their religious engagement. Those who relegate wo/men's religious commitment to "false consciousness" not only overlook the active participation of feminists in biblical religions but also set up agnostic or atheistic feminism as superior to religious feminist struggles.[7] They disregard the fact that for millions of wo/men religion still provides a framework of meaning that is not just alienating and oppressive but also self-affirming and liberating.

Moreover, to reject religion as totally oppressive and to neglect it as a positive source of empowerment and hope in creating a better future for wo/men would mean to relinquish religion to the ownership claims of reactionary, right-wing fundamentalism.[8] The resurgence of such global antifeminist dogmatism and its success not only among men but also among wo/men shows that it plays on people's fear, alienation, and deep anxiety at the vanishing of a world as they have known it. The experience of losing cultural, social, and religious roots in the process of increasing globalization, and a concommitant sense of personal isolation and social marginalization, are matched by a desire for assured certainty, definite security, fixed truth, and a stable picture of the world as guaranteed by G*d. With this desire goes a longing for great leaders and father figures who will take care of us and therefore have every right to require our submission.

Wo/men's traditional cultural and religious socialization to feminine passivity, subordination, and self-negating "love for a man" conditions them to be lured by the appeal of reactionary religious right-wing promises. When such a fundamentalist religious ethos of "feminine" submission allies itself with right-wing political organizations, it is able to harness wo/men's need for financial security and emotional affirmation to conservative, antidemocratic ends. Therefore it is important that feminists engage institutional religions in the struggle to change all situations of oppression. Feminist theory and studies in religion must therefore develop and utilize an analytic of systemic oppression and of wo/men's second-class citizenship.

At this point the objection is increasingly raised that it is no longer justifiable to speak of oppression in general and of wo/men's oppression in particular. According to some postmodern feminist voices, "oppression" belongs together with "sexism," "patriarchy," and "androcentrism," categories whose use is seen as embarrassing because by now they are allegedly outdated and antiquated. Moreover, it is maintained that as a "master narrative," an analytic of oppression revives the old dualisms and other postures of Western thought that seek to give a totalizing explanation of the world.

Yet to abandon the analytical category of oppression and relegate it to the academic dustheap of "jargon" will only serve to keep domination in place. The following actual and not just "textual" incident can illustrate the point I wish to make. Recently Harvard Divinity School interviewed candidates for a senior position in New Testament studies. After the public lecture of the first candidate, one of my colleagues chastised her for supposedly using numerous times in her talk the "analytically fuzzy" and "historically anachronistic" term "oppression." (I immediately realized that this criticism would become the primary strategy of attack in the attempt to torpedo the appointment of a senior woman scholar.) A careful reading of her lecture proved that she had not used the term at all, although she had once in a descriptive way characterized the Roman empire as one of "domination." Hence I could successfully argue that this accusation was a gross misreading of her paper. But what if she *had* used "oppression" as a central analytic category in her argument? The "disciplining" measures of the academy can be severe!

On a political level, both conservatives and progressives argue that in comparison to the poor or the peoples of the Two-Thirds World, wo/men are not oppressed. The wo/men's movement is said to represent the interests of privileged middle-class wo/men. Although this objection might apply to some strategies and articulations of the wo/men's movement in church and society, it nevertheless neglects the fact that not all Western wo/men are privileged. Rather, the majority of the poor all over the world are wo/men and their children. Moreover, this objection overlooks the fact that in every culture, society, and religion, wo/men's status is lower than men's. Nevertheless, it compels one to ask whether the secondary status of wo/men permits one to speak of the oppression of wo/men if not all wo/men are oppressed equally and to the same degree. Here it might be helpful to recall the following five criteria, developed by feminist political scientist Iris Marion Young, to help us ascertain whether and how much a given social group is oppressed.[9]

1. *Exploitation:* International research has documented that wo/men in all countries of the world are exploited economically, culturally, and politically. Internationally wo/men earn only around one- to two-thirds of the income that men of their own class and race receive. Wo/men do the greatest share of unpaid child-rearing and household maintenance work. The unpaid volunteer work of wo/men sustains, for the most part, many cultural and religious institutions.

2. *Marginalization:* Wo/men are underrepresented in all cultural, religious, and scientific institutions. Their participation in cultural life, history, science, and theology is only rarely—if at all—recorded. Wo/men are either not present in religious, political, and cultural leadership positions or they function as "token men" without any power and influence of their own.

3. *Powerlessness:* Although wo/men are able to vote in most countries of the world, they have very few representatives in most governments and not much political, cultural, or religious deci-

sion-making power. Wo/men's interests are not perceived as public interests, and their influence is restricted to private life. Even wo/men who have been leaders of national liberation movements are often pushed aside "after the revolution." According to cultural and religious notions of femininity, wo/men are supposed to exercise manipulative, indirect influence but are not expected to overtly exercise real power.

4. *Cultural imperialism* stereotypes oppressed groups and at the same time makes them invisible. "Women" are not perceived as human persons in their specific particularity but are always seen as *"women."* At the same time, language and scientific knowledge make wo/men invisible as *wo/men* in the accounts of Western culture, which understand the elite white male as the paradigmatic human being and see all other people in relation to him. This Western kyriocentric understanding of language, the world, and humanity then becomes universalized and identified as human culture par excellence.

5. *Systemic Violence:* Violence against wo/men is generally not seen as a violation of human rights. However, studies have shown that wo/men, still today as in the past, are physically and mentally abused, ill treated, battered, tortured, and killed just because they are wo/men. Today, as in antiquity, more girl than boy children have been abandoned; in many cultures, wo/men still receive only the food left over by men; advertising and the mass media objectify wo/men as consumer goods and sexual playthings who allegedly seduce men and provoke sexual abuse and mistreatment. Murder and violence against wo/men have become commonplace everyday events.

Young asserts that if more than one of these criteria applies, one can speak of "wo/men's oppression." The combination of several criteria serves to explicate the specific form and extent of wo/men's oppression. For instance, a white, privileged academic like myself is much less exploited economically, has more influence and possibilities in daily life, is less socially marginalized or stereotypically dehumanized than the wo/man who cleans her office, although both are in danger of being battered or of being raped when they go out at night—or even in their own homes. In comparison to her male colleagues, however, such a professional wo/man receives a lower salary, has fewer chances for professional advancement, and less influence in her field. As a wo/man she is not granted the same respect as her male colleagues and her scholarship is often trivialized, co-opted, or passed over with silence. If her work is not exploited or co-opted, it is likely to be marginalized and to have little power to change cultural and religious institutions.

To these five criteria of wo/men's oppression I would like to add two more that especially apply to wo/men in theology and religion.

6. *Silencing:* Throughout the centuries wo/men have not been allowed to speak in public, to preach, or to have access to the academy. Since the fateful injunctions of Paul and his students that wo/men should be silent in the assembly and that they are not allowed to speak or to teach men, Christian wo/men have been the silenced majority of the people of G*d. Throughout the centuries and still today wo/men are prohibited from ordination, preaching, and official teaching in many churches. Until very recently they have not been allowed to study and teach theology or to define moral and ecclesial policy.

7. *Vilification and Trivialization:* In Western thought wo/men have been seen as the source of all evil and the fountain of all falsehood. Beginning with the Pastoral Epistles, the sin of Eve looms large in the arguments against wo/men's leadership and for wo/men's second-class citizenship. Tertullian is not the only one who has declared wo/man to be "the devil's gateway." Not only the witch-hunts of the Inquisition but also the cosmetic mutilations of today's multimillion-dollar beauty industry have sought to "correct" the deficient and evil nature of wo/men.

Armed with such a complex analysis of the variegated forms and facets of oppression, feminist movements in society and church have brought about substantive change in the past three decades. I want to highlight this with reference to changes in religion. For instance, in the last hundred years or so, wo/men have, in many churches, achieved access to the ordained ministry, and some have even become bishops. Even though some Christian denominations—like my own, Roman Catholicism—still refuse to ordain wo/men, wo/men nevertheless exercise ministerial leadership functions on all levels of church administration, albeit lacking public recognition and official decision-making powers.

As in society, so also in the churches: the work of both ordained and non-ordained wo/men remains underpaid, and clergywo/men are relegated to low-ranking positions. Hence, even after equal access to ordination is achieved, many ordained Christian and Jewish wo/men have begun to see that while this is an important first step in changing kyriarchal structures of exclusion and marginalization, it is just that—a first step. Wo/men's ordination must be accompanied by a change in theological discourses and spiritual visions in order to avoid the appropriation and co-optation of wo/men's religious powers for kyriarchal ends and the engendering of an even greater spiritual violence against wo/men.

Over the last thirty years or so, wo/men in ever greater numbers have achieved access to theological education; today in the United States more than fifty percent of students in liberal Protestant theological schools are wo/men. White European-American wo/men preceded African-, Asian-, and Latin-American wo/men by approximately ten years. However, the number of black, Latina, lesbian or Native American wo/men in biblical studies has remained minuscule. Moreover, wo/men of all colors and denominations are still confronted in many instances with a malestream, Eurocentric religious studies curriculum and sets of doctrines that are either silent about wo/men or negative toward them. Such hegemonic cultural-religious and theological knowledges often lead to the further alienation of wo/men in and through theological education.

Consequently, a critical feminist theology of liberation investigates not only how centuries of wo/men's exclusion from the academy and from theological education has been legitimated, but also how it can be undone. In the last century, wo/men first gained access to intellectual work and academic studies through special courses or schools for wo/men. In this century, wo/men have been admitted to full theological studies and teaching as long as they could prove that they were better than their male colleagues. Despite outstanding qualifications and academic excellence, only a very few wo/men scholars have achieved senior faculty status and theological authority and influence in their own right. But while at first wo/men fought for academic access and excelled in malestream scholarship, in recent decades wo/men scholars have developed feminist studies and theology as alternatives to malestream knowledge and theology. Feminist research and education in theology and religion have brought to consciousness both the complicity of religious knowledge and socialization in wo/men's economic exploitation, societal marginalization, and sexual victimization, and the new field's ability to construct a different world of meaning and a liberating vision that authorizes and empowers wo/men in their struggles for survival, dignity, and self-determination.

The Theoretical Framework of Feminist Studies

The history of feminist theology and studies in religion, as I have argued in the introduction, should not be construed in progressivist developmental terms or assessed in terms of malestream theories. Rather it must be contextualized within critical feminist thought and intellectual practices, which find expression in three or four divergent ways.

Feminist studies methodologically investigate how centuries of wo/men's exclusion from the academy and institutionalized religion has determined religious knowledge and theology. They have shown that the exclusion of wo/men from the university because of their gender, race, class, or ethnicity has produced a system of knowledge and science that is one-sided and biased because it has been articulated from the perspective of elite, educated, mostly Western men.

In general, feminist studies seek to correct and transform such malestream Euro-American scholarship by introducing theoretical perspectives and educational practices that systemically reflect the rich diversity of human experiences. Feminist studies in religion in particular underscore both that wo/men must be recognized as religious and intellectual subjects and that more research needs to be done on wo/men and on the sociopolitical construction of gender.

The academic wo/men's movement began by defining itself as a wo/men's studies movement. *Wo/men's studies*, however, has been developed in two different ways. On the one hand it has come to mean the study of wo/men as objects of inquiry. This approach seeks to complement malestream academic research that does not focus on wo/men. On the other hand, wo/men's studies can also be understood as placing wo/men at the center of its attention, both as subjects of scholarship and research and as critical agents in academic institutions. The former emphasis on wo/men as objects of study has been taken up and further theorized by the field of *gender studies*, which argues that "woman" and "man" are not two independent cultural categories but are correlated and interdependent. Gender categories are not a "natural fact" or "revealed by G*d" but are socially constructed and hence are legitimate subjects of research.

Whereas the disciplinary approach of gender studies stresses the social construction of gender, scholars in the field of *feminist studies* have developed the second aspect of wo/men's studies, which emphasizes that wo/men are intellectual subjects and sociopolitical agents. Critical feminist studies seek to balance and correct the academic-objectivist frameworks of gender and wo/men's studies by developing theory as a critical tool of inquiry into wo/men's oppression. Feminist critical theory seeks not only to understand but also to change our knowledge of the world, and to transform the kyriarchal institutions which produce such knowledge and which are in turn legitimated by it.

In the last decade *gender studies in religion* has appeared as a third discrete approach in religious studies. This approach has emerged from within the academy, and its adherents do not generally position themselves within the various wo/men's movements for political change. Instead, they orient their discourses toward a "scientific," mostly male audience, and seek to win the respect and approval of that audience as a serious intellectual malestream discipline.

For instance, as I have pointed out in *But She Said*, the Canadian scholar Peggy L. Day has advocated a separation between feminist theological studies and gender studies of the bible on methodological grounds; feminist theological interpretation is said to seek out the significance of biblical texts for today, whereas biblical gender studies adopts and applies the critical approaches of "the secular humanities and social sciences to the field of biblical studies."[10]

Yet such a neat division of labor contradicts the goal of feminist studies, which, in the interest of wo/men's liberation movements, seek to use the critical tools of the academy in order to assess the political impact and significance of cultural texts and religious traditions for wo/men today. It also ignores the danger, for both feminist theological and cultural gender studies in religion, that they may accommodate themselves to the reigning "value-neutral" scientistic theoretical paradigm—which in turn puts them in danger of abandoning the very political concerns and practical connections of the wo/men's movements in society and church that have helped biblical wo/men's studies to preserve its feminist political and intellectual integrity. Many feminist scholars have pointed to the depoliticizing tendency of such a shift from wo/men's/womanist/feminist studies to gender studies in the humanities, and we in the field of feminist biblical studies disregard their warnings at our own risk.

Such a move from wo/men's or feminist to gender studies has been facilitated by the adoption of a modified structuralism which is a form of functionalism that tends to satisfy value-neutral scholarship insofar as it describes and accounts for the functioning of a society without making any explicit value judgments and without paying attention to the implicit power imbalance implied in gender constructions. Gender may have replaced "woman" as an object of study because it supposedly communicates the scientific seriousness of a work by suggesting that information about wo/men is of necessity also knowledge about men. Consequently, the claim that gender studies produce a more objective and "neutral" scholarship rests on the uncritical acceptance of malestream theoretical frameworks. Insofar as gender studies isolate gender oppression from other structures of wo/men's oppression such as racism, class exploitation, and colonialism, they are a step backward since they revert to a theoretical frame of analysis that wo/men of all "colors" have challenged as theoretically unsatisfactory and regressive in practice. The diverse resistant discourses of the emerging feminist movements around the world increasingly challenge white Western wo/men's universalistic gender claim, namely that all wo/men have in common a special, essential nature and are defined in their "otherness" to men.

It is debated whether the influx of wo/men of the so-called Two-Thirds World constitutes a fourth approach in feminist studies and whether these new critical voices will be successful in destabilizing the central Euro-American voice of wo/men's, feminist, or gender studies in such a way that feminist studies become redefined in a global or cosmopolitan sense. If wo/men's studies should displace the kyriarchal "politics of otherness," these feminist voices argue, the field can no longer construct wo/men's identity as unitary and universal or establish it in terms of either the exclusion and domination of "the others" or as "the others'" self-negation and subordination. For unraveling the unitary otherness of "woman" from "man" in Western philosophical, political, and religious discourses, the emerging feminist movements around the world focus on specific historical cultural contexts and on historically defined subjectivity as well as on the plurality of wo/men.

By deconstructing the ideological constructs of "woman" and "the feminine," such global feminist discourses elucidate how the identity of wo/men who belong to subordinated races, classes, cultures, or religions is constructed as "other" of the "other," as negative foil for the feminine identity of the "White Lady." As I pointed out in the beginning of this chapter, the African-American feminist Anna Julia Cooper, whose work *A Voice from the South* appeared one hundred years ago, has underscored the significance of wo/men of all "colors" for a feminist movement. Her assertion still holds true today: "The colored woman of to-day occupies, one may say, a unique position in this country. . . . She is confronted by both a woman question and a race problem and is as yet an unknown or an unacknowledged factor in both."[11] In other words, the struggle of the wo/men's movement and its impetus to challenge kyriarchal power relations must be located at the juncture of racial and sexual politics.

However, simply belonging to an oppressed group does not necessarily guarantee the production of emancipatory knowledges. As the African-American literary critic Mary Helen Washington has pointed out, Cooper herself was never quite successful in connecting race, class, and gender issues or in making them pivotal in wo/men's resistance to all forms of subjection. She was not able to do so because she herself could not escape the ideological entanglements of the cult of "true womanhood," or that of the Lady, and its dictates.[12] Writing as a middle-class black woman, Cooper, according to Washington, did not imagine ordinary black working wo/men, sharecroppers, or domestic maids as her audience or as the vanguard of her politics. Rather, like other educated middle-class black wo/men, Cooper had an even greater stake than her white compatriots "in the gentility guaranteed by the politics of true womanhood. . . . Burdened by the race's morality, black women could not be as free as white women or black men to think outside of these boundaries of 'uplift'; every choice they made had tremendous repercussions for an entire race of women already under the stigma of inferiority and immorality."[13]

Although some historians have suggested that the tenets of "true womanhood" represent an incipient form of radical feminism, such a positive assessment of the middle-class cult of femininity overlooks the role of the ideal of the Lady in the dualistic formation of gender-based feminism. Only when, in the words of Cooper, the "darkened eye" is restored, can we begin to "see a circle rather than just a segment" of feminist studies in religion. The insights into the interaction between race, gender, class, and culture which are articulated by feminist discourses emerging around the globe compel middle-class feminists in the so-called First World not to reduplicate the whitemale[14] universalistic discourse of gender dualism. At the same time, they caution middle-class feminists of the Two-Thirds World not to reproduce the neocolonialist discourse on "woman" and "femininity" in attempts to prove their cultural stature and legitimacy.

However, just as in the case of the categories "woman," and "the feminine," so also the term "feminist" has become problematic since it is also often understood in essentialist rather than historical terms. If feminism is understood as a gender theory that concerns itself with the universal and unilateral oppression of wo/men by men, it reproduces the cultural patriarchal discourse on "woman" and "the feminine." Hence for many in the Two-Thirds World the term "feminist" designates a movement of white European and American wo/men, or that of the White Lady. Therefore some have suggested that the qualifier "feminist" should be replaced with a proliferation of names and self-designations, such as "womanist," "mujerista," or Asian/African/Latin American, lesbian, differently abled, elder, Christian, Muslim, Buddist, or Jewish wo/men's perspectives.

While some of the proposed neologisms and self-definitions explicitly claim to be feminist (Alice Walker defines a "womanist" as a "black feminist"), others reject this term as being too radical. Still other feminists of the Two-Thirds World argue to the contrary that abandoning the term "feminism" would be a "mixed blessing" for wo/men of the Two-Thirds World.[15] Not only would it give credence to the notion that the historical achievements of feminism as a worldwide *political* movement were the work of white European-American wo/men alone, it would also relinquish the claim of feminists around the world to shape and continue to define the meaning and practice of feminism in a different key.[16] Instead of rejecting feminism as white and middle-class, these feminists maintain that wo/men of all "colors" have always engaged with feminism or advocated "feminist movement"—to use bell hooks's expression. Hence it is more important for feminists of all "colors," Cheryl Johnson-Odim asserts, to be concerned with participating in shaping

> and defining feminism than with changing the terminology. . . . Since "modern day" feminism is still in the process of incarnation, especially at the international level, I question whether the coining of a new term simply retreats from the debate, running the risk of losing sight of the fair amount of universality in women's oppression.[17]

Rather than reifying "feminist/feminism" as a white supremacist definition by theorizing it in terms of the Western sex/gender system, feminists must question and redefine the meanings of these terms. While it is important that diverse feminist communities use their own self-designations to positively express their own complex cultural religious identities, such a proliferation can easily lead to the balkanization of feminism in the academy and in religion. Such fragmentation is in the interest of established powers because it turns differently articulated feminist movements into "special interest groups." It thereby reenacts the fragmenting tendencies of the modern multiversity, which has splintered knowledge into isolated disciplines and disciplinary languages that speak only to themselves without having a cumulative impact on bringing about change.

The tensions and conflicts between the different formations of wo/men's studies in religion or feminist theology are best understood, I suggest, as symptomatic of structural-systemic problems. Rather than negotiating and debating them only as problems existing *within feminism*, one must analyze them as systemic structural problems engendered by societal, religious, and academic measures of marginalization and oppression. Although all wo/men entering the academy and theological studies face the same disciplining pressures, they experience them quite differently depending on their placement within the overall structures of domination.

Hence it becomes important to critically analyze and identify such institutional disciplining structures as problematic rather than seeing such systemic contradictions primarily as an intra-feminist problem generated by different feminist articulations. In my view, these discursive fragmenting discourses must be reconstituted in political-rhetorical terms by exploring and discussing different feminist interests and articulations. They need to be conceptualized not as forensic arguments in defense of one's own position but as different perspectives and contributions to a deliberative debate that empowers all wo/men who struggle for change and transformation. In order to avoid the debilitating impact of academic and religious fragmentation, as well as the devisive effects of a forensic academic and doctrinal style of discourse, feminists around the globe, I suggest, must conceptualize their debates as open ongoing political discourses.

Only if the terms "feminist" and "feminism" are not reified as fixed essentialist classifications but are understood in rhetorical-political terms can they function as signifiers of an "open-ended" category which is to be questioned, destabilized, and redefined in ever-shifting historical-political situations of domination. For feminist discourses are like the waters of the sea. They can be life-giving or life-destroying. Their combined power washes away all obstacles. Nevertheless they are not all the same. Their colors are

ever-changing, from slate blue to grey, to green, to night black, to
foaming white and dazzling silver, depending on the angle of the
light and the movement of the wind.

Feminist studies in religion must therefore rearticulate again
and again its categories and lenses of interpretation in particular
historical situations and social contexts. Feminist studies should
not subscribe to a single method of analysis nor adopt a single
hermeneutic perspective or mode of approach. Feminist discourse
also should not restrict itself to one single community or audience. Rather, a feminist critical theory should search for appropriate theoretical frameworks and practical ways of interpretation
that can make visible the oppressive as well as the liberative traces
inscribed in Jewish, Christian, and traditional Asian, African, or
indigenous religions. A proliferation of feminist perspectives from
different subject locations that avoids constituting such particular
approaches as exclusive totalizing strategies, I argue, can articulate them as different feminist practices of collaboration for
changing particular relations of domination and alienation.

The Institutional Location of Feminist Studies in Religion

Almost sixty years ago, Virginia Woolf insisted that wo/men have
to set the conditions under which they are willing to join the
"procession of educated men." Wo/men have to ask where this
procession will lead them if they join its ranks. In light of the
overall systemic exploitation and marginalization of wo/men,
feminist liberation theologians have carefully pondered this question as to whether and how to join the procession of (clergy)men
and have explored the conditions under which feminists might
join the hierarchical ranks of church and academy. Many
Catholic feminists, for instance, no longer simply wait for the ar-
rival of wo/men's ordination in their church, since wo/men of
other Christian denominations have been ordained as ministers,
priests, and bishops for quite some time.[18] Rather they ask, What
will ordination do to wo/men and for them in their struggles for
liberation? Is ordination into kyriarchal structures good for
wo/men if it incorporates them into violent and abusive hierarchical situations of domination?

Feminist theologians have come to understand Woolf's conclusion that simply joining the procession of educated men will lead wo/men to war, exploitation, elitism, the greed for power, the degradation of the human race, and the pollution of our natural environment. If one contemplates wo/men's ministry in the context of wo/men's economic exploitation and worldwide poverty, the question seems no longer simply one of wo/men's admission to the kyriarchal hierarchy in and through ordination, but how to prevent wo/men's further exploitation. The central feminist theological problem today, I submit, is the question of whether it is possible to change hierarchical religions and to articulate theology in such a way that it does not continue to foster wo/men's exploitation and self-abnegation. It is no longer "the woman question" that moves feminist studies in religion. Rather it is the question of whether religious institutions and theological disciplines can be changed, redefined, and transformed.

Only if feminist scholars in religion continue to critically explore wo/men's dehumanization in and through theological traditions and kyriocentric sacred language, as well as through the theological politics of wo/men's exclusion from church leadership, will they be able to transform wo/men's lives on the grassroots level in and through the practice of feminist ministry. As more and more Christian wo/men, for instance, become schooled in a feminist liberationist theological perspective they will be committed to ministry in the discipleship of equals. Such feminist ministers will continue to nurture individuals and to empower communities for realizing justice and love as the heartbeat of any religious institution. In liturgy and ritual, in bible study and shelters for the homeless, in preaching and pastoral counseling, in day care centers and town meetings, feminist ministers proclaim and enact the "good news" that wo/men, the weak, and the marginal are "beloved" in the eyes of G*d and therefore must reclaim their dignity, rights, and power in society and church.

In short, feminist theologians and scholars in religion must continue to demand not just the admittance of wo/men to academic studies and professorships but also the recognition of their intellectual religious authority and contributions in the past and present. They must reconceptualize and revise malestream theoretical frameworks, social-ecclesiastical structures, doctrinal ethical teachings, and communicative-educational practices that are based entirely on the experiences and work of "educated [Western Christian clergy]men."

Since the institutional location of feminist studies in religion is that of malestream scholarship, feminists, I argue, must not only deconstruct hegemonic academic discourses but also must construct a different feminist discursive space. They must conceptualize feminist studies as critical rhetorical-political practices for liberation. When one is conscious of wo/men's sociopolitical location in the academy, it becomes apparent what is at stake in the theoretical construction of such a discursive position. Feminists, who as "outsiders" or "aliens" engage in religious studies in order to transform the patri-kyriarchal discourses of church and academy, can do so only if they can manage to both become qualified *residents* within religious institutions and remain *foreign speakers* at one and the same time.

Although the number of wo/men studying religion and enrolling in seminaries has increased worldwide in the past decade or so, no equivalent change in institutional practices has yet taken place.[19] Consequently, wo/men entering theological and religious studies still have to adopt the language and discourse of those clerical and academic communities that have silenced them, have excluded them as the "other" of the Divine, marginalized them as the "other" to the scientific "Man of Reason,"[20] and relegated them to the status of social, religious, and intellectual nobodies. In order for feminists to enter into hegemonic theological discourses as equals, the systemic interrelation of theological-religious knowledge with global oppression must become conscious and the "gendered character" of religious and theological studies must be rendered explicit.

The dominant paradigms of religious studies must therefore be critically scrutinized for their emancipatory aims, for their impact on the formation of a critical consciousness, and for their ability to produce radical democratic discourses. For scholars are always constrained by the theoretical frames of reference and the interpretive communities to which they belong.[21] If the malestream academic community acts in some ways like a police force that

defends against "unacceptable" scientific practices, then it becomes important to reflect on the different social and institutional
locations of critical feminist studies within departments of religion and schools of theology. For whenever liberation discourses
are displaced from their social location in emancipatory movements and become integrated into the institutional practices of religion or the academy, they become subject to the disciplinary
pressures and requirements of these interpretive communities.

For almost two hundred and fifty years, academic religious studies
in the United States were understood as a "discipline" for the training
of elite white men in "religious and moral piety."[22] In the nineteenth century a paradigm shift took place that introduced as the new
model for higher education that of German scientific research.
This transformation of the humanities curriculum replaced religion
with science. This change resulted in a galaxy of separate "disciplines" and "departments" that accredited persons for a particular kind of professional work. The unifying ethos of the emerging
scientific academy, which insisted on an objectivist method, scientific value neutrality, and disinterested research, unseated the cen-
trality of the bible and religion in the Western academic universe.

This scientific positivist ethos has engendered not only the privatization and "feminization" of religion, but also the "masculin-
ization" of all other disciplines within the university as "hard"
sciences.[23] Yet feminist studies have shown that despite such
rhetorical claims to value-neutral objectivity, virtually every academic discipline operates on the unreflected "commonsense" assumption that equates male reality with human reality.
Intellectual histories and other "canonized" cultural and academic texts have generally assumed that the elite educated man is
the paradigmatic human being. At the same time they have
claimed that "natural" or essential differences exist between
wo/men and men. Consequently they have defined wo/men and
other colonized peoples as rationally inferior, marginal, sub-
sidiary, or derivative "feminine others." Wo/men intellectuals who
have shown leadership and claimed independence have been
judged to be unnatural, aggressive, and disruptive. As Adrienne
Rich has put it, "There is no discipline that does not obscure and
devalue the history and experience of women as a group."[24]

The Contradictory Location of Wo/men Scholars

Wo/men scholars find themselves in a contradictory and conflictual position: in order to become speaking theological subjects, they must "master" the clerical and academic discourses of the fathers, which have been fashioned to exclude wo/men. For, in Thomas Kuhn's terms, to become members of the community of scholars, students have to internalize an entire constellation of beliefs, values, techniques, shared worldviews, and systems of knowledge as maps or guidelines for thinking and speaking in a "scholarly" way.[25] In the course of this socialization process, wo/men students experience severe contradictions, which they often internalize as personal failure. If they "master" these conflicts between their own social or religious life-worlds and those of their discipline they will finally speak and think in the professional idiom. Such a process of acquiring the insider's language and public persona can be likened to the process of socialization into an alien culture.

This process of socialization, of becoming a Harvard, Stellenbosch, Humboldt, or postmodern "man," is even more alienating for those wo/men students and faculty who do not share the racial, social, cultural, or religious background of those elite white men who have shaped and continue to shape the academic disciplines. Black wo/men, for instance, suffer from much greater contradictions between their own cultural languages and experiences and those of academic theological or religious studies disciplines than white wo/men do.[26] Wo/men of non-elite backgrounds also experience acute self-alienation, having to move between two language worlds and feeling out of place in both.[27] Given the long history of the silencing of wo/men in religion and the academy, it remains very difficult even for committed feminists to understand themselves as subjects speaking with authority or as theory-producing scholars who must occupy resistant subject-positions in the dominant discourses of the discipline.

Although critical feminist liberation theologians and scholars in religion speak from within the disciplinary discourses of academy and church, we must do so, I have suggested, from the sociopolitical location of *resident aliens*. The notion of resident alien positions one as both insider and outsider: insider by virtue of residence or family affiliation to a citizen or institution; outsider in terms of language, experience, culture, and history. The metaphor of "resident alien" seems an apt figure for a feminist movement and politics that seek to open up a theoretical space and sociopolitical position from which critical feminist scholars in religious studies can speak.

Since the White Lady has been the civilizing channel and feminine "glue" of Western domination,[28] white middle-class wo/men, who are fairly recent "immigrants" in academy and ministry, must continue to struggle against pressures to function as elite wo/men and prized tokens who are "loyal to civilization" (Adrienne Rich's phrase). Hence white feminists must refuse to mediate or teach religious studies and theological knowledges which legitimate intellectual and religious discourses that dehumanize and vilify wo/men and other "nobodies" by justifying practices of exclusion and the languages of hate.

However, feminists must remain aware that the malestream academy will respond by declaring alternative feminist knowledges that contest those of dominant biblical scholarship to be marginal, anomalous, or ideological claims. Malestream scholarship rarely grants that feminists produce alternative knowledges that are equally valid although based on a different procedure of validation. Hence the malestream academy continues to insist that feminist work must be measured by the prevailing intellectual standards of excellence. Pioneering work by black feminists, for instance, is often put down as "unscientific," while mediocre research that fine-tunes established methods and approaches is pronounced to be excellent and worthy of prestigious awards.

Feminists seeking to change religious studies, therefore, must explicitly challenge malestream standards of scientific and professional validation and unmask those that are partial, biased, or formulated in the interests of one particular group in society and religion. Like feminists in other academic disciplines, so feminists in religion must question dominant modes of reasoning, especially the Eurocentric malestream paradigm of knowledge that separates reason from feelings and emotions in order to produce detached impartial knowledges.[29]

Speaking from the subject-position of the resident alien, feminist students and faculty can confront this malesteam ethos as well as its dominant modes of theological argument and pedagogy. Wo/men students who have been silenced by traditional theology must learn to demystify the dominant frameworks and structures of knowledge production if they are to find their own theological voices, exercise personal choices, and achieve intellectual satisfaction in their work.

Feminist studies have therefore sought to develop a *different model of intellectual discourse*, one that does not reinforce the kyriarchal patterns of knowledge production but which seeks to construct a democratic mode of producing and communicating knowledge. Such a radical democratic feminist paradigm will enable students and faculty to find their own intellectual theological voices by developing discourses of critique, empowerment, and possibility. It also seeks to engage in the complex process of redefining knowledge by making wo/men's experience a primary resource for insight, by conceptualizing wo/men as active agents in the creation of knowledge, and by including wo/men's perspective on and perception of the world of G*d. If one sees gender, race, class, and colonialism as fundamental to the articulation of knowledge in Western thought, all knowledge claims will be changed.[30] In such a critical democratic feminist model of education, students would begin with the systemic exploration of their own experience, commitments, and questions as well as a critical analysis of their theological presuppositions and frameworks.[31] At stake here is a theoretical shift from the pedagogical paradigm of domination to one of radical equality.[32]

In the past two decades, I submit, political or liberationist rather than gender-based feminism has offered the most dynamic examples of such an academic counter-discourse. Liberation feminism has constituted a public arena for generating critical analyses of oppression and for articulating feminist interests and visions. Still, insofar as the feminist movement as a whole has projected itself as a single oppositional front which has been articulated largely in terms of the sex/gender system and has generated a universalizing critique of sociopolitical structures from the standpoint of Euro-American elite "Woman," it has tended to constitute its feminist counter-public as a hegemonic sphere of privileged, white Western wo/men.

Recent feminist work that positions itself within the ethical-political space of the radical democratic paradigm seeks to theorize such a public feminist space from whence to speak differently. In order to move away from essentialist notions such as "wo/men's perspective," Chandra Talpade Mohanti has suggested the concept of the "imagined community" as the kind of space that is needed for Two-Thirds World oppositional struggles.[33]

Situating feminist theorizing and theologizing within the logic of radical equality rather than within that of female/ethnic identity allows one to contextualize so-called "natural" binary sexual arrangements, together with those of race, ethnicity, or class, as sociopolitical ideological constructions. Wo/men live in structures and institutions that are not simply pluralistic; wo/men are stratified into differentiated social groups of unequal status, power, and access to resources, traversed by pervasive axes of inequality along the lines of class, gender, race, ethnicity, and age.[34] By insisting in their own discourses on the *theoretical* visibility and difference, for instance, of black, poor, colonial, lesbian, or working wo/men, feminist theory and theology can make it clear that "wo/men" do not have a unitary nature and essence but represent a historical multiplicity, not only as a group but also as individuals.[35]

In short, I argue that in order to minimize the possibility of their co-optation in the interests of relations of domination, feminist theology and studies in religion must place at the center of their attention particular analyses of the multiplicative structures of wo/men's oppression and everywo/man's struggle to survive and to transform these structures. Instead of focusing their gaze primarily on malestream texts, traditions, institutions and authorities, they must ask their questions and shape their intellectual frameworks in light of wo/men's struggles for survival and liberation. Since throughout the centuries patriarchal theology and church have silenced and excluded wo/men from religious institutions of authority, feminist theology must seek to empower wo/men to become religious subjects, to participate in the critical construction of biblical-theological meanings, and to claim their authority to do so. Whenever feminist scholars of religion succeed in such a process of intellectual conscientization and in the production of radical democratic emancipatory knowledges, they are apt to rewrite religious scholarship in such a way that they change the discipline rather than become disciplined by it.

Christian wo/men have entered the emerging field of religious studies and the house of theology from which they were excluded for centuries. In the last twenty years, an explosion of research in wo/men's, gender, queer, womanist, mujerista, Africana, Latina feminist studies in religion and theology has taken place. I can illustrate this with reference to my own experience. In the late sixties I was able to read every publication that appeared in the area of feminist studies, in the seventies I could read all the new publications in the field of feminist studies in religion and theology, and in the eighties I could still do the same for feminist publications in biblical studies. However, over the past couple of years the flood of feminist research in religion has increased to the point that it is no longer possible to keep up with its pace and insights.

Nevertheless, as in other academic disciplines, the knowledge produced by feminist studies in religion remains marginal to the overall curriculum. Most often it appears as a "special interest" topic and remains restricted to those who are already converted. Hence the ever-present temptation to define oneself in malestream terms—as a cultural, ideological, or postmodern critic rather than as a feminist one. Wo/men students still have to do "double duty"—or "triple duty," if they belong to a minority group. They study feminist Latina, black, or Asian theology because these forms of theology speak to their own experiences; however, their professional competence is judged by whether they know malestream intellectual work in "theology" as such.

In light of continuing discriminations and exclusions,[36] as well as in light of the ongoing struggles of wo/men for change and transformation, feminist scholars, I argue, must continue to insist that it is not enough to seek integration into a male-dominated academy and church or to fashion feminist theory and theology in the mold of malestream theories and theologies, be they traditional or avant-garde. Nothing less than the transformation of all academic disciplines and religious practices is necessary.[37] Church

and academy will be changed into institutions that cease to produce misogynist theologies of exclusion and one-sided malestream
knowledge only if and when they allow for the full intellectual
participation and decision-making citizenship of wo/men.

Wo/men's theological silencing and exclusion from the academy is only one side of the story. The other side is the "dangerous
memory" of wo/men's religious agency as prophets, teachers, and
wise wo/men, not only in Christianity but also in Judaism, Islam,
and non-biblical religions. Such wo/men emerge from historical-
religious memory as paradigms for feminist theologians today.
Throughout the centuries, wo/men of Wisdom have not only been
victims of oppressive religions, they have also shaped and defined
biblical and other religions, although most often historical records
either do not mention them or refer to them as marginal figures.
The mere fact that the names of wo/men prophets, religious leaders, and wise wo/men have survived in antiheretical or colonial
records indicates that wo/men have always been religious leaders,
teachers, and theologians. It is this intellectual and theological
tradition of wo/men who have gathered around Wisdom's table
all those who have been excluded, marginalized, and dehumanized
that feminist liberation theologians seek to reclaim today. Both
sides of the story—that of wo/men's dehumanization, co-optation,
and silencing, and that of their courage and agency—must be held
together if wo/men are to find their intellectual theological voices
today.

Wisdom prospered their works by the hand of a holy prophet.
They journeyed through an uninhabited wilderness,
and pitched their tents in untrodden places.
They withstood their enemies and fought off their foes.
When they were thirsty, they called upon you,
and water was given them out of flinty rock,
and from hard stone a remedy for their thirst.

WISDOM 11:1–4 (NRSV)

The Works of Wisdom-Sophia: The Ambiguous Heritage of *The Woman's Bible*

CHAPTER 3

ADRIENNE RICH OBSERVES: "One serious cultural obstacle encountered by any feminist writer is that each feminist work has tended to be received as if it emerged from nowhere; as if each of us had lived, thought, and worked without any historical past or contextual present. This is one of the ways in which women's work and thinking has been made to seem sporadic, errant, orphaned of any tradition of its own."[1] Reading Mary Pellauer's dissertation on the religious thought of Elizabeth Cady Stanton, Susan B. Anthony, and Anna Howard Shaw provided for me a moment of recognition, a "breakthrough" experience, which in the early days of feminist theology was called a "click" or an "aha" experience. When I began to theorize the image of the *ekklēsia* of wo/men as a radical democratic biblical symbol in order to provide an alternative image to the then prevalent either/or dualistic choice—either exodus from institutionalized religion or defense of institutionalized religion—I was unaware that in its struggle for justice the suffragist movement had already developed the idea of democracy as a religious biblical vision. Mary Pellauer has made a convincing case that leading suffragists spoke of democracy in religious terms.[2]

Although they chose quite different political and religious paths, Pellauer argues that their struggles against misogyny and for justice were rooted in an ethos shaped by the conjunction of their sociopolitical analysis and their religious-moral perspective. Thus Anna Howard Shaw, for instance, even speaks of the democracy of the gospel:

> The democracy of the gospel must permeate the democracy of our land and we must learn that as the hand cannot say to the foot, or the ear to the eye—"I have no need of thee." Neither can the educated say to the uneducated—"I have no need of thee"; nor the rich to the poor—"I have no need of thee." Each has need of the other; each must live and grow together, or else the survivors must be chained to the diseased and corrupt body of the outcasts. We cannot separate ourselves from them.[3]

The Historical Location of Feminist Biblical Interpretation

As the historical theologian Elisabeth Gössmann has warned, we must not make the mistake of assuming that wo/men's biblical interpretation came into being only in the past twenty-five years.[4] The practice of wo/men's biblical interpretation is not merely a recent fashionable feminist trend but can be found in all centuries. Just as other oppressed people have done, so have Christian wo/men challenged religion and society, and attempted to change them. In the struggle they have always referred to the bible, quoting and relying on certain biblical texts in order to authorize their attempts at reform. Christian wo/men have pointed to the great female figures of the bible, especially the Israelite and early Christian prophets, in order to argue for their rights to education, to speak in public, and to be admitted to ordination. Through reference to sacred scripture they have legitimated their critique of exclusivist clericalism and societal exploitation. The abolition of slavery and the recognition of the human dignity of so-called savage people were preached by women as a biblical demand.

This type of use of the bible in liberation struggles either refers selectively to liberating biblical texts identified with biblical wo/men, or it uses biblical texts and images as part of the language of a liberation rhetoric. Since in modernity the bible was used in the battles against the emancipation of slaves, the suffrage of wo/men, and the recognition of the human dignity of colonized peoples, Western emancipation movements have again and again resorted to using and quoting liberating biblical texts. They have emphasized that freeborn educated clergymen and theologians have misused the bible in their own interests.

Conversely, the defenders of the status quo have also argued again and again from the divine authority of the bible. They have deemed those who have advocated radical equality and justice in religion and society to be either heretical or unscholarly and naive because they have attempted to question established dogmas, behaviors, thought processes, and argumentative patterns. In short, reactionary ecclesiastical and societal powers have supported attacks against the rights and human dignity of wo/men and other oppressed peoples with biblical quotations.

In the United States today, in the realm of politics, science, economics, and the church, voices again emerge to argue against the self-definition, self-determination, and equality of wo/men, homosexuals, and immigrants, and to insist on promoting the "biblical values" of the Western world. Kyriarchal biblical texts, that is, domination-legitimating texts, are preached from numerous pulpits and on fundamentalist television programs as the directly revealed word of G*d. The emancipatory struggles and liberationist intentions of feminists, workers, the homeless, or illegal immigrants are often denounced as "godless humanism" or "Western secularism," both of which allegedly undermine the basic Christian values of state and family.

Christian feminists use the same hermeneutical methods when they defend against such attacks with biblical quotations in order to avoid explicitly challenging the authority of sacred scripture. However, such an apologetics—which declares the antifeminist bible quotations to be "time conditioned," a misuse of scripture, or a false way of quoting the bible—misses the central problem of feminist biblical interpretation; it mystifies the fact that texts of sacred scripture can be used against democratic emancipation movements not just because they are understood wrongly but because they were originally written with the intention of inculcating kyriarchal relations of domination and to legitimate these relations as ordained by G*d. The bible as sacred scripture has sanctioned oppression throughout the centuries not just because it was falsely interpreted but because in many ways it preaches oppressive relations of domination and it has helped to form Christian identity decisively along those lines.

The problem that Christian feminist interpretation must confront, therefore, is a fundamental theological question: Does a conflict exist between being a wo/man and being a Christian? Is this a basic contradiction that can only be overcome if one of these poles of identity is relinquished for the sake of the other? Or is it possible that both poles— being a Christian and being a feminist—can be kept in a fruitful tension, so that my being a Christian supports my liberation struggle, and, conversely, my being a feminist supports my Christian engagement for the realization of justice and love? Christian feminist biblical interpretation has tended to respond to this question in two different ways, by declaring the bible to be totally patriarchal or by seeking to defend the authority of scripture over and against feminist attacks. However, neither a total rejection of it nor a feminist apologetics of the bible can foster a fruitful dialectical engagement with the biblical heritage, a spiritual heritage that does not necessarily undermine feminist liberation struggles against kyriarchal structures of oppression but can support them.

The story of feminist biblical interpretation can be told in different ways. *The Woman's Bible*, edited by the Anglo-American

Elizabeth Cady Stanton,[5] has always been an important starting point for contemporary feminist scholarship in religion, beginning with the first sessions of the American Academy of Religion's "Women and Religion" section. Yet *The Woman's Bible* was not the first or the only such feminist work. Recently Cynthia Scheinberg pointed out to me that Grace Aguilar (1816–47), a British Sephardic Jew, published in around 1830 a two-volume work, *The Women of Israel*, that predates *The Woman's Bible* by more than six decades.[6] For a symposium celebrating the centennial of *The Woman's Bible* in 1995, in Vienna,[7] Marie-Theres Wacker researched the history of biblical interpretation by German-speaking wo/men. She points out that in Germany the first woman to receive a doctorate was Carola Barth, who in 1908 was promoted with a dissertation in New Testament studies.[8] Hence, if I elaborate on this history here by focusing on the contributions of *The Woman's Bible*, this should not be understood as if only *The Woman's Bible* were significant.

Over the course of several years, in preparation for the one-hundredth birthday celebration of *The Woman's Bible* in 1995, I initiated and organized panel discussions to explore the critical dimensions of Cady Stanton's project. (These took place under the aegis of the Society of Biblical Literature's "Women in the Biblical World" section.)

This attempt to critically reflect on the ambiguous heritage of *The Woman's Bible* and to conceptualize it anew has engendered two new incarnations of *The Woman's Bible*. *The Women's Bible*, edited by Carol Newsome and Sharon Ringe, depends strongly on the model of Elizabeth Cady Stanton's *Woman's Bible*, but differs from it by including commentaries on all the books of the so-called Old and New Testaments, not just the passages on women.[9] Moreover, *The Women's Bible* has a similar theoretical framework as *The Woman's Bible* in that its editors explicitly invited each contributor to read biblical texts *as a woman*.

The second project, *Searching the Scriptures*, was edited by me and has appeared in two volumes.[10] It adopted a liberationist starting point, one that is critical of kyriarchal oppression and malestream theoretical frameworks of interpretation and seeks to recast the heritage of *The Woman's Bible*. *Searching the Scrip-*

tures was conceptualized as an international, interreligious, and interconfessional project. Although the work clearly speaks from a Christian feminist cultural place, it invited scholars with or without religious alliances to participate. The first volume discusses the hermeneutical and methodological problems of a critical feminist biblical interpretation. The commentators of the second volume do not limit themselves to the canonical writings of the Christian Testament but also interpret Jewish and extra-canonical writings of the time in order to critically analyze and explore them as biblical roots. The contributors to both volumes were chosen because they represent a broad spectrum of feminist theoretical perspectives and approaches, and not because they belong to a religious tradition.

African-American Wo/men's Interpretation

The first hermeneutical and methodological volume of *Searching the Scriptures* is dedicated to the memory of the African-American suffragist Anna Julia Cooper. Cooper was a linguist, writer, and teacher who was educated at the Sorbonne in Paris and known as a fighter for the well-being of her people. Her most important work, *A Voice from the South*, also appeared a little over one hundred years ago (1892). Cooper's essential contribution to feminist biblical interpretation consists, in my view, of her articulation of an inclusive vision and a radical democratic interpretive framework. Cooper not only emphasizes the right of wo/men to speak publicly but also stresses that the whole world needs to hear the voices of wo/men. In the passage quoted in the previous chapter, wo/men's struggles are linked with "every wrong that needs a voice." Since the world's vision has been one-sided, the world, like a man with one eye, has been limping along with a wobbling gait. When finally the bandage will be removed from the other eye, the whole body will be filled with light: "It sees a circle where before it saw a segment. The darkened eye restored, every member rejoices with it."[11] Such a vision is exceptionally important for feminist liberation hermeneutics, but it has not, in my opinion, been sufficiently explored in feminist theory.

However, Anna Julia Cooper was by no means the first American wo/man to argue for the right of wo/men to speak in public. The first American to do so probably was, as far as we know, Maria W. Miller Stewart, who spoke in Boston in 1832 before a mixed audience.[12] Miller Stewart was a freeborn black wo/man and impoverished household worker whose feminist speeches preceded those of the Grimké sisters by around five years. In her public addresses she challenged wo/men to organize, to become economically independent, and to get an education because they must know that knowledge is power. "Have the spirit of men courageous and daring without fear and unintimidated. Demand your rights and privileges. Know the reason why you do not get them. Exhaust them with your insistence."[13]

In a speech given in Boston in 1833, she defended the right of wo/men to speak publicly, and to fight for the liberation of slaves, by utilizing a reference to the leading wo/men of the bible.

> What if I am a woman; is not the God of ancient times the God of these modern days? Did he not raise up Deborah to be a mother and a judge in Israel? Did not Queen Esther save the lives of the Jews? And Mary Magdalene first declare the resurrection of Christ from the dead? . . . If such women as are here described have once existed, be no longer astonished then, my brethren and friends, that God at this eventful period should raise up your own females to strive, by their example both in public and private, to assist those who are endeavoring [against] the strong Current of Prejudice that flows so profoundly against us at present. No longer ridicule their efforts, it will be counted as sin.[14]

The point of departure for African-American wo/men in the nineteenth century was not primarily the struggle for wo/men's individual emancipation and personal self-development. Rather, African-American wo/men heard and read the bible in the context of their experience of slavery and liberation. The womanist ethicist Katie Cannon has underlined that in the last century racial slavery was the sociopolitical context not only of African-American but also of white malestream biblical interpretation. She identifies three ideological constructs that made it possible for white Christians to justify the chattel slavery of Africans. As property, slaves were seen as not fully human, as Africans they were classed as heathen savages to be saved through enslavement, and as Christians they were expected to believe that slavery was divinely willed in the bible.[15] Within this context, Africans used the bible as a "matrix" for the transformation of meaning. Sarah Parker Redmond summarizes their argument against slavery as follows: "God is our father and the creator of us all, whatever your skin color, your appearance, your race, or your country is. We are all equal in the sight of God."[16]

Just as Anglo-American suffragists did, African-American wo/men sought valorization and authentication from the bible. However, unlike white wo/men, black wo/men such as Maria Miller Stewart spoke from a doubly disadvantaged location. As blacks they had to address white audiences who doubted that African-Americans had the human capacity for learning and religious salvation. As wo/men they had to address audiences, black and white, who questioned both their ability to exercise authority and the legitimacy of their speaking in public.

Since slaves were prohibited from learning how to read and write, their biblical interpretation did not so much focus on the explanation of texts. Instead, they freely engaged the stories and images of the bible to illuminate their sociopolitical experience. Interpretation was therefore "controlled" by the freeing of the collective consciousness and imagination of the African slaves as they heard the biblical stories and retold them to reflect their actual situation as well as their visions for something different.[17] Such an Afracentric reading of the bible incorporates texts that affirm the dignity of the African person in the face of dehumanization, rejecting those texts that can be used to legitimize slavery. Read in the rhetorical space of the struggle for liberation from slavery, the bible offered enslaved Africans dignity, equality, and citizenship. "Redemption and salvation incorporated economic and political empowerment and a restoration to civil status."[18]

The womanist theologian Jacquelyn Grant has therefore justly emphasized that the source for the understanding of G*d and for the mission-consciousness of black wo/men in the nineteenth century was not primarily the bible.[19] Just as Maria Miller Stewart did, so other black wo/men spoke of the direct experience of the presence and powerful help of G*d or Jesus, and they read the bible in light of this experience. Since they read the bible in the context of their own experience of liberation they did not primarily criticize or defend biblical texts, but reclaimed the bible's authority in order to legitimate their own dignity and demands for justice.

It is this divine authorization that compelled African-American wo/men to transcend the limits imposed upon them by the kyriarchal gender-race-class system of slavery. The critical interplay between "spiritual" experience and authorizing interpretation of scripture leads to an implicit privileging of sociopolitical experience. The following much-quoted statement by Howard Thurman's grandmother, a freedwo/man who could not read or write, articulates how slave wo/men used their own experience as a critical measuring rod for assessing scripture:

> During the days of slavery, she said, "the master's minister would occasionally hold services for the slaves. Always the white minister used as his text something from Paul. 'Slaves be obedient to them that are your masters . . . as unto Christ.' Then he would go on to show how, if we were good and happy slaves, God would bless us. I promised my Maker that if I ever learned to read and if freedom ever came, I would not read that part of the Bible."[20]

On grounds of the experience of slavery, passages of scripture and their critical interpretation are shown to be either liberating or oppressive. Rejection of scripture is not total and does not apply to the whole of scripture but only to those parts, for instance the Pauline letters, that were experienced as oppressive. This hermeneutical principle of selection remained at work in the black church in America insofar as certain biblical texts were quoted again and again, preached and elaborated narratively whereas other texts were overlooked and not recognized. However, such a selective approach is hardly unique; it is a typical practice in all Christian churches and communities insofar as they generally do not read the whole bible from beginning to end but select only certain of its texts for proclamation in worship. Unusual and exceptional in this practice of the black church is only that Afracentric biblical interpretation measures all biblical texts against the principle of human dignity and social liberty for all people without exception. This selection principle allows one to reject texts which advocate oppression and slavery as not being the word of G*d.

The Woman's Bible

The second volume of *Searching the Scriptures*[21] is dedicated to the memory of Elizabeth Cady Stanton and especially to the anniversary of *The Woman's Bible*, which appeared in two volumes, in 1895 and 1899. The hermeneutic of *The Woman's Bible* grew out of the Anglo-Saxon wo/men's suffrage movement and its struggles. Elizabeth Cady Stanton insisted on the basic right of wo/men to interpret scripture; she also translated this demand into practice with the publication of *The Woman's Bible*.

In an article published in the *Woman's Tribune* on February 7, 1891, Cady Stanton argued that the American social order is segmented in four ways—it is divided into the areas of family, society, politics, and religion. By comparing these four domains to the four strands of a rope, she articulated a complex vision of wo/men's oppression:

> Here then is a fourfold bondage, so many cords tightly twisted together, strong for one purpose. To attempt to undo one is to loosen all. . . . To my mind, if we had at first bravely untwisted all the strands of this fourfold cord which bound us, and demanded equality in the whole round of the circle, while perhaps we should have had a harder battle to fight, it would have been more effective and far shorter.[22]

Religion is an important strand in the rope of kyriarchal oppression. Although in Cady Stanton's view every form of religion has degraded wo/men, it is especially biblical religion, she insists, that has kept wo/men in subjection throughout the centuries. Hence no serious reform of society in the interest of wo/men's emancipation will be successful if it does not seek to advance also the reform of biblical religions. If suffragists believe that they can neglect the revision of the bible because there are more pressing political issues at stake, Cady Stanton argues, then they do not recognize the impact of religion and the bible upon society, and their continuing power especially in the lives of wo/men.[23]

This critical feminist insight regarding the force of religion in wo/men's lives has been simultaneously espoused and neglected by the so-called second wave of the wo/men's movement in the last thirty years. Although feminists have indicted education, the law, and the academy as patriarchal institutions, they have not given up attempts to change them. Yet feminist discourses often see biblical religions as totally patriarchal and hence judge attempts to change theology and church as at best a waste of time and at worst a noxious collaboration with the enemy. Like Cady Stanton, they tend not to distinguish between emancipatory and reactionary forms or functions of religion and therefore take the oppressive character of religion for granted. Hence they do not see institutionalized religions as a feminist site of struggle for change. While feminist scholars in religion and theology carefully discuss and confront feminist research and theories in other disciplines and intellectual areas,[24] feminist scholars in other disciplines still fail to recognize religion and theology as significant areas of feminist struggle for wo/men's rights and full citizenship.

It was Mathilda Joslyn Gage who, in 1878, at the annual meeting of the National Woman's Suffrage Association, introduced a resolution which demanded the right of wo/men to interpret scripture. She maintained that this was a fundamental principle of the Protestant Reformation. She argued that the individual conscience and judgment used in the interpretation of scripture, which heretofore had been exercised by men alone, should now be claimed by wo/men. Since false interpretation of scripture gives wo/men only duties and responsibilities but no rights and power, it has humiliated and degraded "woman and humanity," she argued; therefore wo/men must insist that they have been created as free, responsible human beings, "equal to men in rights, powers, duties, and obligations."[25]

While Gage insisted on the fundamental right of Protestant

wo/men to interpret Scripture, Elizabeth Cady Stanton and the editorial committee she called together translated this demand into feminist practice by publishing *The Woman's Bible*. Seeking to respond to those who use the bible against wo/men's emancipation, Cady Stanton and her coworkers conceptualized their project in scientific terms—that is, in order to investigate and to elaborate accurately what the bible says about the subjection of wo/men. The impulse for the publication of *The Woman's Bible* derived from the realization that throughout the centuries the bible has been invoked both as a weapon against and as a defense for subjugated wo/men in their struggles for access to citizenship, public speaking, reproductive rights, theological education, and ordained ministry.

In these often bitter debates the opposing parties have claimed—and still do so today—biblical normativity and revelatory authority not only for and against wo/men's full ecclesial participation and religious leadership but also for and against the full citizenship of freeborn wo/men, for and against the emancipation of slave wo/men, for and against the rights of lesbians and gay men, as well as for and against economic equity for older or poor wo/men and their children.

Opposing sides in these debates have appealed—and continue to appeal—to the bible as the revealed "Word of G*d" for legitimating their arguments for and against wo/men's civil and religious emancipation. In short, *The Woman's Bible* and its interpretive traditions remain positioned within the space defined by kyriarchal argument and wo/men's apologetic responses to it, although the actual intention of Cady Stanton's "Revising Committee" was to produce a "scientific" commentary on the biblical passages speaking about wo/men, and hence to utilize a different hermeneutic.

In publishing *The Woman's Bible*, Cady Stanton sought to interrupt the conservative trend in the suffrage movement. The National Woman's Christian Temperance Union (WCTU) had adopted a suffrage plank and its members swelled the ranks of local and national suffrage associations. Cady Stanton tried to force the National American Woman's Suffrage Association (NAWSA) to engage in a public discussion of this conservative social trend, with its narrow political focus on the ballot rather than on a complete emancipation of wo/men from "the woman's sphere."[26]

In response to those who contended that a suffragist critique of the bible was a waste of time or a political mistake, Cady Stanton argued that one cannot reform one area of society without reforming all the others at the same time; since "all reforms are interdependent," one cannot attempt to change the law, education, and other cultural institutions without also seeking to change biblical religions.

Moreover, she insisted, it is important that wo/men interpret the bible because scripture and its authority is and has been used against wo/men struggling for emancipation. In addition, one must keep in mind that not only men but also wo/men have internalized misogynist biblical teachings as divine revelation. Hence she and her collaborators sought to utilize the historical-critical scholarship of the time to free wo/men from such false beliefs by proving that the bible is the word of men who have projected their own selfish interests onto it. In this view, texts that speak negatively about wo/men are either mistranslated, misinterpreted, antiquated relics of a past time, or they are not true because they contradict the principles of reason and science. Since throughout the centuries men were the bible's authoritative interpreters, wo/men must now claim their right to biblical interpretation.

Although *The Woman's Bible* had as its goal a revision of Protestant exegesis and dogma, the individual contributors to it took a diversity of hermeneutical positions. Some authors intended to eliminate all patriarchal biblical texts, others argued that such passages could still claim authority if they were read not only in a historical-critical but also in a feminist-critical way. Others rejected the historical critical methods of liberal Protestant exegesis and instead argued for esoteric interpretations such as astrology. Some attempted, with the methods of comparative religion, to undermine the conservative Christian doctrine of the divine truth and authority of the bible.

The Reception of The Woman's Bible

In the end, the project of *The Woman's Bible* proved to be very unpopular because of its radical political and theological implications. In fact, Cady Stanton's strategy backfired. Not only did she have great difficulty in finding contributors to her project of biblical revision, she also failed to garner sufficient support for it because of the fear that *The Woman's Bible* would engender an antisuffrage backlash in the churches. Rather than disturbing the alliance between nonreligious political pragmatists and religious conservatives, *The Woman's Bible* consolidated it. In 1886, NAWSA publicly distanced itself from the project. More importantly, as a consequence Cady Stanton's call for a feminist political engagement with biblical religion was widely disregarded not only in the nineteenth century but also by the second wave of the wo/men's movement in this century.

Nevertheless, *The Woman's Bible* was unpopular not only because of its political implications but even more so because of its radical intellectual perspective. Its hermeneutics sought to expand and replace the apologetic argument of other suffragists who maintained that the bible *correctly understood* does not preach wo/men's subordination. Because in their view the true message of the bible was obstructed by faulty translations and biased interpretations of clergymen, apologetic feminists argued that wo/men should learn the original languages in order to fashion their own interpretations. Although Cady Stanton agreed with them that the translations and interpretations of the bible reflected male bias, she nevertheless insisted that the bible has not just been misinterpreted but that it is in itself biased in the interests of men.

Over against those who held to the notion of plenary inspiration of the bible as the direct word of G*d, Cady Stanton stressed that the bible was written by men and reflects the male interests of its authors because "no man ever saw or talked with God." By treating the bible as man-made and not as a fetish, and by denying divine inspiration to its degrading ideas about wo/men, *The Woman's Bible* has shown more reverence for G*d than have the clergy or the men of the church. Hence *The Woman's Bible*, Cady Stanton insists, comes to the ordinary reader "like a real benediction." It tells her that "the good Lord did not write the Book."[27] If that is the case, every biblical statement that speaks about "woman" must be carefully analyzed and assessed with respect to its male bias.

Such a radical critical demythologization of the bible theoretically solidifies, however, a double dualism: it not only distinguishes between "good" and "bad" texts, it also works with a Western universalizing gender construct that understands "woman" as essentially different from "man." In following its example, feminist biblical interpreters have felt compelled to center their discourses on the significance of biblical authority and normativity for changing wo/men's societal and ecclesial positions without recognizing that gender is only one element in the operation of the multiplicative structural oppressions of wo/men.

Against the advice and opposition of her suffragist friends, Cady Stanton asserted the political importance of wo/men's biblical interpretation and therefore, together with her collaborators, initiated and completed the pathbreaking project of *The Woman's Bible*. Hence she deserves our respect and honor, although we must not forget that she could not overcome the limitations set by her race and class privileges. For, as Toni Morrison has argued so forcefully, racial ideology does not just have "horrific results on its objects" but also on the minds, imagination, and behavior of the masters who perpetuate it.[28]

Like other Anglo-Saxon suffragists and social reformers (and as we are today), Elizabeth Cady Stanton was very much formed and limited by her social status and class position. For her argument that elite wo/men's suffrage would buttress the numbers of Anglo-Saxon voters, she resorted to anti-immigrant sentiments and anti-Catholic prejudice. When she exhorted "American women of wealth and refinement" to action, she did not shy away from appealing to ethnic and racial prejudices: "If you do not wish the lower orders of Chinese, Africans, Germans, and Irish, with their low ideas of womanhood to make laws for you . . . demand that woman, too, shall be represented in the government."[29]

Moreover, unlike her contemporary Clara Colby, for instance, Cady Stanton did not concern herself with the problems of the working class or with the different needs and struggles of African-

American and Native American wo/men. Finally, *The Woman's Bible* uncritically repeats many of the anti-Jewish patterns and stereotypes so prevalent in Christian popular and scholarly discourses of the time. For example, Cady Stanton judges that the Pentateuch is stamped as "emanating from the most obscene minds of a barbarous age."[30] Her commentary to Numbers 31 crystallizes the anti-Jewish arguments which still influence Christian biblical interpretation:

> We see from this chapter that Jewish women, as well as those of other nations, were held in a condition of perpetual tutelage or minority under the authority of the father until married and then under the husband. . . . That Jewish men appreciate the degradation of woman's position is seen in a part of their service in which a man says on every Sabbath day: "I thank Thee, oh Lord, that I was not born a woman" and the woman meekly responds: "I thank Thee, oh Lord, that I am what I am according to Thy holy will."[31]

Although Elizabeth Cady Stanton and the white elite suffragist movement must be taken to task for their shortcomings and prejudices, we still need to honor, albeit critically, their contributions to the feminist movement and feminist thought. We must do so in the awareness that just as those of our foresisters were, our own visions and practices are partial and subject to kyriarchal deformations.[32]

The Ambiguous Inheritance of The Woman's Bible

I would like to summarize and crystallize the following four rather ambiguous arguments of Elizabeth Cady Stanton, which, as far as I can see, have determined all subsequent feminist biblical interpretation:

First: Wo/men have not only the authority and the right but also the duty to interpret sacred scripture and to investigate it critically as to its prejudices. For such a critical evaluation of the bible, Cady Stanton appeals to sound human reason, faith in progress, and the natural law of justice which is innate to the soul.

However, whereas feminist biblical interpretation today rejects for the most part Cady Stanton's faith in ongoing progress, many feminist interpreters still accept her appeal to "sound," "normal" feminine reason or "commonsense" feminine experience.

Second: If the bible is not the word of G*d but the word of man, it must not only be read with a critical feminist lens, it must also be investigated with objective scholarly methods as an historical and religious work. In this effort, however, Cady Stanton did not question but rather took over the rationalist positivism of the biblical scholarship of her time. Just as her opponents did, she preferred a literalist historical reading of the bible, since she feared that allegorical or metaphorical interpretations would explain away the dehumanizing impact of biblical texts on wo/men.33

Third: Cady Stanton argues for the necessity of feminist work on the bible because not only men but also and especially wo/men still believe in the supremacy of the bible and have internalized its authority claims. A critical interpretation of scripture is therefore not just a Christian but a feminist duty. However, Cady Stanton's negative judgment of the bible, which strongly influenced later wo/men's movements, prevented her from working positively with this insight. Consequently, the wo/men's movement as a whole has not avoided the danger of seeing religious wo/men as "bad feminists" and of accusing them of "false consciousness."

Fourth: The bible does not serve only religious but also and especially political right-wing interests that deny democratic rights and human dignity to wo/men. If wo/men want to change society and state, then they cannot stop before church doors. Bible, religion, and church are important institutions which must be changed.

In the last twenty-five years, feminist biblical scholarship has taken up these hermeneutical insights of Elizabeth Cady Stanton and explicated them in a theoretical fashion. Whereas established critical biblical scholarship has shown that the language and content of the bible is politically and culturally limited and conditioned, feminist biblical scholarship has especially pointed out that the bible is the word of men conditioned by a kyriarchal culture and functioning in its interests. Very different feminist analyses agree today not only that the bible is written in androcentric—or, better, kyriocentric—languages and symbols, but also that it is deeply entrenched in kyriarchal cultures and societies.

Contemporary feminist biblical scholarship has for the most part questioned not only Cady Stanton's positivistic and rationalist understanding of scholarship and progress but also her selective methods of interpretation and her piecemeal or cutting-up approach. Since texts are not simply androcentric but kyriocentric, feminist biblical interpretation, I have argued, should not limit itself to texts *about wo/men*, texts that have marginalized wo/men religiously and historically. Rather, we must recognize that all biblical texts are rhetorical texts which must be understood in terms of their sociohistorical situation. Finally, today feminist scholars in religion take it for granted that wo/men are not just objects of biblical studies but that they are subjects of biblical interpretation. Therefore they pay special attention to the processes of interpretation and their sociocultural locations.

Such attempts to appropriate Cady Stanton's achievement and to construct a positive history of feminist biblical interpretation on this basis, however, must not overlook or neglect the negative consequences that contemporary feminist biblical studies have inherited from *The Woman's Bible*. Such problematic aspects and prejudices must be exposed and critically appraised in and through a hermeneutics of suspicion. I would like to single out the following four points for further discussion:

First: Although feminist biblical interpretation has critically explored the assumptions of established biblical scholarship, it is still, for the most part, in danger of continuing uncritically the approaches and strategies of malestream biblical studies. This can be seen not only from the fact that the number of books about wo/men in the bible is again increasing rapidly but also from the fact that androcentric or kyriocentric language is still either seen as reflecting historical reality or understood in terms of a closed system of language. Although, in general, feminist scientific interpretation no longer concentrates on isolated texts about wo/men, it often fails to proceed to a kyriarchal critical analysis but tends instead to reify the linguistic and cultural kyriarchal constructions of the bible.[34]

Second: Cady Stanton's dualistic either/or alternative and hermeneutical pattern—either the bible is liberating or the bible is oppressive, either wo/men as Christians accept biblical authority or as feminists they must reject biblical religion—still dominates many feminist theological and hermeneutical discussions. This either/or alternative overlooks, for the most part, the tradition of a feminist liberation hermeneutics, a tradition which was elaborated by African-American wo/men in the last century and today is advocated by liberationist feminists around the world. Such a critical feminist hermeneutic of liberation does not only attempt to show why and how the bible has been and still is used as a weapon against the liberation of wo/men; it also attempts to ask positively whether and how the bible has served and still serves as authorization and means of survival in wo/men's struggles for the abolition of kyriarchal structures of domination.

This hermeneutical perspective on the bible has been emphasized again and again, especially by womanist scholars and wo/men of the so-called Two-Thirds World, because in a minority situation of rampant oppression, the bible and its interpretation have again and again functioned to express the affirmation of human dignity and rights for oppressed peoples. My own approach has taken up this hermeneutical challenge and theorized it in the context of a critical feminist theology of liberation.

Third: In my view, the most detrimental heritage of *The Woman's Bible* is its anti-Jewish framework. Negative commentaries about Judaism in *The Woman's Bible* are concentrated in discussions of the so-called Old Testament, especially in relation to the claim of the Jewish people to be the elect of G*d. This anti-Jewish tendency of *The Woman's Bible* has been taken up in this century and is still found in many scholarly and popular books, be they feminist or not.[35] However, it must not be overlooked that Cady Stanton does not set Christianity over and against Judaism in order to prove that Jesus and the early church were feminist, as has often been done by feminist apologetics that follow her lead.

Fourth: Equally disturbing is the negative impact that Cady Stanton's Anglo-Saxon elitism seems to have had not only on the history of the wo/men's movement as a whole, but especially on contemporary feminist theoretical frameworks. Such racist ethnocentrism is found especially in Cady Stanton's later writings. Since after the American Civil War suffrage was given to black and uneducated European immigrant men—"Patrick and Sambo and Hans and Yung Tung"—but not to wo/men of the upper classes, Cady Stanton again and again contrasts immigrant men with the educational refinements achieved by the white Anglo-Saxon Lady.

This racist and ethnocentrically determined rhetoric shows that Cady Stanton and other suffragists identified "woman" de facto with the educated Anglo-Saxon Lady, although they ostensibly claimed to demand universal rights for all wo/men. In Cady Stanton's later work, this ethnocentric framework is often connected with the ideology of "true womanhood" or with the theory that sex and gender determine the soul and the "essence of woman."

This feminist essentialism, which advocates an idealized female nature and a culturally defined feminine being as hermeneutical framework and key, still exerts a determining influence on feminist discussions and biblical interpretations today. This framework is continued and reified, for instance, in those feminist biblical interpretations in which "feminine" ways of writing, feminine virtues, and ideal femininity are taken as evaluative criteria or as hermeneutical frames of reference for feminist biblical interpretation. This "femininity" approach in feminist biblical studies has had and still has grave consequences insofar as it compels feminist biblical interpreters to adopt as their theoretical framework a dualistic notion of patriarchy rather than a complex analysis of kyriarchy.

The insight that Elizabeth Cady Stanton's work is both racist and egalitarian compels us to appreciate the political engagement of her work and at the same time warns us not to adopt the theoretical framework of *The Woman's Bible*, a framework which consists of a universalizing notion of womanhood and an essentialist construction of gender. Because of its concentration on "woman" and femininity, a feminist gender-based analysis that understands patriarchy as the domination of all men over all wo/men equally cannot foster a complex analysis of wo/men's oppression, an analysis which would be able to explore and to research the multiplicative structures of racism, class elitism, heterosexism, and colonialism.

A methodological approach which reads the bible "as a woman" or "from the perspective of a woman" remains equally caught up in such a dualistic gender framework. Interpretation of the bible from the perspective of "woman" or from a "feminine" point of view, therefore, cannot be automatically seen as a feminist interpretation. This approach does not question the culturally determined elite image of wo/men and cannot see wo/men who are multiply oppressed.

Instead of assuming the "common sense" notion that feminine ways of thinking and knowing are liberating, I continue to argue that a truly feminist biblical interpretation must explore methodologically and hermeneutically how the biblical texts about wo/men and the wo/men characters of the bible inculcate kyriarchal values and worldviews, and how they, as gender constructions, mirror and/or mystify kyriarchal relations of domination. However, one must not overlook the fact that one's own powers of imagination and fantasy are also kyriarchally damaged because wo/men—not only men—have internalized cultural and religious values of femininity.

If, however, neither "woman" nor "feminine essence" nor a dualistic gender framework can provide the epistemological basis and methodological approach for a critical feminist liberationist interpretation of the bible, then one must search for a different framework of interpretation which can historically articulate and methodologically explore the multiform differences between wo/men and within individual wo/men. As such an interpretative framework and epistemological approach I have advocated the image of the *ekklēsia* of wo/men, which is at once a feminist reality, construct, and vision. The concept of *ekklēsia* of wo/men— which is best translated as "congress" of wo/men and not as "church"—must not, however, be reduced to "wo/men-church" or be limited to wo/men. Rather, with this neologism I attempt to articulate a radical democratic vision as the basis and goal of feminist emancipatory struggles that seek to radically change kyriarchal society and church. A feminist biblical interpretation interested in liberation therefore privileges hermeneutical approaches and methods which are able to underscore not only the kyriarchal rhetoric of the bible and its interpretations but also the radical democratic biblical values and visions of the *ekklēsia* of wo/men.

It was Anna Julia Cooper and not Elizabeth Cady Stanton who in the last century articulated such a critical hermeneutical horizon. At a congress in 1892 she insisted,

> Let women's claim be as broad in the concrete as in the abstract. We take our stand on the solidarity of humanity, the oneness of life, and the unnaturalness and injustice of all special favoritism, whether of sex, race, country, or condition. . . . The colored woman feels that women's cause is one and universal and that not till the image of God whether in parian or ebony, is sacred and inviolable; not till race, color, sex, and condition are seen as accidents, and not the substance of life; not till the universal title of humanity to life, liberty, and the pursuit of happiness is conceded to be inalienable to all; not till then is woman's cause won—not the white woman's, nor the black woman's, nor the red woman's, but the cause of every man and every woman who has writhed silently under a mighty wrong. Woman's wrongs are thus indissolubly linked with all undefended woe and the acquirement of her "rights" will mean the final triumph of all right over might, the supremacy of the moral forces of reason, and justice, and love in the government of the nations of earth.[36]

Hence the radical democratic vision of the *ekklēsia* of wo/men continues the nineteenth-century vision of the African-American suffragist Anna Julia Cooper more than it does that of Elizabeth Cady Stanton. As Karen Baker Fletcher has pointed out, equality and freedom were not simply physical states or states of mind for this African-American theorist, but rather political-spiritual realities.[37] Cooper believed that democratic progress was "a shadow mark of the Creator's image" derived "from the essential worth of humanity." She envisioned a future for humanity governed by the principles of equality, freedom, and democracy, which she conceptualized as ontological universal aspects of human nature, "an inborn human endowment—a shadow mark of the Creator's image, or if you will an urge-cell, the universal and unmistakable hall-mark traceable to the Father of all."[38]

Cooper understands democracy in religious terms. She broadens the white suffragist ethos of struggle for full citizenship when she insists that democratic equality and freedom are G*d-given, inborn, ontological capacities of every human being regardless of race, sex, class, or country. Against those suffragists (Cady Stanton among them) who claimed democracy, equality, and freedom as the property of the superior races of Western European civilization, Cooper argues that these are inherent in the fact of being human and hence could never be suppressed. The key metaphor for G*d in Cooper's religious discourse, according to Baker Fletcher, is a "singing something" which in every nation cries out for justice. As Baker Fletcher puts it: "What makes one human is one's inner voice, the voice of equality and freedom that is directly traceable to God. The voice of God, in this sense, sings through the human spirit and calls humankind to action, growth, development and reform. There is movement involved in the act of vocalization."[39]

While my own radical democratic understanding of the ekklēsia of wo/men is theorized quite differently and speaks to a different rhetorical situation and historical context,[40] it is nevertheless a part of and continues this nineteenth-century tradition. Critics have not connected my work with this feminist tradition, however. Instead, my theoretical-theological framework and proposal is usually assessed as to whether and how much it is stamped by or in line with the intellectual tradition of the "great men" or "fathers" of hermeneutics, rhetorics, or dogmatics. Whereas reviewers have suggested that the intellectual framework of my work is articulated in dialogue with or dependence on one or another of the "masters" of hermeneutics, such as Gadamer, Bultmann, Ricoeur,[41] the Frankfurt School,[42] Dworkin,[43] or the American pragmatist philosophical tradition,[44] they have not inquired as to its intellectual "foresisters."[45]

Such an evaluation of feminist work in terms of malestream hermeneutical discourses not only neglects that feminists have independently and differently theorized many of the questions raised by postmodernism, it also overlooks that as a critical theoretical inquiry, feminist biblical hermeneutics must be evaluated in terms of its own theoretical frameworks and practical goals, which determine its selective use or "quilting" of those hermeneutical theories upon which it draws. By constructing the genealogy of feminist hermeneutics primarily in light of malestream biblical hermeneutics, or by spanning it into the procrustean bed of the "great fathers" of hermeneutics, feminist scholars are in danger of collaborating in the continuing kyriarchal silencing and marginalizing of feminist theoretical work.

The submerged and often forgotten feminist intellectual tradition of wo/men's religious agency in biblical interpretation, in which my own work stands, has claimed and continues to claim the authority and right of wo/men to interpret experience, tradition, and religion from their own perspective and in their own interests. This tradition has insisted again and again that equality, freedom, and democracy can not be realized if wo/men's voices are not raised or not heard and heeded in the struggle for justice and liberation for everyone regardless of sex, class, race, nationality, or religion. Although this feminist tradition of wo/men's religious authority and theological agency remains fragmented and has not always been able to escape the contextual limitations and prejudicial frameworks of its own time and social location, its critical knowledge and continuing vibrancy, I submit, remains nevertheless crucial for contemporary feminist theology and studies in religion.

In order to be able to transform kyriarchal religious and theological traditions of silencing, dehumanization, and exclusion, feminist theologians and scholars in religion—as I have argued in the preceding chapter—must remain resident immigrants or resident aliens in academy and church. We must resist the temptation to continue to be motherless daughters who are proud to be "firsts" among wo/men and to have sprung from the heads of the fathers.[46] To prove our intellectual brilliance and religious faithfulness by demonstrating our "fit" with malestream theories and theologies means to disqualify other feminist work, deprives us of our roots, and diminishes our power for change. White Western wo/men in particular must cease to perform the civilizing role of the White Lady, who is expected to mediate the cultural and religious kyriarchal knowledges of elite white Western Man. Only if we firmly plant our feet in a critical feminist hermeneutical and theological tradition that insists on the rights, dignity, and power of all will we be able not only to critically analyze the oppressive mind-sets and ideological frameworks of our academic or religious fathers but also to change them in the interest of every wo/man in the global city.

I love those who love me,
and those who seek me diligently find me.
Riches and honor are with me,
enduring wealth and prosperity.
My fruit is better than gold, even fine gold,
and my yield than choice silver.
I walk in the way of righteousness,
along the paths of justice,
endowing with wealth those who love me,
and filling their treasuries.

PROVERBS 8:17–21 (NRSV)

The Love of Wisdom-Sophia:
Biblical Interpretation as a Site of Struggle

CHAPTER 4

AS A LEGACY of suffragist interpretation of scripture in the last century, feminist biblical studies has inherited the Enlightenment's either/or paradigm: either scripture is oppressive or it is liberating. In its search for justice and liberation, feminist biblical interpretation thus confronts two seemingly contradictory hermeneutical insights. On the one hand, the bible is written in androcentric language, has its origin in the patriarchal cultures of antiquity, and has functioned throughout its history for inculcating misogynist mind-sets and oppressive values. On the other hand, the bible has also been experienced as inspiring

75

and as authorizing wo/men and other non-persons in their struggles against patriarchal/kyriarchal oppression.

Christian liberationist studies from the perspective of wo/men have underscored this latter point by stressing that the bible and religion have not served only to oppress wo/men. Rather, in the experience of their communities, religion and scripture have also authorized and energized wo/men in their struggles for liberation. Whereas those feminist scholars who seek to defend biblical religion tend to downplay its androcentric-kyriarchal character, postbiblical feminists tend to declare that the contention that the bible has been and is read by wo/men in a liberating way is an instance of "false consciousness." In one way or the other, feminist biblical studies still presupposes and continues to wrestle with this either/or alternative.

Feminist Biblical Interpretation as a Site of Struggle

A critical feminist interpretation for liberation, I have argued in my own work, must not deny this conflict but reconceptualize it as a site of struggle. Religion, theology, and biblical interpretation are best understood as feminist places of struggle over the production of either oppressive or liberative meaning and authority. Hence feminists in religion may neither abandon nor defend kyriarchal religions. Rather they must articulate the religious-theological agency of wo/men and their authority to participate in the critical construction and assessment of religious, biblical, and theo-ethical meanings. In reclaiming the authority of wo/men as religious-theological subjects for shaping and determining biblical religions, my own feminist work has attempted to reconceptualize the act of biblical interpretation as a moment in the global praxis for liberation.

Since it takes the contradictory feminist evaluation of the bible seriously, a critical feminist interpretation for liberation adopts a doubled strategy, arguing that the bible must be read in both a deconstructive and a reconstructive mode. To that end I have developed a hermeneutical model which employs seven and not just four[1] hermeneutical moments and strategies: a hermeneutics of experience that socially locates experience, a hermeneutics of domination, a hermeneutics of suspicion, a hermeneutics of assessment and evaluation, a hermeneutics of reimagination, a hermeneutics of reconstruction, and a hermeneutics of change and transformation. These strategies are not to be construed simply as successive and progressive but must be understood as corrective, repetitive and interactive.[2]

In addition, this critical hermeneutical model does not work simply with a dualistic and objectivist-positivist model of interpretation which understands the text as object and the interpreter as subject, or with a dualistic dialogical model, according to which the reader/interpreter "dialogues with" or is shaped by the text. Rather it adopts a process model of interpretation that has not just three[3] (interpreter, text, ideology) but four (interpreter, text, world, ideology) hermeneutical poles among which meaning circulates.[4] Hence the seven hermeneutical strategies work on all four levels of meaning. They moreover operate with a "doubled" historical rhetoric: on the one hand they target the language systems, ideological frameworks, and socio-political-religious locations of contemporary readers in kyriarchal systems of domination. On the other hand they investigate the linguistic and sociohistorical systems of biblical texts, and their sociopolitical worlds and symbolic universes, as well as their historical impact and effects.

These seven hermeneutical strategies of a critical feminist interpretation for liberation are rhetorical discursive practices which seek to *displace* positivist and depoliticized academic practices of reading, practices which seem to have gained ground even biblical wo/men's studies. In developing such a complex interactive model, I have sought to challenge the prevalent positivist ethos of biblical studies and its rhetoric of inquiry in order to transform both of them.

Consequently, a critical interpretation for liberation does not commence by beginning with the text and by placing the bible at the center of its attention. Rather it begins with a reflection on one's own experience and sociopolitical religious location. For such a reflection it utilizes a critical systemic analysis of those kyriarchal oppressive structures which shape our lives and which are inscribed in biblical texts and interpretations. When reading biblical texts, I have consistently argued, a critical feminist perspective must focus on those wo/men who struggle at the bottom of the kyriarchal pyramid of domination and exploitation. It must locate its hermeneutical "standpoint" with them because their struggles reveal both the fulcrum of dehumanizing oppression threatening every wo/man and the power of Divine Wisdom at work in our midst.

Hence a feminist critical interpretation for liberation insists on the hermeneutical priority of feminist struggles in the process of interpretation. It does so not only in order to be able to disentangle the ideological (religious-theological) practices and functions of biblical texts for inculcating and legitimating the kyriarchal order but also in order to identify their potential for fostering justice and liberation.[5] Biblical readings that do not prioritize wo/men's struggles against multiplicative oppressions but privilege the biblical text itself or malestream frameworks of interpretation cannot but be either recuperative or deconstructive.

Consequently, a critical feminist interpretation for liberation has to position itself within the theological paradigm shift engendered by critical theories and liberation theologies. This paradigm shift articulates, first of all, a change in the aims and goals of biblical interpretation and theology. The task of interpretation is not just to understand biblical texts and traditions but to change Western idealist hermeneutical frameworks, individualist practices, and sociopolitical relations. Hence liberation theologies of all "colors" take the experience and voices of the oppressed and marginalized, of those wo/men traditionally excluded from articulating theology and shaping communal life, as the starting point of hermeneutical reflection.

Long before postmodern theories, liberation theologies not only recognized the perspectival and contextual nature of knowledge and interpretation but also asserted that biblical interpretation and theology are—knowingly or not—always engaged for or against the oppressed. Intellectual neutrality is not possible in a world of historical exploitation and oppression. Yet such a position does not reinscribe Western dualism, as some postmodern critics have argued, insofar as it does not assume the innocence and purity of the oppressed. It moreover does not see wo/men as victims only but also as agents for change. Such a shift from a modern Western malestream to a critical liberation theological frame of reference seeks to engender a fourfold change: a change of interpretive assumptions and goals, a change of methodology and epistemology, a change of individual and collective consciousness, and a change of social-ecclesial institutions and cultural-religious formations.

If I were to identify a key interpretive metaphor for such a critical feminist approach, I would choose that of struggle. I remember quite vividly one of the many academic panel discussions on *In Memory of Her*, when the book was criticized for being either too "Germanic" because of its many footnotes, too difficult for students because of its scientific rigor, or too much tinged with "male" rationality. At the height of the discussion, an African-American woman in the audience got up to defend my work. "I don't understand what you all are complaining about," she chided my colleagues on the panel. "I'm only a first-year seminary student but I had no difficulty understanding the book. Although I had to look up many of the academic words, I could not put it down until I finished it. When I went off to college my mother told me, 'Believe in and respect yourself, stand up for your dignity and rights, and always remember the struggle.' Isn't that what the book is all about?" She had gotten it right! The notion of wo/men's emancipatory struggles for dignity, authority, and self-respect are key to the epistemological/hermeneutical frame of meaning that determines my work.

A critical feminist interpretation for liberation that reads the bible with the lens of and in the context of wo/men struggling for survival and for change, I continue to argue, must be distinguished from both a Christian "apologetic" feminist biblical interpretation and a dualistic academic gender studies approach. Popular and academic biblical readings by female readers, reading the bible "as a woman" and "from the perspective of woman," as well as biblical interpretation in terms of gender, are not simply identical with a critical feminist hermeneutics of liberation, insofar as these modes of reading do not problematize their preconstructed religious and cultural gender lenses of interpretation.

Liberation theologies of all kinds do not derive their lenses of interpretation from the modern individualistic understanding of religion and the bible; rather they shift attention to the politics of biblical interpretation and its sociopolitical contexts. Hence they must place wo/men as historical agents at the center of attention. To that end, one needs to develop and engage not only a deconstructive but also a (re)constructive methodology of interpretation.[6] The feminist coin, if it should retain its currency, must have two sides: deconstruction and reconstruction!

Site of Struggle Over Authority

It is this methodological contention and my attempt to displace the inherited feminist either/or approach by dialectically constructing, as a third term, "wo/men's historical agency" that has been most disputed. Since my critical hermeneutical model has sought to replace both malestream theological and positivist "scientific" authority claims with a critical feminist hermeneutical-rhetorical model of interpretation that engages in both deconstruction and reconstruction, it remains controverted. Objections against such a two-pronged critical feminist model of interpretation, which insists on both deconstructive and reconstructive movement, seem to be based on a basic misunderstanding of how I theorize a hermeneutics of suspicion.

For instance, Dorothy Lee has argued that a critical feminist liberation theological interpretation remains entrapped in the doubt and skepticism of the Enlightenment. She alleges that it moves from a "hermeneutics of suspicion" to a "reclaiming of the text" rather than starting with "reading a text naively, opening ourselves to its dynamic in the way children listen to stories."[7] Instead of putting the proverbial feminist label on all biblical texts "caution, could be dangerous to your health and survival", Lee seeks to rehabilitate the mode of "faithful" biblical reading, admonishes feminists to make a contribution to the renewal of the Christian tradition, and warns, "If we begin reading Scripture in a suspicious frame of mind presupposing its androcentrism (or whatever), our interpretation can become entrapped, at best in a 'neutral' reading that ignores the place of faith and the Spirit, and at worst in negativity, prejudice, self-projection, and the desire for control."[8]

Such a warning does not recognize that a "hermeneutics of suspicion" has its roots not in the rationalism but in the emancipatory struggles of the Enlightenment. It also does not discern that a "hermeneutics of suspicion" is inspired by Christianity's emancipatory impulses as well as by the theological acknowledgment of sinful structures and people. Moreover, Lee's warning overlooks the careful distinction between androcentrism/kyriocentrism understood as a symbolic/linguistic system and patriarchy/kyriarchy conceptualized as a sociopolitical system of dominations and subordinations. Since "androcentrism" is a property of biblical language, grammar, and text, feminist critical readings do not presuppose "androcentrism (or whatever)" but seek to recognize, analyze, and interpret it in the act of reading.

Mary Fulkerson in turn objects that a critical feminist approach is not able to respect the biblical interpretation of conservative wo/men because it rejects biblical texts and readings that advocate kyriarchal values. She alleges that a critical feminist hermeneutics operates with biblical essentialism, which in turn is defined as ascribing sexism to biblical texts; because of such essentialism it allegedly does not respect the positive "meaning making" of conservative wo/men who derive self-worth and respect from reading such biblical texts.[9]

This objection overlooks one of the key insights of a critical liberation hermeneutics. The Brazilian educator Paolo Freire pointed out long ago that the oppressed have internalized their own oppression and are divided within and among themselves: "The oppressed, having internalized the image of the oppressor and adopted his [sic] guidelines, are fearful of freedom. Freedom would require them to reject this image and replace it with autonomy and responsibility. Freedom . . . must be pursued constantly and responsibly."[10]

Since both the oppressed and their oppressors are "manifestations of dehumanization,"[11] the methodological starting point of a critical liberation hermeneutics cannot be "commonsense" experience alone—it must be systemically analyzed and reflected-upon experience. Since wo/men have internalized and are shaped by kyriarchal "commonsense" mind-sets and values, the hermeneutical starting point of critical feminist interpretation can

only be wo/men's experience of injustice as it has been critically
explored by a hermeneutics of suspicion in the process of "conscientization."

Insofar as biblical readings of conservative wo/men do not start
from a critical consciousness and with a critical feminist analysis
of kyriarchal sociopolitical and ecclesial-religious subordination
and wo/men's second-class citizenship, they tend to construe the
respect and dignity of wo/men in terms of their internalized cultural ideological frameworks of femininity and "true womanhood." Consequently, such conservative readings cannot but keep
the ideological structures of wo/men's oppression in place. By
continuing to insist that such readings are not feminist or liberationist and by disagreeing with their often antifeminist interpretations, one does not deny agency and respect to individual wo/men
but rather names these frameworks for what they are.

However, I agree very strongly with one point of this feminist
critique. Feminist biblical interpretation, I have argued for quite
some time, must shift its attention away from the kyriocentric
text to consider the ways wo/men read and internalize *authoritative* texts. This would enable wo/men to become conscious not
only of the ways their readings are determined but also of what
kind of values they internalize in the process of reading. As long
as scripture is used not only against wo/men struggling for emancipation and in support of kyriarchy[12] but also for shaping
wo/men's self-understandings and lives, feminist biblical interpretation must seek to enable wo/men to engage texts critically, to reclaim their own spiritual authority for adjudicating what they
read, and to value the process of biblical readings as a process of
conscientization.

Because Christians understand the bible as the revealed word
of G*d, readers of biblical texts learn early on to develop strategies of textual valorization and validation rather than hermeneutical skills for critically interrogating and assessing scriptural
interpretations and texts along with their visions, values, and prescriptions. If the literary canonization of texts in general places a
work outside of any further need to establish its merits on its own
grounds, the canonization of sacred scriptures as G*d's word in
particular generates even more uncritical acceptance. Canoniza-

tion compels readers to offer increasingly more ingenious interpretations, not only in order to establish "the truth of the text itself" or a "single sense" correct meaning of the text, but also in
order to sustain allegiance and submission to the authority of the
bible as sacred scripture.

People often take such teachings at face value. They are often
unaware that Christian churches which continue to insist on the
authority of the bible for Christian life and community face the
rhetorical problem of how such authority can be maintained in
the face of critical biblical studies. These studies have underscored
the bible's pluriformity, historicity, and "linguisticality," and have
proven its theological relativity and ideological function in the interest of relations of domination. Today, a Christian dogmatic
hermeneutic that many have internalized confronts the theological
problem of how to articulate revealed authority and authoritative
truth in the face of critical biblical scholarship. A theological
hermeneutic that intellectually rules out fundamentalist literalism
and plenary inspiration needs to come to terms with this challenge. If biblical norms and traditions are not only historically
conditioned but also distorted, then one must ask how one can
determine the normative truth of the bible or derive canonical
principles from a human document that is limited by its ancient
linguistic and historical horizon. It is not just feminist theology
that raises these questions. What kind of authority does the bible,
as a historically and theologically determined and limited book,
have for believing communities today?

At least since the last century, feminists have intensified this crisis of biblical authority insofar as they have pointed out that the
bible has been written not simply by human hands but by the
hands of elite men. Not only is it the product of kyriarchal past
cultures, but it has been used to instill the dehumanizing violence
of such cultures as the "word of G*d." Protestant theological
hermeneutics in particular, with its emphasis on *sola scriptura*,
faces this problem of how to articulate the authority of scripture.
As Mary Ann Tolbert has pointed out,

> For Protestants, the central and unavoidable problem-
> atic posed by the role of Scripture is its *authority* but

exactly what that authority entails varies from denomination to denomination and indeed is often a hotly
contested issue within denominations. . . . Scripture,
then, for Protestants becomes the primary medium of
communication with God; if Catholics commune with
God mainly through participation in the sacraments,
and especially the Mass, Protestants commune with
God through Scripture.[13]

If for Christians the bible is "not primarily a source of knowledge about" G*d but "rather a source for *experiencing*, hearing,
God or God-in-Jesus in each present moment in life,"[14] then the
question of criteria for judging the truth claims of such experiences becomes especially pressing. This question is not a problem
for Protestantism alone. Although traditional Roman Catholic
theology has insisted that the teaching authority of the church defines biblical norms and criteria, such an assertion does not provide a way out of the problem because the teaching authority of
the hierarchy remains bound to the norms of scripture. Hence
Protestant and Catholic theological hermeneutics have had to develop differing approaches to the problem of authority raised by
the insight into the historicity and linguisticality—the historical
and linguistic character—of scripture.[15] Approaches to the question of biblical authority vary not only in terms of confessional
dogmatics but also in terms of sociopolitical interests.

One widely known proposal holds that scripture itself, or the
canon as a whole, is the norm of truth; texts that mandate the
submission of slaves, for instance, are corrected by texts that
stress the dignity of people. Another approach isolates a canon
within the canon as the revealed center of scripture; the Pauline
teaching of justification by faith, for instance, is offered as such a
central canonical criterion of truth.

A third approach is that of the "hermeneutics of correlation,"
which seeks in a continuous to-and-fro to relate a particular
revealed principle within the canon to a particular ethical-
theological principle today. For instance, this interpretive strategy
correlates the critical-prophetical principle of scripture with the
feminist critical principle of wo/men's full humanity.[16] A similar

hermeneutical approach personifies the biblical text or scripture as a pilgrim who has been the conversation partner of believing communities throughout the centuries and still is so today.[17] Such a conversation between scripture and believer is ongoing, mutually corrective, and of reciprocal benefit.

It is obvious that my work joins the discussion on theological hermeneutics from an intellectual location within post–Vatican II European Catholicism, which is quite distinct from American immigrant Catholicism. After decades of resistance to critical biblical scholarship, the Council's document on *Divine Revelation* embraced critical exegesis with its attendant recognition of the linguisticality and historicity of biblical texts. This Vatican II document recognizes that the bible "*contains* revelation, namely in the form of a written record; but that not all of Scripture is revelation."[18] In line with Augustine and Thomas, Vatican II articulated a criterion that limits revealed truth to matters pertaining to salvation: the bible teaches "firmly, faithfully and without error that truth which God wanted put into sacred writings for the sake of our salvation."[19]

Although the Council "fathers" probably intended to state that the truth revealed in scripture for the sake of our salvation is comprehensive and sufficient, one can read this text against its grain as asserting that the theological criterion "for the sake of our salvation" allows one to measure everything said in scripture as to whether it fosters human—that is, wo/men's—well-being. It is obvious that such a formal evaluative criterion must be spelled out concretely in ever-new situations. A critical feminist hermeneutics of liberation reads "our salvation" to include wo/men's salvation. Therefore it insists that this criterion must be spelled out by feminist theologies in contemporary struggles for justice and liberation, recognizing at the same time that these feminist struggles are always already inspired by biblical and cultural notions of justice and well-being.

In the last analysis, my critical feminist lens is, strictly speaking, shaped neither by malestream Catholic nor by Protestant understandings of authority. Rather its chosen sociotheological location and hermeneutical starting point is liberationist and feminist. Neither the teaching authority of the Catholic hierarchy nor the Protestant principle of *sola scriptura*, in my view, have articulated "revealed truth" given for the sake of *wo/men's salvation*. Moreover, what is "revealed" for the sake of wo/men's salvation, liberation, and well-being cannot be articulated once and for all. The criterion of "wo/men's salvation" is principled and pragmatic at one and the same time. It is also a formal criterion that needs to be "spelled out" in ever new socio-political-religious situations of struggle. It is not inherent in the biblical text nor in the individual subjectivity of the reader but must be articulated again and again in the practice of biblical interpretation and within particular historical contexts.

In short, the principle for testing and assessing biblical texts and traditions is to be spelled out again and again in the context of actual religious experiences of liberation and particular struggles for wo/men's well-being. Historical and religious meaning is always sociopolitically constructed insofar as biblical interpretation is located in social networks of power/knowledge relations that shape society, university, and biblical religion. Hermeneutical theological discourses that remain unconscious of their rhetorical functions and abstracted from their socio-political-ecclesial contexts do not produce a more objective criterion of truth. Rather they are less critical insofar as they hide and deny the social constructedness and relativity of their claims to divine revelation.[20]

Hence I continue to insist that practitioners of a critical feminist interpretation for liberation must read the bible in the horizon of and with the *ekklēsia* of wo/men as their hermeneutical center. Wo/men have the authority to assess and evaluate scholarly interpretations and the biblical texts themselves. Such a stress on wo/men's authority and agency stands in tension with both traditional teachings on scriptural authority and the dominant positivistic paradigms of academic scholarship. It seeks to render problematic and undermine the doctrinal-theological, the scientific-historical/literary, and the cultural-postmodern models of reading.

By making conscious the fact that the dominant symbolic "frame of meaning" determining all readings is *kyriocentric*, a critical feminist interpretation seeks to empower wo/men as reading subjects who construct meaning while at the same time they become conscious of such a process of construction. By showing how gender, race, and class affect the way we read, a critical interpretation for liberation underlines the importance of the reader's particular sociocultural location. Reading and thinking in a kyriocentric—master/lord/father/husband—centered symbol system entices readers to identify not only with what is culturally "male" but also with what is elite male. Thus biblical readings intensify theologically wo/men's internalization of a cultural system whose misogynist, racist, and Western supremacist values alienate us both from ourselves and from each other if they maintain that all biblical texts are the inerrant word of G*d.

The feminist emancipatory tradition of religious agency, justice, and equality for wo/men, in which my own work stands, has claimed and continues to claim the authority and right of wo/men to interpret experience, tradition, and religion from their own perspective and in their own interests. This tradition has insisted that equality, freedom, and democracy cannot be realized if wo/men's voices are not raised or are not heard and heeded in the struggle for justice and liberation for everyone regardless of sex, class, race, nationality, or religion. Although this feminist tradition of wo/men's religious authority and theological agency remains fragmented and has not always been able to escape the contextual limitations and prejudicial frameworks of its own time and social location, its critical knowledge and continuing vibrancy remains, nevertheless, crucial for feminist biblical studies.

In short, a critical feminist model of reading for liberation engages in biblical interpretation not only as a theological but also as a cultural-religious practice of resistance and transformation.[21] To that end, not only does it utilize historical- and literary-critical as well as ideology-critical and theo-ethical evaluative methods which focus on the rhetoric of the biblical text in its historical contexts. It also employs methods of storytelling, role play, bibliodrama, poetry, pictorial arts, dance, music, and ritual for creating a "different" religious imagination.

By taking the experience and analysis articulated in feminist struggles for transforming kyriarchy as its point of departure,[22] feminist biblical interpretation claims the authority of wo/men struggling for survival and liberation for contesting the kyriarchal

authority claims and oppressive values encoded in Christian scriptures. Hence a critical feminist interpretation for liberation is akin
to the ancient sophialogical practice of "discerning the spirits" as
a deliberative rhetorical spiritual practice. As theological subjects,
wo/men, I continue to argue, must insist on their spiritual authority to assess both the oppressive as well as the liberating imagination of particular biblical texts. They must do so because of the
kyriarchal functions of authoritative scriptural claims that collude
with Western cultural discourses in inculcating inferiority, obedience, and subordination. By deconstructing the all-encompassing
religious kyriarchal rhetoric and politics of subordination, critical
feminist discourses are able to generate new possibilities for the
communicative construction of biblical identities and emancipatory practices.

Site of Struggle Over Language and Theory

Today the theoretical struggle over a critical deconstructive and
reconstructive feminist model of interpretation for the most part
does not center on theological hermeneutics but on issues of language and theory. Nevertheless, this debate revives again the inherited feminist either/or alternative but now does so on
methodological grounds. It insists that a truly critical feminist
hermeneutics must be deconstructive. Hence it rejects the positive
moment of reconstruction. Whereas I continue to argue that the
critical "feminist coin" must have two sides, a deconstructive *and*
a reconstructive one, the postmodern objection maintains that
any attempt to "reconstitute the world" (Adrienne Rich's phrase)
loses its critical edge and rehabilitates the andro-kyriocentric language world of the text. Any reconstitutive biblical interpretation
allegedly reinstates hegemonic kyriocentric discourses. Such an
objection seems to be based primarily on a misunderstanding of
the concept of a hermeneutics of suspicion as I have developed it.
At the same time it works with a different theory of andro-
kyriocentric language, as well as with a different understanding of
the relation between text and history. In order not to be accused of
building up a "straw woman" as a target for my argument, I will
refer to two concrete examples. Since I invited and published the

contributions of advocates of such alternative readings in the second volume of *Searching the Scriptures*, I hope my discussion will be seen as an attempt to sharpen the theoretical issues at stake rather than as a deconstructive critique of their work.

To begin with, the objection against the hermeneutics of suspicion is most succinctly stated by the Collective of the *Postmodern Bible*:

> The hermeneutics of suspicion remains very much a hermeneutics, that is, a mode of knowing that employs an ontology of discovery assuming that there is some order in the world that stands on its own and that can be discovered or at least approached by human knowing. Truth is something discovered by employing a hermeneutics of suspicion, wherein one is suspicious of the various disguises one can use to cover up and distort reality.[23]

However, this objection does not read a hermeneutics of suspicion as I have developed it, in terms of liberation theology. Such a hermeneutics of is aptly described by Stephen Breck Reid. He argues that the African-American community of slaves is a "stepchild" of the Enlightenment which

> constructs a world where the "natural" view is Euro-centric and the "natural children" are of European origin. . . . As the stepchildren of the Enlightenment African-American scholars/preachers employ a hermeneutics of suspicion to which they add hope. . . . The stepchild learns through deciphering texts and experience that the natural child's view of truth is based on a lie. . . . Their hermeneutics of suspicion formulates new readings to replace what the dominant group calls the "accepted reading." It clears away the debris of conventional reading and moves to a different style of deciphering.[24]

However, Breck Reid seeks to align such a hermeneutics of suspicion with the "masters of suspicion," Freud and Marx, as working away at the layers upon layers of cultural sediment which hide or repress a "deeper truth." In a similar fashion, as Laura Donaldson has pointed out, the gynecentric feminist reading approach developed by the literary critics Sandra Gilbert and Susan Gubar also follows in the steps of the "masters of suspicion." For Gilbert and Gubar, Donaldson states, "the masculinist literary tradition hides the feminine 'truth' of the woman's text palimpsest."[25] However, according to Donaldson, in their view such social or sexual repression has a positive function; it enables the female voice "to survive the crushing weight of an overtly hostile literary tradition."[26]

In distinction, my own understanding of a hermeneutics of suspicion does not just address the "lie" of dominant readings or seek to uncover a "feminine/female truth" in the text or the tradition. Rather it is predicated on the theorizing of kyriocentric language in sociopolitical, cultural terms. In my view a hermeneutics of suspicion does not have the task of unearthing or uncovering historical or theological truth but of disentangling the ideological workings of andro-kyriocentric language. Grammatically andro-centric language is not a closed system of signs but is historically and socially constructed. The term "grammatical gender" derives from the Latin *genus*, which means "class, kind, or category in general." The grammatical noun classification system masculine/feminine is said to have been introduced by the fifth-century Sophist Protagoras. If Protagoras had used a different classification system, such as, for instance, long/short, the devastating conflation of grammatical gender with biological sex in Western languages might have been avoided. Many non-Western cultures have grammatical systems that are not gendered but structured according to status or function.

According to the grammarian Dennis Baron, the association of grammatical gender with human generation was developed by medieval grammarians in Latin as "species,"[27] an association which later grammarians imposed on Old English by arguing for it in cultural-religious terms.[28] For instance, Baron quotes James Beatie's *Theory of Language*, published in 1788, which argues on theological grounds for the distinction of biological sex as the primary basis for noun classification:

> Beings superior to man, although we conceive them to be of no sex, are spoken of as masculine in most of the modern tongues of Europe, on account of their dignity; the male being according to our ideas, the nobler sex. But idolatrous nations acknowledge both male and female deities; and some of them have even given to the Supreme Being a name of the feminine gender.[29]

Or, to give another example of the sociopolitical and historical construction of language: in 1850 the British Parliament passed an act declaring that henceforth the pronoun "he" would be used as including reference to women as well as to men, thereby replacing the use of "they" as generic with the pseudo-generic "he."

This Western linguistic sex/gender system functions to reify and naturalize sociopolitical cultural gender constructs. In such a linguistic system, masculine terms function as "generic" language in which man/male/masculine/he stands for human *and* male whereas woman/female/feminine/she connotes only femaleness. Grammatically androcentric "generic" Western languages that are based on the classical grammatical systems of Greek and Latin explicitly mention women only as the exception to the rule, as problematic, or specifically as particular individuals. In all other cases one has to adjudicate in light of contextual linguistic markers whether wo/men are meant or not.

Kyriocentric language operates simultaneously on four discursive levels: the linguistic-grammatical, the biological-natural, the social-political, and the ethical-symbolic levels. The categories "man" and "woman" do not signify dualistic opposites or fixed linguistic gender slots but socio-political-cultural-religious discursive practices. Anatomical physical differences are discursively constructed and socially maintained as cultural sex differences. Different cultures construct the meaning of anatomical differences differently. For instance, one could argue that boy and girl children are physically more alike than are girls and nursing mothers. Moreover, biological differences would receive different signification if they were discursively constructed on a continuum rather than in terms of a dualistic classification.

Social relations that give rise to gender differences are relations of domination which are codified in language. In other words, the social world is determined by relations of domination; gender is an integral part of the relations of ruling that also ground other divisions such as class and race. Such kyriarchal relations of domination and subordination come to be understood as biological differences, as natural or G*d-given, because of the linguistic-symbolic processes that "naturalize" gender, race, and class differences and reify them into "commonsense" assumptions. They reinscribe again and again the cultural-religious prejudices and social-kyriarchal relations that in turn undergird their own disciplinary practices.

Moreover, Western androcentric languages and discourses do not just marginalize women or eliminate them from the historical cultural-religious record. They also construct the meaning of being "woman" differently. What it means to be female/woman/feminine does not so much depend on one's sex but rather on one's location in the socio-symbolic kyriarchal system of multiform oppressions. The meaning of "woman" is unstable and ever-shifting,[30] depending not so much on its sex/gender relation but on its socio-systemic contextualization.[31] The category "woman" today is used interchangeably with female/feminine and thus has become a "naturalized" generic sex-based term, although until very recently it was utilized as an appellation for lower-class females only. Today, the slippages, cultural constructedness, and historical ambiguity of the meaning of "woman" can be much more easily perceived with reference to the term "lady" than in the use of the term "woman." Since "lady" has been restricted to wo/men of higher status or educational refinement and has signified "true womanhood" and feminine refinement until very recently, it readily "reveals" its race, class, and colonial prejudice because a statement such as "slaves were not wo/men" offends "commonsense" meaning, whereas a statement such as "slaves were not ladies" seems to make perfect sense.

In Western kyriocentric language systems the lady/mistress/mother is the "other" of the lord/master/father, whereas all other wo/men who are marked as "inferior" by race, class, religion, or culture are the "others of the other."[32] Hence they are not mentioned in historical kyriocentric records at all. Read in a kyriocentric way, for instance, the famous text Galatians 3:28, which states that in Christ there is "neither Jew nor Greek, . . . slave nor free, there is neither male and female," is usually interpreted as referring to three different social groups: "Jew" and "Greek" are understood as religious-ethnic characterizations, "slave" and "free" as sociopolitical determinations, and "male" and "female" as gender designations. However, such a reading does not take into account the obfuscating strategies of kyriocentric language when it tacitly infers, on the one hand, that "Jew," "Greek," "slave," and "free" are terms referring only to men and, on the other, tacitly assumes that only the third pair, "male" and "female," refers to gender.

Moreover, reading "as a woman" perpetrates and naturalizes the notion that wo/men and men are essentially different and that masculine and feminine represent antagonistic or complementary archetypes of being human. In so doing, it reifies and stabilizes sociocultural gender constructs as natural, essential, or "G*d-given." Such a reading unifies and naturalizes gender identity by obfuscating or denying that the subjectivity of wo/men readers is traversed by multiple structures of oppression. For instance, Tina Pippin proposes to read the Book of Revelation in terms of gender:

> The ideology of gender in the text is a neglected area in studies on the Apocalypse, so a focus on gender and misogyny is partially justified by the history of the neglect of these topics. But in this reading for gender I am promoting a western, white feminist reading and hermeneutic. Gender oppression has to be linked with other forms of oppression that women experience. Since I am not Third World or living in poverty or in the midst of war, my voice is limited. In my gender analysis of the Apocalypse I cannot claim to speak for any women readers of this text except myself. The majority of women suffer multiple oppression—sexism, racism, ableism, classism, ageism, heterosexism, colonialism. I am not listing these oppressions just to be "politically correct." Rather, I am called by women of color to face my own role in their multiple oppressions and our mutual enslavement.[33]

This confessional statement at one and the same time assumes and elides responsibility for its construction of white elite woman's agency and identity as universal. It unwittingly reinscribes the privileged position of the white educated elite woman, the White Lady. It does so by privatizing and individualizing its theoretical "reading as a *woman*." Thereby it mystifies the fact that it produces its readings from the position of the White Lady for readers who are differently positioned in the kyriarchal systems of oppression.

Without question, every feminist voice is limited and none can speak for all wo/men, but insofar as we do speak we always speak to and seek to communicate *with* others. Hence feminist discourses must treat as problematic and critically explore the interests of white educated wo/men that are at stake in a one-dimensional gender reading "as a woman." Rather than, for instance, evaluating Revelation's depiction of Babylon and its destruction simply in terms of gender, one must explore why and how an identification with the image of Babylon, the Great City, could have had a liberating cathartic effect if the hearer or reader were, for example a Roman slave or a freeborn Jewish wo/man of the first century.

Pippin sums up her reading in this way: "Having studied the evils of Roman imperial policy in the colonies, I find the violent destruction of Rome very cathartic. But when I looked in the face of Rome, I saw a *woman*."[34] Gender remains the overarching lens of interpretation. The difference of meaning produced by feminist political interpretation that I have in mind comes to expression in Julia Esquivel's poem "Thanksgiving Day." When Julia Esquivel, a Guatemalan refugee, looks into the eye of Rome symbolized in Revelation 17 and 18, she sees the U.S. imperial power that has been so destructive of all native peoples.

> In the third year of the massacres
> by Lucas and the other coyotes
> against the poor of Guatemala
> I was led by the Spirit into the desert
> And on the eve
> of Thanksgiving Day
> I had a vision of Babylon:

the city sprang forth arrogantly . . .

Each day false prophets
invited the inhabitants
of the Unchaste City
to kneel before the idols of gluttony
money
and death:
Idolaters of all nations
were being converted to the American way of life . . .

The Spirit told me
in the River of death
flows the blood of many peoples . . .
the blood of the Indian's ancestors
who lived on those lands, of those who
even now are kept hostage in the Great Mountain
and on the Black Hills of Dakota
by the guardians of the beast.[35]

In short, a hermeneutics of suspicion, as I have developed it, investigates how the andro-kyriocentric text constructs, silences, eradicates, positions, and elaborates not only gender, woman, and the feminine but also other sociopolitical and cultural marginalizing or dehumanizing codes in the interest of maintaining kyriarchal oppressions. The hermeneutics of suspicion is an interpretive activity through which thinking "escapes the power of the linguistic even while it is itself linguistically constituted."[36] Hence a hermeneutics of suspicion interrogates not only the text but also the reader as to how each is linguistically constituted. It does not reduce text or reader to an ahistorical core—the "truth" or "human nature"—but seeks to understand both as produced in the context of kyriarchal relations of domination.

In sum, a hermeneutics of suspicion insists that practices of understanding "the world"—such as speaking, writing, reading, or reasoning—are never outside of language or outside of time and history; that is, they are never transcendentally located outside of "the world." Hence this approach focuses on the ambiguity and instability of grammatically gendered language and text, and works with a theory of language that does not assume linguistic determinism. Rather it understands language as a convention or tool that enables writers and readers to negotiate linguistic tensions and inscribed ambiguities and thereby to create meaning in specific contexts and sociopolitical locations.

In this understanding, language is not a straitjacket into which our thoughts must be forced, or a naturalized, closed, gendered linguistic system, but rather a medium that is shaped by its sociopolitical contexts, one which changes in different sociopolitical locations. This hermeneutical approach understands that grammatically androcentric language can function either as "natural," as gender-specific, or as generic-inclusive language. In their interactions with kyriocentric texts, readers decide how to read them in their specific sociopolitical situations and "ideological" cultural-religious contexts. How meaning is constructed depends not only on how one reads the social, cultural, and religious markers inscribed in the text but also on what kind of "intertexts," "frames of meaning," or "reading paradigms" readers utilize when interpreting linguistic markers and textualized symbols.

If texts are not "closed" systems that force readers into predetermined reading slots but rather invite readers' sociopolitical negotiations and (re)constructions of meaning, then the interpretation of texts depends greatly on readers' choices of intertexts, reading paradigms, and frames of meaning. Hence a feminist reading must first of all critically examine the inscribed sex/gender system of the text and deploy a hermeneutics of suspicion in order to analyze its inscription. Most readers negotiate texts in terms of a "commonsense" meaning of reality and language. The tendency to "naturalize" gender and to read it in terms of archetypal masculinity and femininity bespeaks such a hegemonic commonsense construction of reality. A *gynecentric* gender reading that simply seeks to replace or turn the hegemonic andro-kyriocentric interpretation of the world on its head cannot help but naturalize and reinscribe the very linguistic system that it seeks to undermine.

In *But She Said* I made a distinction between an understanding of language that is pragmatic-communicative and one that is deterministic, one which espouses a kind of textual positivism that is the mirror image of historical positivism. A deterministic theory of language understands the cultural asymmetrical sex-gender system that is reproduced in androcentric, grammatically masculine language as a self-contained and self-evident "given" linguistic structure. It identifies grammatical gender with natural gender and thereby reifies sociocultural gender constructs as natural, commonsense, and self-evident.

This distinction between two different theories of language presently operating in feminist biblical studies is of crucial importance if feminist biblical interpretation is not to lose its political power in the endless play of deconstruction. The Collective of the *Postmodern Bible* has objected, however, that I do not define my understanding of language as deterministic but instead use the characterization in a totalizing way. They suggest that I may be referring to a view of language as the ubiquitous framework and mediator of experience, a view embraced by a wide range of critics loosely grouped together as postmodernists.[37]

Against my claim that by employing a totalizing gender analysis certain feminist readings are in danger of reinscribing the feminine kyriarchal gender positions of the text, the authors of *The Postmodern Bible* object (in a somewhat un-postmodern fashion) that such readings are only descriptive but not prescriptive. Of course this skirts the issue, since every description inscribes a politics of interpretation. The question is not *whether* but *what kind* of politics a given interpretation reinscribes. In other words, there is no "innocent" description. The following three examples may help to clarify the issue.

In various publications, Lone Fatum has polemicized against one form of feminist historical reconstruction based on a hermeneutics of suspicion. She argues that the Pauline letters are not only written in androcentric language, but also are male communications to a male community, clearly defined by androcentric values and social conventions and organized in terms of social patriarchal structures. Fatum uses 1 Thessalonians as a prime example:

> Paul's man-to-man communication with his Thessalonian sons and brothers leaves no trace of Christian women's presence, let alone their status and activity as

free and active members of a democratic discipleship. An attempt to discover such a trace to reconstruct a discipleship of women cannot rely on the literary and historical evidence before us; it requires feminist creativity and wishful thinking. Such an approach, I submit, will have to do violence not only to the text of 1 Thessalonians but also to the whole androcentric construction of Christian consciousness which is intrinsically and inseparably bound up with the androcentric consciousness of patriarchal antiquity.[38]

The battle lines are drawn: any reconstructive attempt is declared to be "wishful thinking," to read the text against the grain is doing "violence" to the text, and historical "evidence" must be relied on and taken as "self-evident."

However, the contradictions in Fatum's text indicate that such a totalizing reading is not without fissures and problems. While at first Fatum asserts that in Thessalonica "there seem to be no women to silence and no women's active commitment to curb," she concludes

that the Thessalonian women converts of Paul's time— probably 49–50—were a homogenous group, conforming to patriarchal social custom and established gender ideology. . . . In relation to the community they seem embedded in men's life, just as in society in general their lives were embedded in men's lives. Thus we may conclude that although women were surely among the converts in Thessalonica, they were not among the brothers as members of the community. Because they were defined and qualified as women, they were not seen as Christians and their socio-sexual presence among the brethren was virtually a non-presence.[39]

We have come full circle. Malestream scholarship has always known that wo/men did not count—that, if present, they must have been there as wives, mothers, or daughters, because of and through their affiliation with men. Now this very same patriarchal assumption is argued in the name of feminist scholarship!

Fatum's "realistic" narrative covers over the contradictions in her texts and naturalizes the commonsense assumption that wo/men have no presence in their own right. The androcentric text becomes a script and blueprint of "how it actually was." The silences, gaps, omissions, and partial truths of the text are filled out with reference to the laws, habits, and practices of patriarchal society, which are taken for granted. Catherine Belsey has identified such a reading as "expressive realism," which reigns in the period of industrial capitalism.

> The strategies of the classic realist text divert the reader from what is contradictory within it to the renewed recognition (misrecognition) of what he or she already "knows," knows because the myth and signifying systems of the classic realist text re-present experience in the ways in which it is conventionally articulated in our society.[40]

For my second example I want to return to Tina Pippin's work, which is an original and creative attempt to reread the Book of Revelation in and through the unmasking of its gender codes. Nevertheless, Pippin remains within the naturalizing gender system when she identifies the book's female/feminine symbols and images—such as mother, whore, and bride—with "real women." She repeatedly states that she wants to focus on "real women" in order to uncover the misogynism of the text. However, she then goes on to read the female images of the Apocalypse as feminine archetypes[41]:

> I want to focus on the clearly identified women in the text who are destroyed and on the general "apocalypse of women" brought about in the utopian vision of the New Jerusalem. By the "apocalypse of women" I mean the misogyny and disenfranchisement that are at the root of gender relations, accompanied by (hetero)sexism and racism along with violence, poverty, disempowerment and fear. . . . The text of the Apocalypse, with its female archetypes of good and evil, virgin and whore is an account of a political and religious and also gender crisis of the end of the first century C.E.[42]

My objection to such an approach is not directed against a deconstructive reading that brings to the fore the gender inscriptions of the text. Rather, my objection is and has been that such a deconstructive reading does not go far enough if it is combined with an archetypal structural reading that reinscribes and naturalizes the andro-kyriocentric feminine representations of the text as a self-evident and self-contained totality. By establishing a one-to-one relationship between female/feminine language and symbol on the one hand and actual wo/men on the other, Pippin's reading does not destabilize but rather literalizes the gender inscriptions of the Apocalypse. Although she recognizes the "mixed" character, for instance, of the image of Babylon, she nevertheless insists that it is the image of a "woman." Such a literalization and naturalization of the book's gendered images and language does not comprehend the vacillation and ambiguity of a text that slips and slides between feminine and urban characterization, between masculine and beastly symbolization, between images of war and justice, violence and salvation, defeat and hope, ethical struggle and divine predestination. It is this ambiguity and slippage inscribed in the text, I would suggest, that "reveals" an unresolved political, religious, and gender crisis at the end of the first century.

To reify such ambiguity into a closed system of antagonistic dualism produces a linguistic-religious determinism that does not allow for resistance and change. It ends up in the same place as a literalist religious, historical, or linguistic positivism does, one that negates the possibility of ethical decisions and resistance insofar as it does not leave a space for reading the Apocalypse "otherwise." Although Pippin delights in the postmodern language of multiplicity, surplus of meaning, and play of desire, her interpretation does not allow for a *different* feminist reading of the Apocalypse's symbolic world.

By contrast, a symptomatic reading in terms of the multiplicative sociopolitical and cultural-linguistic systems of patriarchal kyriarchy is able to reject the privatization of the female voice and to problematize the construction of wo/man's position as that of the White Lady. Hence the personifications of the female in the Apocalypse as mother, virgin, or whore must be considered problematic not only in terms of gender but also in terms of the systemic structures of race, class, and imperialist oppression. A systemic analysis can show that language does not produce and negotiate just *androcentric* but also *kyriocentric* relations of domination, not only *between women and men* but also *between wo/men and wo/men*. It is able to comprehend that in the Apocalypse, the sexual metaphor of "whoring" does not speak about a female person and actual historical wo/man but must be read as a conventional metaphor for idolatry, thereby "transforming" gendered language into language which needs to be scrutinized not so much for its misogynist but for its religious exclusivist bias.

To Speak from an Alternative Place

What is at stake in this argument between a purely deconstructive reading and one that insists on both deconstruction and reconstruction comes to the fore in the title of a splendid article by the feminist philosopher Andrea Nye, "The Hidden Host: Irigaray and Diotima at Plato's Symposium."[43] I am not concerned here with arguing that Nye's interpretation does more justice to the text than Irigaray's reading. Rather I am interested in arguing that we need both reading strategies if we want to see "the hidden host" who funds and caters biblical texts and interpretations. Such a combining of critical feminist readings does not seek to "uncover the truth" but to reinscribe the truth that feminist knowledge produces: wo/men are not and have not been an absence but a presence in all human affairs.

Both Nye's close reading of the philosophy of Diotima inscribed in Plato's text and Irigaray's deconstructive reading of Diotima provide a brilliant analysis of why a purely deconstructive reading is not able to comprehend Diotima's teachings. According to Nye, Diotima is not marginal or an anomaly in Plato's discourse if placed in her own historical context. Rather she is the "hidden host" of Plato's banquet who is speaking from a Minoan and pre-Socratic tradition of female power that was still alive in classical Greece during the time in which she lived. Nye insists that Diotima's philosophy of love must not be read in a Platonic fashion. Diotima's teaching of love differs, according to Nye, from both the "theory of forms" in Plato's *Republic* and from the "mystical Pythagoreanism" of the *Phaedrus*.

> Diotima sees bodily love as the metaphor and concrete
> training ground for all creative and knowledge-produc-
> ing activities. . . . The beauty-in-itself that the initiate in
> Diotima's philosophy may experience as the culmina-
> tion of her training is not a transcendent Platonic
> Form. The initiate glimpses no universal abstracted
> from imperfect particulars, but an indwelling immortal
> divine beauty, an attracting center that foments fruitful
> creation in all areas of existence. Diotima identifies this
> center with the pre-Hellenic Cretan goddess Eilethia,
> goddess of childbirth, and with her attendant spinner
> of fate, Moira (206d). To be in touch with this divinity,
> she says, is to live a new enlightened existence and to
> be a lover of the divine.[44]

Understood within this historical context, Plato turns out not
to be the founder of Western philosophy and thought. It is not
surprising, therefore, that classical scholars have preferred a different reading, one that understands Diotima as a Platonist. But
what is surprising, Nye points out, is that an astute feminist critic
would misread Diotima in the same fashion. For Irigaray, Diotima
is "not the mistress of her own home but an alienated troubler of
dichotomous categories" and her success depends "on being
clever enough to subvert Plato's logic." Irigaray's own commitment
to this "feminine operation," Nye suggests, "prevents her from
understanding Diotima's teaching and its relation to Platon-
ism."[45] In Nye's view, Irigaray cannot understand Diotima because of her ahistorical method of reading. However, the
assumption of feminine marginality and "lack" forms the conceptual infrastructure of her thought, which draws for its method on
Derrida and stages its readings on Lacan's ground.

Nye explicates the Sausurrian view of language as a system of
signs internally related, Derrida's method of the deferral of meaning, and Lacan's understanding of language not as a means of
communication but as entering "a fixed system of meanings"
which is structured around the Phallus and the "Name of the Father" as the master signifier. According to this theory, to which
Irigaray is beholden, there is no "reality" outside of language that

language may correctly or incorrectly represent. History, literature, culture, everything that is human is a text. Since there is no
non-textual situation and "no woman" outside masculine appropriation, Irigaray's method cannot comprehend that Diotima
speaks with her own authority. When applied to Diotima, Irigaray's method fails because there is no masculine presence nor
feminine absence to deconstruct.

> The a-historical character of Irigaray's intellectual in-
> heritance prevents her from seeing the difference. In
> Lacanian and Derridean metaphysics the distinction be-
> tween material and/or historical reality and the linguis-
> tic terms we use to interpret, represent or criticize that
> reality is dissolved. To learn to speak is not to learn to
> express sensations or articulate intersubjectively consti-
> tuted experience but to enter the world of the
> symbolic.[46]

In short, Nye ascribes Iriagary's failure to understand Diotima
differently to her adopted method of reading and the frame of
thought undergirding this method. A deconstructive reading á la
Derrida, Lacan, or Irigaray, Nye argues, is only able to crash and
parody the male text and tradition but cannot comprehend
wo/men as speaking subjects with authority and power. This
method of textual practice and its underlying theory of language
is very useful for deconstructive ends but cannot engage in reconstruction because it cannot speak from the alternative place of
wo/men's presence, authority, and power.

Critical feminist biblical interpretation, I have argued in this
section, must not only adopt a theory of language that allows for
wo/men's voice, creativity, and agency in interpretation—in speaking, writing, and reading. It also must be careful not to construe
malestream tradition and method as all-pervasive in a totalizing
fashion. This does not mean feminist interpretation cannot utilize
malestream methods and theories. It only means that it must do
so critically and eclectically, and integrate them into a feminist
method and theory based on wo/men's agency. Feminist historical
readings have the task of elaborating the assumption of wo/men's

presence in ever-new historical situations rather than positing "woman" as a lack or absence. However, feminist interpretation may not then turn around and understand the historical presence of wo/men in an essentializing fashion. Rather it must elaborate their presence and power in political-historical terms.

To sum up my argument, I have attempted to sort out the points of difference and disagreement between confessional theological hermeneutics, critical postmodern reading approaches, and a critical feminist interpretation for liberation. I have done so by staging a debate between various feminist biblical scholars and myself, using their critique of my work to clarify the issues. I was not so much concerned to show whether I believe their readings are right or wrong but to exemplify a critical instance of the debate in the *ekklēsia* of wo/men which discusses and deliberates the present and future welfare and well-being of all inhabitants of the global *polis*.

In my view, the feminist biblical scholar and historian must have the "perverse" will to "reconstitute the world with no extraordinary power" (Adrienne Rich's words). This, I suggest, constitutes the decisive point of difference between a critical liberationist and a critical postmodern feminist hermeneutics. The insistence on wo/men's authority for doing so marks the difference between a postmodern, a "confessional" theological, and a critical liberationist feminist hermeneutics.

Does not Wisdom call,
and does not understanding raise her voice?
On the heights, beside the way,
at the crossroads she takes her stand;
beside the gates in front of the town,
at the entrance of the portals she cries out:
"To you, O people, I call,
and my cry is to all that live."

PROVERBS 8:1–4 (NRSV)

The Public of Wisdom-Sophia:
Reading the Bible in a Global Context

CHAPTER 5

A CRITICAL FEMINIST INTERPRETATION must be both deconstructive and reconstructive at the same time. It must unmask both the kyriarchal discourses of contemporary culture and those of the biblical text itself; it must also rewrite them by asserting the presence and agency of wo/men in kyriarchal texts, cultures, and religions. With Alicia Suskin Ostriker, who identifies herself as "critic and poet, as Jew, woman, and (dare I say) human being," I would therefore insist:

I am engaged both theoretically and practically in the

question of what will happen when the spiritual imagination of women, women who may call themselves Jews or Christian, pagans or atheists, witches or worshippers of the Great Goddess, is released into language and into history. . . . I feel desperately fractured much of the time, as anyone in a pathological culture must. But I strive for healing. And so I must confront what is toxic—but I must do more than that.[1]

She goes on to argue for a revisionist reading of the bible that no longer posits a simple adversarial relationship between male text and female "re/writers" and points out that "woman's re-imaginings" of the bible are "both forbidden and invited by the very text and tradition" she is challenging. In her view, such a revisionist reading consists of "three sometimes overlapping forms: a hermeneutics of suspicion, a hermeneutics of desire and a hermeneutics of indeterminacy."[2] She reasons that a hermeneutics of desire can be characterized as "you see what you need to see," and has always been practiced by traditional biblical exegesis. She maintains that a hermeneutics of indeterminacy that fosters plural readings will be most significant for the future:

> Human civilization has a stake in plural readings. We've seen this at least since the eighteenth century when the notion of religious tolerance was invented to keep the Christian sects from killing each other. The notion of racial tolerance came later. . . . Most people need "right" answers, just as they need "superior" races. . . . At this particular moment it happens to be feminists and other socially marginal types who are battling for cultural pluralism. Still, this is an activity we're undertaking on behalf of humanity, all of whom would be the happier, I believe, were they to throw away their addiction to final solutions.[3]

Whereas in the preceding chapter I have argued that a hermeneutics of suspicion and reconstruction are the two sides of the same feminist coin, in this chapter I would like to approach the same question by utilizing two key concepts of Alicia Suskin

Ostriker—a hermeneutics of desire and a hermeneutics of indeterminacy. By reading them in conjunction with the notion of the *ekklēsia* of wo/men, I intend to investigate and contextualize a hermeneutics of desire in public biblical discourses and political struggles. I do so in order to explore the practical grounds and political limitations of a hermeneutics of indeterminacy. Such a hermeneutics, I argue, must be accompanied by deliberation and critical evaluation if it is to retain its subversive edge and engender transformation and change. For that reason, a hermeneutics of indeterminacy must position itself within the theoretical space of radical democracy which I have named the *ekklēsia* of wo/men, understood as a discipleship of equals.

Religious-Political Contextualization

Economists such as former U.S. Secretary of Labor Robert Reich have pointed out that it is not the erosion of American values but the depletion of economic resources that fuels the anxiety and insecurity of the American people. In his book *The Wealth of Nations*, Reich has argued that in a global economy only the upper, highly skilled fifteen to twenty percent of the population will be able to maintain the American dream, whereas the other eighty percent of all the world's citizens will more and more be relegated to the status of the working poor, the unemployed, and recipients of welfare.[4] For instance, I was told that in Manila two-thirds of the inhabitants live below the poverty line and thirty-five percent of them are slum dwellers, the majority of whom are wo/men and children dependent on wo/men. The economic and educational erosion of the "middle classes" engenders a similar economic-political situation around the world. The neocapitalist ethos of unrestrained profit increasingly draws the dividing line between the so-called First and Third Worlds, and between the haves and the have-nots, but now the gap between those living in the same city, county, or country becomes ever wider. In other words, my neighbor who works for an international computer firm has more in common with her counterparts in Europe, Latin America, or Japan than with the wo/man on welfare who lives three blocks away.

The response to the increasing economic insecurity and deadly

violence has been a global political shift to the right, which promises to mitigate public anxiety and insecurity by appealing to unacknowledged fears and scapegoating the weakest among us. The
severe crisis which confronts us today presents stark alternatives:
either we will be able to fashion a worldwide ethos and practice
of a radical democratic world community that is governed by the
economic-political well-being of all, or the global village will turn
into a tightly controlled dictatorship of multinational corporations, a dictatorship that concentrates all economic and cultural
resources in the hands of a few and relegates the majority of the
world's people to a permanent, impoverished, and dehumanized
underclass. In this struggle religion and church will either serve to
keep the "dream of freedom" alive before the eyes of the disenfranchised or they will be used to encourage a nationalistic
"bunker mentality" and for the abandonment of the disadvantaged by the well-to-do.

Many people around the globe experience the complexity of
their situation because of increasing globalization not only as very
confusing but also as very threatening, as a loss of the familiar
world. Fundamentalist discourses address this insecurity and anxiety by promising certainty in a sea of change, by delineating exclusivist group boundaries, by formulating clear-cut identities,
and by promising emotional stability in an ever-changing world.[5]
To that end they stereotype "others" as deviant and rigidly defend
their own prejudices as "orthodox" tradition. By identifying "the
enemy" and scapegoating the "other," they seek to alleviate their
own helplessness in a world that seems to be coming to an end.

How then is the bible read in such a global context? How
should it be studied and used? Those who quote the bible most
often are neoconservative Christians who read the bible in the
context of proliferating fundamentalist movements around the
globe. Such fundamentalist movements—whether the electronic
churches of the United States, technologically sophisticated Is-
lamic fundamentalism, the ultra-right movement of Rabbi Ke-
hane, biblicist and revivalist movements in Latin America,
emergent Hindu fundamentalism in India, or fundamentalist Shin-
toism in Japan—all exhibit common traits: they employ modern
media technology in very sophisticated ways and generally advo-

cate nationalist or religious exclusivism and the subordination of wo/men. While they embrace modern technological science as well as modern industrialism and nationalism, they reject many of the political and ethical values of modern democracy—basic individual rights, pluralism, freedom of speech, equal rights for wo/men, the right to housing, health-care, and work, equal compensation for equal work, social market measures, a democratic ethos, sharing of power, and political responsibility.

However, such a biblicist fundamentalism not only reads the bible with the theological lenses of individualized and privatized bourgeois religion, it also militantly asserts that its approach is the only legitimate Christian way of reading the bible. It thereby neglects not only the fact that different Christian communities and churches use the bible differently but also the fact that throughout the centuries different models of biblical interpretation have been and still are being developed by Christians. Although such literalist biblicism berates mainline churches for succumbing to modernity and secularization, it has adopted its particular, equally modern understanding of religion and the bible as the only approach that is truly Christian.

Right-wing fundamentalist interpretations of scripture set out to produce feelings of security and certainty by asserting philological, historical, or theological literalism—a form of positivistic scientism—which rejects hermeneutics and stresses verbal inspiration. Doctrinal literalism understands the bible as the direct, inerrant word of G*d which Christians must accept without question. This emphasis on verbal inerrancy asserts that the bible and its interpretation transcend ideology and particularity. It obscures the interests at work in biblical texts and interpretations and reduces faith to intellectual assent rather than a way of life. Such revelatory positivism promotes belief in the bible rather than faith in G*d.

Although fundamentalism combats modern liberal religion, it is itself a modern phenomenon. Insofar as it seeks to recreate inside the religious world all that is no longer viable in the outside world, it offers a modernist integrative meaning system within the process of globalization that dislocates traditional worldviews and belief systems. As the sociologist John Coleman puts it, "The challenge is to see how fundamentalists have entered an important vacuum of meaning about globalization as a process and about the particular identities of peoples and nations and societies as this new inter-dependence grows devoid of any deeper meaning system."[6]

This situation, which is determined by the increasing globalization of poverty and the fundamentalistic response to it, cries out for alternative liberating biblical readings. Is biblical scholarship able to step into this ever-larger vacuum of meaning and hope generated by a globalization process that relativizes the particular identities of peoples, societies, and nations? As this new global interdependence grows, it summons Christians to overcome their exclusivist parochial identity formations and, together with other religious people, to articulate a religious vision that can contribute to a world vision and discourse of radical democratic human community and well-being for all.

In a global situation in which venture capitalism and information highways exist side by side with tremendous poverty, all religious persons are challenged to articulate and realize a liberating spiritual vision of justice. Feminist biblical interpretation must participate in weaving together the heterogeneous strands of the emancipatory visions of the world's religions into a multicolored tapestry of different ethical-religious spiritual visions. The field of biblical studies must be rethought in such a way that it can contribute to the articulation of spiritual understandings that envision human dignity, justice, inclusivity, and diversity in new ways.

Otherwise, the postcolonial moment that demands the transformation of Eurocentric cultural canons, North-American political hegemony, and Western Christian supremacy is in danger of being subverted by the forces of dehumanization. Such forces include not only the capitalist processes of economic and cultural colonization, ethnic cleansing, and divisive balkanization but also religious fundamentalist exclusivism.[7] In attempting to find resources and criteria for biblical spiritual visions that can meet this challenge, feminist biblical scholarship must steadily focus its hermeneutical gaze on the struggles of wo/men at the bottom of the global kyriarchal pyramid of oppression and begin by affirming the knowledges of every subjugated wo/man around the globe.

However, biblical scholarship, I submit, is not equipped to address this global crisis of meaning because it has its roots in the individualistic and relativistic discourses of modernity,[8] and shares with fundamentalism modernity's positivist scientific and technological character. In spite of its critical posture, academic biblical exegesis is, in a certain sense, akin to fundamentalism insofar as it insists that scholars are able to produce scientific, true, reliable and non-ideological interpretations of the bible. They are able to do so as long as they silence their own interests and abstract from their own sociopolitical situations. Insofar as academic scholarship insists that it has methods that produce scientific certainty and can isolate the "facts" or the universal "truth" from the bible's multivalent and often contradictory meanings, it denies its own particular hegemonic perspectives and indebtedness to the European Enlightenment. By objectifying and privatizing scripture it is in danger of playing into the hands of fundamentalist biblicism. Thus "scientific" positivist biblical studies in their modern historical or literary textualist forms are not able to provide an alternative interpretive frame of meaning to that of fundamentalist biblicism.

Instead, a critical feminist interpretation for liberation, I suggest, can provide such an alternative because it does not understand biblical texts in positivist but rather in rhetorical terms. Such a critical rhetorical understanding of interpretation investigates and reconstructs the discursive arguments of a text, its socioreligious location, and its diverse interpretations in order to underscore the text's oppressive as well as liberative performative actions, values, and possibilities in ever-changing historical situations. It understands the bible and biblical interpretation as a site of struggle over authority and meaning. Its hermeneutics of desire seeks for radical democratic biblical visions that will contribute to the fashioning of a spiritual vision of liberation. For, as Alicia Suskin Ostriker suggests, there are such visions to be found:

> It is a common dream, sprung from an old promise.
> For the Moses of Exodus exclaims, "Would God that
> all the Lord's people were prophets" (Numbers 11:29).
> If the Bible is a flaming sword forbidding our entrance
> to the garden, it is also a burning bush urging us to-

ward freedom. It is what we wrestle with all night and from which we may, if we demand it, wrest a blessing.⁹

The biblical political vision of the *ekklēsia* of wo/men and the associated theological notion of a *discipleship of equals* aims to articulate and theorize a hermeneutical center for such a critical biblical reading.

A Hermeneutics of Desire: The Discipleship of Equals

If the vision of the *ekklēsia* of wo/men—understood as *the congress of full decision-making citizens*—is to articulate a sociopolitical religious horizon for biblical interpretation, it must be spelled out both in sociopolitical and cultural-religious terms. *Ekklēsia* is not just a Christian religious notion; rather it expresses a sociopolitical radical democratic vision. The expression does not refer primarily to "church" but seeks to convey the notion of radical democracy. This egalitarian vision has never been fully realized in history since in Western traditions wo/men have not been accorded full citizenship and self-determination.¹⁰

Thus the radical democratic belief that all are created equal, together with the notion of the *ekklēsia* as the *decision-making congress/assembly of full citizens*, stands in conflictive tension with the reality of classical and modern kyriarchy.¹¹ This alternative vision of *ekklēsia* understood as radical democracy—"as the form of politics that brings people together as citizens"¹²—becomes embodied and realized again and again in debates and emancipatory struggles to change relations of domination, exploitation, and marginalization. This same tension between radical democratic and malestream kyriarchal socioreligious visions and projects still comes to the fore in the linguistic notion of "church."

The Greek word *ekklēsia* is usually translated as "church," although the English word *church* derives from the Greek word *kyriakē*—belonging to the lord/master/father/husband. Accordingly, the translation of *ekklēsia* as "church" is misleading. *Ekklēsia* is best rendered as "democratic assembly/congress of full citizens." The translation process which transformed *ekklēsia*/democratic assembly into *kyriakē*/church, indicates a history that has privileged the kyriarchal/hierarchical form of church over that of a democratic congress or discipleship of equals.

Thus the word *church* in English entails two contradictory meanings: one derived from the patri-kyriarchal household of antiquity which was governed by the lord/master/husband/father, to whom freeborn women, freeborn dependents, clients, workers, and slaves (both women and men) were subordinated. The other meaning of church— *ekklēsia*—connotes the equality of its members in terms of citizenship and friendship. This meaning of "church" evolves from the vision of democracy in antiquity and modernity.

Does the democratic vision of radical equality still surface as a "dangerous memory" in a critical feminist reading of scripture? Do biblical theologies offer a religious vision and communal practice of radical democracy that can intervene in, inspire, and empower these struggles? This is the key question, I submit, that feminist and other liberation theologies must urgently raise today in the face of increasing global exploitation and religious dogmatism.

Together with the neologism *ekklēsia* of wo/men, the notion of the *discipleship of equals* as I have developed it in my own work aims to articulate such a biblical vision. It seeks to overcome the separation between church and world by theorizing a radical democratic vision of society and church which is rooted in biblical traditions. The modification of the word "discipleship" with that of "equals" must not be understood as advocating sameness under the guise of universality. Rather it seeks to underscore *equality in diversity* as the central ethos of discipleship.

However, to construe the relation between the *ekklēsia* of wo/men and the discipleship of equals as a simplistic continuity overlooks the creative space in between the reality and the vision or interpretive center and normative horizon inhabited by the *ekklēsia* of wo/men. It also does not appreciate the contradiction and conflict between egalitarian practices of community and the dominant reality of patriarchal kyriarchy.112

Only a theoretical model that comprehends the ongoing conflicts and struggles between the vision and emancipatory practices of radical democracy, on the one hand, and those of kyriarchal social systems on the other, I argue, is able to make visible or conscious the submerged knowledges of the oppressed and to provide for a fragile historical continuity of emancipatory struggles. Indeed, feminist emancipatory biblical studies must be positioned within both this history of conflict and struggle for human freedom, dignity, and well-being (the *ekklēsia*) and the biblical vision of the basileia, G*d's different society and world without poverty, hunger, suffering, homelessness, murder, and injustice.

If one wants to speak of a discipleship of equals, one has to argue that wo/men have both equal status, dignity, and rights as images of the Divine and equal access to the multifarious gifts of the Spirit, Sophia. Each and every person enriches the discipleship community of equals with different experiences, vocations, and talents. In short, the notion of discipleship of equals seeks to map a radical democratic vision and reality that articulates an alternative to biblical kyriarchal structures of domination.

Reconstructions of the Jesus movements in Palestine have underscored that these movements are best understood as inner-Jewish emancipatory movements that proclaimed the gracious goodness of the Sophia-Creator G*d who wills the well-being of everyone without exception. Well-being and inclusiveness are the hallmarks of the gospel, that is, the good news. As far as we can still see, the followers of Jesus did not all conform to the kyriarchal ethos and structures of their own society and religion. But neither did they all conform to a radical democratic ethos, for the texts that transmit this ethos are frequently prescriptive texts indicating that not all the disciples observed such a radical ethos of equality.

The inclusive ethos of the Jesus movements allowed wo/men, the poor, the rich, and the cultically unclean as well as strict observers of the Torah to become disciples. Wo/men such as Mary of Magdala were among the most prominent and faithful in this discipleship of equals. So-called church fathers still acknowledge Mary of Magdala as a key apostolic witness when they call her the "apostle to the apostles."

This ethos of the discipleship of equals was antipatriarchal insofar as it required the breaking of household relationships. Those who followed the Jesuanic *basileia* vision were promised a new familial community in return.[13] This new "family" of equal disciples was prohibited from calling anyone "father" (Mt 23:8–11) or according status on the grounds of motherhood (Lk 11:27–28). Insofar as this new familial community has no "fathers" it implicitly rejects patriarchal socioreligious power and status.

Rather than reproducing the kyriarchal status relationships of the household in antiquity, this ethos of the Jesus movements demands a radical break with them. The child or slave, who occupied the lowest place within ancient kyriarchal structures, becomes the primary paradigm for true discipleship. Such discipleship is not measured by the honor and respect given to the father/lord/master position but by that of the child/slave, as is stressed in the paradoxical Jesus saying "Whoever does not receive the *basileia* of God like a child/slave shall not enter it" (Mk 10:15). This saying is not an invitation to childlike innocence and naiveté but a challenge to relinquish all claims to the power of domination over others.

The actual political context of the Jesus movements' good news about G*d's different society and world was the Roman form of imperial domination. Whereas the "pax romana," the "new world order" of imperial Rome, created opportunities for people in the cities of the empire, it intensified the colonial oppression of rural populations.[14] The colonial situation of first-century rural Palestine was characterized by the tension between the urban ruling elites, aligned with the Roman occupation, and the ninety percent of the rural population whom they exploited through heavy taxation. The Jesus traditions are best contextualized in a situation of colonial oppression that favored the Herodian or Roman elites and exploited the bulk of the people.[15]

In this sociopolitical colonial context the Jesus movements proclaimed a radical Jewish democratic vision. It is the vision of the *basileia*, of G*d's alternative society and world that is free of domination and does not exclude anyone. The term *basileia*, usually translated as "kingdom" or "rule," belongs to a royal-monarchical context of meaning that has as its sociopolitical referent the Roman empire. But *basileia* is also an ancestral symbol of Second Temple Judaism and so appeals to the democratic traditions of ancient Israel.[16] These traditions, which are located in the prophetic milieu of the north, assert a democratic counter-meaning to the royal meaning of the term. According to these northern traditions, Yahweh saved the children of Israel from Egypt (Josh 24:7) and made a covenant with the people (e.g., Ex 3:9–13), who are called "a *basileia* of priests and a holy nation" (Ex 19:4–6).[17] These traditions are critical of kingship and monarchy (cf. the Jotham fable in Jgs 9:8–15). Because monarchy engenders militarism, economic exploitation, and slavery, they regard it as a rejection of G*d's commonweal (1 Sm 8:1–22). By asking for a human king (1 Sm 12:16–20), the people have rejected G*d, who liberated and delivered them from "all the kingdoms that have oppressed" and "saved [them] from all their misery and distress" (1 Sm 10:17–27, especially v. 18f; Hos 8:4, 9:15). In this tradition, kingly rule or *kyriarchy* is not a divine but a human institution.[18]

However, the proclamation of the basileia of G*d[19] did not allude only to a range of ancestral democratic-religious traditions which proclaimed G*d's liberating power. It also functioned as an anti-imperial political symbol that appealed to the oppositional imagination of Jewish and other peoples victimized by the Roman imperial system. The gospel of the *basileia* envisioned an alternative world free of hunger, poverty, and domination. It summoned the people in the local villages, the sinners, tax collectors, debtors, beggars, prostitutes, and all those wo/men exploited and marginalized (Mt 15:24, 10:6). Its *shalom*, that is, its liberation and salvation, was at work in the healing and liberating practices of the Jesus movements, in their inclusive table-sharing as well as whenever the disciples practiced domination-free kinship relations. In distinction to democratic forms of Greco-Roman kyriarchy, the ethos of the Jesuanic *basileia* movements did not secure their identity by drawing exclusive boundaries but by welcoming all the people of G*d, even tax collectors and sinners,[20] as children of the Divine Creator, Wisdom.

Traces of the discipleship of equals that surface as "dangerous memory" in a critical radical democratic reading of the Jesus traditions are also inscribed in the Pauline correspondence. Although they are articulated here differently, they still indicate that the ethos of the discipleship of equals was also at work in the *ekklēsia*—the public assembly or congress of the Christ movements in the Greco-Roman urban centers. The key symbols of their self-understanding were *soma*, or body/corporation of Christ/Messiah, and *ekklēsia*, or democratic assembly.[21] Both terms evoke an emancipatory political symbolic universe and vision. The metaphor of the messianic body must not be understood in anthropological individual terms.[22] Rather it is best contextualized within the popular political discourses of antiquity, which understood the *polis* or city state as a "body politic"[23] that has a multiplicity of members who are different but interdependent.[24] The metaphor of the body (*soma* in Greek, *corpus* in Latin) describes "being in Christ" with the political language of the day. A translation that seeks to explicate the sociopolitical language of the text would read as follows:

> For just as the *soma* [or corporation] is one and has many members, and all the members of the [corporation], though many, are one [corporation], so is it with Christ. For in the one Spirit we were all baptized into one [corporation]—Jews or Greeks, slaves or free [both wo/men and men]—and we were all made to drink of one Spirit. (1 Cor 12:12–13)[25]

In the messianic body politic all have equal access to the gifts of the Spirit. This equality in the Spirit does not mean that all are the same. Rather, the gifts of the members vary and their individual functions are irreplaceable. Yet no one can claim to have a superior function because all functions are necessary and must be equally honored for the building up of the "corporation."[26] Solidarity and collaboration are the "civic" virtues in the political order (*politeuma* of Christ), which is best characterized as a "pneumatic" or "charismatic" democracy.

"In Christ"—that is, in the body politic, the messianic sphere of power—socioreligious status inequalities no longer pertain. Equally, social status inequalities and privileges between Jews and Gentiles, Greeks and barbarians, slave and free—both women and men—are no longer defining those who are "in Christ" (Gal 3:28).[27] Those within the Christian (that is, messianic) movements in Greco-Roman cities understood themselves as equally gifted and called to freedom. G*d's Spirit was poured out upon all, sons and daughters, old and young, slaves and free, both women and men (cf. Acts 2:17–18). Those who have been baptized are "pneumatics," that is, spirit-filled people (Gal 6:1). They are a "new creation"(2 Cor 5:17). They are all called, elect, and holy, adopted children of G*d.[28] All without exception: Jewish, pagan, slave, free, poor, rich wo/men, those with high status and those who are "nothing" in the eyes of the world. Their equality in the Spirit is expressed in alternating leadership and partnership,[29] in equal access for everyone, Greeks, Jews, Barbarians, slaves, free, rich, poor—both wo/men and men. They therefore call their assembly with the democratic name *ekklēsia*. Such a political elaboration of the *ekklēsia* seeks to defend against the common idealistic misunderstanding fostered by the Book of Acts that all conflicts ceased and all were "one heart and one soul."

The full decision-making assemblies of Christians who were exiles and resident aliens in their societies (1 Peter 2:11)[30] and constituted a different political order (*politeuma*) (Phil 3:20) met in private houses. House-churches were crucial factors in the missionary movements insofar as they provided space and actual leadership in the Spirit.[31] Women played a decisive role in the founding, sustaining, and shaping of such house-*ekklēsiai*. They could do so because the classic division between private and public spheres was transformed in the *ekklēsia* that assembled in the "house." In the Christian *ekklēsia* the private space of the house is the public sphere of the *ekklēsia* -church.

Christians were neither the first nor the only group who gathered together in house-assemblies. Religious cults, voluntary associations, professional clubs, and funeral societies, including the Jewish synagogue, gathered in private houses. These organizations did not adopt the structures of the patriarchal household but utilized rules and offices of the democratic assembly—the *ekklēsia* of the *polis*. Such assemblies were often socially stratified but conceded an equal share in the life of the association to all their members.

Just like other private associations, the Christian *ekklēsia* was considered with suspicion and as potentially subversive to the dominant kyriarchal-imperial order of Rome.[32] Insofar as the Christian associations admitted individual converts as equals, independent of their status in the kyriarchal household, membership in the Christian *ekklēsia* often stood in tension with the structures of household and state. Such hegemonic kyriarchal structures were legitimated in the first century especially through Neoplatonic[33] and Aristotelian political philosophy. These philosophical legitimizations found their way into Christian scriptures in the form of the so-called household code texts, which are kyriarchal injunctions to submission.[34]

The contradiction between Greco-Roman sociopolitical structures of domination and the radical democratic vision of the *ekklēsia* as the "alternative discipleship community of equals" and G*d's "new [social] creation" engendered struggles for liberation in the past and still does so today. The struggles of freeborn wo/men and slave wo/men to maintain their authority and freedom in the Christian *ekklēsia*, therefore, are to be seen as an integral part of the struggle between the emerging Christian movement and its vision of equality and freedom, on the one hand, and the kyriarchal ethos of the Greco-Roman world advocated by other Christians, on the other.[35] As those with kyriarchal interests gained more power and influence, freeborn wo/men's and slave wo/men's leadership in the *ekklēsia* —envisioned as a charismatic democracy—was partially submerged again, transformed or pushed to the margins of malestream churches.[36]

Like that of the *basileia*, so too the democratic construction of the Christian *ekklēsia* constitutes a partial reality and provides an enduring vision. Such a radical democratic vision of the discipleship of equals is not simply a given fact, nor is it just an ideal. Rather it is an active process[37] moving toward greater equality, freedom, and responsibility as well as toward communal relations free from domination. All wo/men silenced and marginalized by kyriarchal-hierarchic structures of domination are crucial in this *ekklēsial* process of radical democratization inspired by the *basileia* vision of a society and world free of exploitation, domination, and evil.

In sum, early Christian discourses still allow one to glimpse the practical and theological struggles of wo/men who sought to realize the radical democratic religious vision of the discipleship of equals in a sociopolitical and religious context of Roman colonial imperialism. Such a reconstruction in terms of a hermeneutics of desire must, however, not be misunderstood as a factual transcript of egalitarian Christian beginnings or as a theological legitimization of Christian origins. Rather it must be seen as a *reconstitution* of those early Christian beginnings that have engendered radical egalitarian Christian visions and movements throughout the centuries. The reality of the discipleship of equals is already and not yet. It is the eschatological project of the *basileia*, the intended society and world of G*d, which must be realized again and again in and through the continuing struggle against the dehumanizing kyriarchal powers of oppression which are theologically named as structural sin.

However, one would be ill-advised to tackle the question as to whether scripture supports a radical democratic church, society, and the full citizenship of wo/men in an apologetic fashion. For it is not possible to "prove" methodologically that the bible advocates egalitarian democracy rather than kyriarchal monarchy since both forms of social organization are inscribed in the sociosymbolic universe of biblical writings. Contrary to popular opinion, the bible does not speak for itself. Rather, interpretations of biblical texts and reconstructions of early Christian history are shaped by the contemporary interests of the biblical historian, theologian, or general reader just as much as they are by historical realities. For our experience functions as what the anthropologist Clifford Geertz calls a model of reality.[38] The notions and beliefs we hold today inform how we read the texts of the past.

Without such "alternative" models or "imaginative designs" we would have no basis for comprehending the past, which requires interpretation. It is not simply there in the text, waiting for us to discover how things really were or what Jesus really said. In other words, those biblical interpreters who favor a "discipleship of equals" model of church will emphasize the radical democratic elements inscribed in biblical texts and those who favor a "hierarchical" one will stress the kyriarchal aspects advocated by biblical writers. Interpreters can do so because variations of both models of church are inscribed in biblical traditions and available as models of reality for today.

As the controversies around *The Woman's Bible* and the resulting either/or feminist alternative have shown, it is important, however, for such a hermeneutics of desire that it does not fall into the trap of apologetic defense, which does not change the assumptions and frameworks of its opponents but seeks to refute them without changing the terms of the argument. What is crucial, therefore, is that a hermeneutics of desire rewrite biblical discourses in such a way that the terms of the debate are shifted and a new approach is staked out. For that reason a hermeneutics of desire needs to be balanced by a hermeneutics of indeterminacy lest it be construed in a fundamentalistic theological or positivistic historical-textual fashion. In the following section I will stage such a hermeneutics of indeterminacy with reference to a particular text, the story of the Syrophoenician wo/man, in order to exemplify how biblical interpretation is understood as a debate within the *ekklēsia* of wo/men. I will do so in order to underscore the fact that the text's possibilities of interpretation and plurality of meanings call for a hermeneutics of critical evaluation.

A Hermeneutics of Indeterminacy: The Syrophoenician Wo/man

A cursory rereading of the story of the Syrophoenician wo/man (Mk 7) and its diverse interpretations may serve as an example for biblical interpretation as a site of struggle over meaning. My reading seeks to engage a hermeneutics of indeterminacy in order to engender a process of critical conscientization.

> From there he set out and went away to the region of Tyre. He entered a house and did not want anyone to know he was there. Yet he could not escape notice, but a woman whose little daughter had an unclean spirit immediately heard about him, and she came and bowed down at his feet. Now the woman was a Gentile, of Syrophoenician origin. She begged him to cast the demon out of her daughter. He said to her, "Let the children be fed first, for it is not fair to take the children's food and throw it to the dogs." But she answered him, "Sir, even the dogs under the table eat the children's crumbs." Then Jesus said to her, "Because of

this word, you may go—the demon has left your
daughter." So she went home, found the child lying on
the bed, and the demon gone. (Mark 7:24–30)

This text is best read as an *ideo-story*, whose "representational
makeup promotes concreteness and visualization" for rhetorical
ends.[39] Since the narrative of an ideo-story is not closed but open,
it allows readers to elaborate the main characters in an imaginative and typological fashion.

Whether one situates this story's rhetorical practice in the life
of Jesus or in that of the early church, or limits its present narrative context in Mark's or Matthew's gospel, Jesus is seen in the
story as engaging in an argument that discloses religious prejudice
and exclusivist identity because he is quoted as saying, "It is not
right to take the children's bread and throw it to the dogs." The
wo/man, in turn, is characterized ethnically and culturally as a religious outsider, one who enters kyriocentric theological argument, turns it against itself, overcomes the prejudice of Jesus, and
achieves the well-being of her little daughter.

Two different forms of this story are found in the gospels of
Mark and Matthew. It is absent in the gospel of Luke, even
though Luke is generally praised in malestream exegesis for favor-
ing stories about wo/men. In Mark 7:24–30 the wo/man's identity
is marked through linguistic-cultural (Greek) as well as national-
racial (of Syrophoenician origin) characterizations. The text does
not recognize the wo/man either by her own name or by that of
her father or husband. Rather she is characterized by her cultural,
religious and ethnic location as an outsider who enters the house
into which Jesus has withdrawn.[40] Her daring and disruptive ini-
tiative is fueled by her interest in the well-being of her daughter.
However, the story in its present form does not tell the miracle
but centers on the argument of Jesus rejecting the wo/man's peti-
tion because she is a cultural, religious, and national outsider.
Nevertheless the wo/man does not give in but takes up Jesus' in-
sulting words and uses them to argue against him. She wins the
controversy because Jesus, convinced by her argument (*dia touton
ton logon*), announces her daughter's well-being.

A critical-historical reading that traces the transmission of this story in the pre-Markan tradition makes it possible to see how rhetorical arguments may have shaped the genesis of this narrative. The story might have begun as a simple Galilean miracle story which was told about a wo/man asking Jesus to exorcise her daughter, with Jesus granting her request. In the process of the retelling of this miracle story at a second stage, the opposition between Syrophoenician/Greek/female on the one hand and Jesus/Galilean/male on the other was probably introduced. Moreover, the parabolic saying about food/children/table/dogs now plays on an "ironic" double meaning, in the case that Jesus speaks of street dogs and the wo/man of house dogs. The addition of this saying not only inscribes the opposition between Jew and Gentile, it also ascribes an offensive, exclusivist attitude to Jesus, an attitude that the argument of the Syrophoenician wo/man challenges and overcomes. At a third stage of transmission, this story probably was taken over by Mark and tied into the gospel narrative through the introduction in verse 24 and the qualifying addition of "first" in verse 27.

Another version of this story is found in Matthew's Gospel. In Matthew's version (15:21–28), the two protagonists remain embroiled in the argument about food/children/master's table/house dogs. Matthew changes the story's theological dynamics in significant ways both by adding the saying "I was sent only to the lost sheep of the house of Israel" and by identifying the disciples as those who want to get rid of the wo/man. Thus in Matthew both the characterization of the protagonists and the plot of the story are changed. The wo/man is consistently rebuffed not only by Jesus but also by his disciples. She is characterized with the archaic term "Canaanite," which reminds the reader of Israel's long struggle with Canaan's cultic heritage. The wo/man not only enters the public domain, but she does so speaking loudly. The Greek word for her public outcry, *krazein*, may also carry cultic overtones.

Matthew's text concludes with Jesus praising the wo/man's "great faith," and Mark's ends with Jesus announcing that her daughter is freed from the demon because of her word or because of her teaching. Although this is one of the few gospel stories in which a female character is accorded "voice," the final promise in both versions gives the last word to Jesus and underscores that the authority of these texts rests with the "master" voice of Jesus. Her argument serves to enhance its discursive resonance. Standard scholarly commentaries also tend to engage in an apologetic defense of the "master" voice of Jesus,[41] if they comment at all on the wo/man and her significance. Thus they not only amplify the marginalizing tendencies of the biblical text but also reinscribe it into critical scholarship.[42]

Read in a kyriocentric, that is, a master-centered frame, the story functions as one more variation of "woman" as outsider in the symbolic worlds and social constructions of male discourse. A substantial part of the Markan manuscript tradition seeks to portray the wo/man as an example of humble submissiveness by inserting "yes" into the text,[43] to play down the "but" of the wo/man, so that the text now reads, "But the woman answered and said, 'Yes, Lord'" (Mk 7:28). Moreover, both gospel texts contrast the wo/man outsider with the master figure of Jesus, who, according to Mark, has withdrawn inside the house, while in Matthew he is surrounded by his disciples. Whereas Matthew calls her by the antiquated scriptural name Canaanite, Mark elaborately characterizes the wo/man as a Greek who was a Syrophoenician by birth. Not only by virtue of her gender, but also because of her ethnicity and cultural-religious affiliation, the wo/man enters the site of canonical male discourse as a "triple" outsider.

HISTORY OF INTERPRETATION

The history of interpretation of this story is variegated.[44] To my knowledge, the first retelling of the story in the early church emerges in a lesser-known Jewish-Christian extra-canonical writing called the Pseudo-Clementine Homilies. The Pseudo-Clementine Homilies are thought to have been composed during the third and fourth centuries, but probably incorporate older traditions.[45] They tell the story of Clement of Rome, who accompanied Peter on his missionary journeys. In their retelling of the Syrophoenician wo/man's story (Ps. Clem. Hom. II, 19, 1–3), the wo/man, for the first time, receives a name. She is called in Latin "Justa," which means "the just one" and is characterized as a well-educated upper-class wo/man. In this version of the story, Justa is joined by the disciples in asking Jesus to heal her daughter. But Jesus replies in the negative: "'It is not permitted to heal the gentiles who are similar to dogs in that they use all kinds of food and do all kinds of things, since the table in the *basileia* is given to the children of Israel.'" The text underscores that the wo/man responds positively: "But hearing this she wanted to participate in the table like a dog, namely in the crumbs from the table, abandoned her previous customs, in that she ate in the same manner as the 'sons of the kingdom' and achieved, as she desired, the healing of her daughter." Although Justa does not persuade Jesus to change his prejudice, she is persuaded by Jesus to change her lifestyle. Justa converts to Judaism. She becomes the righteous one.

In the subsequent history of interpretation, two rhetorical strategies compete with each other. The *salvation historical* approach employs the allegorical method of interpretation. In this reading, the healing from a distance corresponds to the situation of the pagans, the dogs under the table are analogous to the gentiles, the children stand for Israel, the bread of the children signifies the gospel, and the table is sacred scripture. Such allegorical interpretations spiritualize and theologize the story in such a way that it can be read in a salvation historical sense. The wo/man is seen as a proselyte interceding for the salvation of the gentiles, who are saved not through the encounter with the historical Jesus but through his word. This interpretation carries anti-Jewish overtones. Whereas the Jews were the children and the gentiles were the dogs in the days of Christ, now, in the time of the church, the opposite is the case: the Jews have killed the prophets and Jesus, and have become dogs. Thus the salvation historical interpretation is closely intertwined with anti-Judaism.

While the salvation historical reading is anti-Jewish, the *exhortative* reading approach focuses on the paradigmatic behavior of the wo/man, especially on her exemplary faith, which is differently understood in different confessional historical contextualizations. Interpretations of the early church, in medieval times, and in the Catholic Counter-Reformation understand faith as a virtue that is expressed as modesty, perseverance, reverence, prudence, trust, and especially as meekness and humility. According to this interpretive strategy, the wo/man's faith comes to the fore as humbleness, especially in Mark 7:27, where she does not reject Jesus' calling her a dog but accepts it, saying, "Yes, Lord." Yet, whereas medieval exegesis thought that her humble behavior exhibited a "masculine" stance, modern exegesis stresses that her humble acceptance of grace expresses her "feminine soul." The Reformation also stresses the wo/man's faith but understands it as feminine surrender rather than as humility. Now the story becomes a doctrinal discourse on the topic of submissive faith. Faith consists in the unconditional surrender to the Lord, which expresses itself in repeated intercessions and persevering prayer. It consists in the recognition that the self is nothing except for its trust in Jesus, the Lord.

Finally, missionary discourses have underscored the wo/man's subservient behavior as an example to be imitated. In her new book *Discovering the Bible in the Non-Biblical World*, the Chinese scholar Kwok Pui-Lan, for instance, points to the use of this story for colonialist ends.[46] She highlights that just as the gentile wo/man, so also colonialized peoples were expected to be as subservient, obedient, and loyal as a "devoted dog would be." The Western feminine construction of the alien "other" relies on stories of biblical wo/men and the upholding of "feminine" virtues in order to inculcate Western values of domination. Moreover, Kwok argues, such a colonialist interpretation contrasts Jesus' attitude toward wo/men with the understanding of womanhood in non-Christian cultures in order to prove their inferiority and the superiority of Christianity. Such a colonialist use of biblical wo/men's stories parallels their anti-Jewish interpretation in Christian apologetic discourses.

CONTEMPORARY INTERPRETATIONS

Most contemporary commentators are troubled by the response of Jesus in Mark, a response that reveals his biased partiality. Their interpretations are concerned with changing the prejudicial tenor of the story by either declaring Jesus' response as historically inauthentic, by explaining away his religious-ethnic prejudice and exclusivity, by resorting to features of the Matthean version, or by adducing anti-Jewish or folklorist considerations. They argue, for instance, that Jesus did not intend to insult the

wo/man but only wanted to test her faith, that he rebuked her because he needed his meal and rest, that he was instructing his disciples and not the wo/man, that he muttered this harsh word
under his breath, or even that it was the wo/man who first mentioned dogs since she knew how Jews regarded her people, and
that Jesus merely responded to her own words. Others suggest
that the saying about children and dogs might have roots in rab-
binic oral teachings or reflect a Jewish proverb ordering who eats
first in a Jewish household. Some in turn explicate that Jesus used
the diminutive of "dog" (*kynarion*) in order to soften this allegedly widely known Jewish label for gentiles or that the wo/man
is thereby characterized as a cynic philosopher. All these arguments seek to diminish the insult of the saying on the lips of Jesus
by giving good reasons for Jesus' prejudicial words. In short,
rather than critically assessing and ethically evaluating the patriarchal politics of the text for Christian identity formation, they
try to explain away its cultural-religious bias.

   In *In Memory of Her* I have engaged in a *tradition-historical*
reading and proposed that the story's controversy is best situated
historically in Galilean missionary beginnings. Although the Syrophoenician respects the primacy of the children of Israel, she
nevertheless makes a theological argument against limiting the Jesuanic inclusive table-community to Israel alone. That such a historical argument is placed in the mouth of a wo/man gives us a
clue to the historical leadership of wo/men in opening up the
Jesus movement to gentiles. Thus the story of the Syrophoenician
makes wo/men's contributions to one of the most crucial transitions
in early Christian beginnings historically visible. Although I still
believe that such a historical reconstruction of an inner-Christian
debate about the mission to gentiles is plausible, I also need to
point out that it has been construed in an anti-Jewish fashion and
has been used for deflecting a critical theological discussion and
ethical evaluation of the prejudice and discriminatory stance ascribed to Jesus.

   The Japanese interpreter Hisako Kinukawa suggests a *cultural-
ethnic* contextualization. She reads the story of the Syrophoenician not within debates on the equal participation of gentiles in
early Christian beginnings but within Israelite purity regulations.

She does so in order to draw out parallels between the understanding of ethnic exclusivism and national integrity in first-century Judaism and in Japan today. Kinukawa rejects other feminist interpretations that emphasize the audacity of the wo/man and instead stresses her alien status. She points out that the Israelites "excluded foreigners from their ethnic borders in order to retain their purity of blood. . . . Geographically they were defenseless against foreign invasions and were invaded by one foreign power after another. Thus it seems natural for Jesus as a Jew to defend his people and not to want to dilute their ethnic integrity."[47] Yet, by drawing out the structural socioreligious parallel between the situation in early Judaism and that of contemporary Japan, the danger exists that, at least for Western readers, the Christian prejudice against Jewish purity laws will be reinscribed.[48] In Western contexts this interpretive strategy may serve, albeit unintentionally, in the interest of theological anti-Judaism.

A *sociohistorical* reading, as developed by the German scholar Gerd Theissen, in turn contextualizes the story of the Syrophoenician not in terms of early Christian theological debates or Jewish purity laws, but rather in terms of inner-Jewish ethnic and class conflicts. This socio-critical reading emphasizes that the story's first teller and audience were familiar with the tensions between Jews and gentiles in the villages of the Tyrian-Galilean border regions. The description of the Syrophoenician as Greek characterizes her as an educated upper-class wo/man who asks Jesus for help. This characterization underlines the "social" clash between her and Jesus, who is portrayed, by contrast, as an itinerant preacher and exorcist from the backwaters of Galilee.

In the context of such social status difference, Jesus' retort must have been heard, so Theissen argues, as follows: Let the poor people in the Galilean backwaters be satisfied, for it is not just to take away food from the poor people in the Galilean villages and to give it to rich gentiles from the cities. This reading situates the story of the Syrophoenician within an inner-Jewish debate, the conflict between poor Galilean villagers and rich gentile citizens. It does not exculpate Jesus, however, because he is still seen as expressing the resentment of the underprivileged population. By avoiding confronting ethically and theologically the prejudicial saying ascribed to Jesus, this reading ascribes it to the resentment of the underprivileged.

Whereas this sociocultural contextualization stresses the contrast between poor villagers and rich city folk, the *gender* reading of Sharon Ringe focuses on the wo/man as widow, divorcee, or never married, as totally alone and isolated from family support. When we meet her she is left with only a daughter who is a further liability in her society's terms. Nevertheless, for the sake of her daughter, the Syrophoenician breaks custom and stands up to the visiting rabbi and miracle-worker. Such a single-minded focus on gender relations rejects the interpretation of the original story in terms of either cultural, class, or early Christian missionary conflicts. Instead, Ringe argues that the story's significance is christological. The story could not have been invented by the church because of its shocking portrait of the man Jesus. Rather than inventing such a story, it is more likely that the early church tried to make the best out of a bizarre tradition which must have preserved the memory of an incident in the life of Jesus "when he was caught with his compassion down."[49] Only in the Markan retelling, according to Ringe, does the story become a story about Jews and gentiles.

To sum up my exercise: I hope to have shown that a critical evaluative process of interpretation for liberation does not reduce the historical and textual richness of the bible in general and of the story of the Syrophoenician in particular to abstract theological or ethical principles, timeless norms, or ontologically immutable archetypes which are to be accurately repeated and translated from generation to generation. I hope that I have succeeded in showing how a critical feminist interpretation for liberation explores, questions, and assesses different reading paradigms and hegemonic interpretations. Its goal is to unmask biblical texts and readings that foster an elite "feminine," racist, exclusivist, dehumanizing colonialist, or Christian anti-Jewish inscription of cultural-religious identity. Thus it re-visions biblical interpretation as an argumentative, persuasive, and emancipatory praxis that destabilizes, proliferates, and energizes critical readings for liberation in particular sociohistorical-religious contexts. In so doing, it seeks to undermine a fundamentalist mode of biblical reading that claims to be the only correct or true one. It thereby attempts to overcome a kyriarchal identity formation which invokes the authority of G*d for biblical texts that rein-scribe prejudice and dehumanization.

Many more interpretations of this story could be cited and many additional ones have been offered.[50] However, my point here is not to be comprehensive but to be illustrative. I have attempted to display the hermeneutics of indeterminacy at work in the interpretation of a particular text. Since all meaningful inter-pretations require some closure and their representations are given in narrative form, one cannot produce such an account without framing the understanding of the text. By shaping the multiplicity of interpretations as responses to a difficulty of mean-ing inscribed in the text, I have directed the attention of readers toward the need for a hermeneutics of evaluation.

A Radical Democratic Hermeneutics of Transformation

In shaping my representations of the interpretations of this one biblical story, I have operated with a basic ethical-political and re-ligious assumption that prejudice is wrong and must be chal-lenged. This assumption has as its critical frame of reference or background theory both a systemic kyriarchal analysis and the al-ternative vision of radical equality. It has allowed me to critically evaluate and assess the different possible interpretations in light of such a frame of reference. In other words, indeterminacy must be affirmed in order to escape a literalist fundamentalist interpre-tation. If, however, it is not to result in an endless play of meaning in which each reading has equal standing, one must articulate a scale of values and visions for adjudicating the hermeneutical in-determinacy of the text and its meanings.

If the hermeneutics of indeterminacy and its pluralism of read-ings is not to be understood in the sense of liberal pluralism, di-verse interpretations must be evaluated as to whether they advocate kyriarchal or liberationist values and whether they rein-scribe patterns of prejudice and discrimination or other, emanci-patory visions of transformation. Such criteria of assessment or such a scale of values cannot be articulated once and for all but must be formulated in ongoing feminist debates and deliberations. The moral space and hermeneutical center for such ongoing deliberations, I have argued, is the *ekklēsia* of wo/men both as a political-cultural and religious-theological reality and as a vision. How does such a theoretical conceptualization and practical vision operate to sustain both a hermeneutics of indeterminacy and a hermeneutics of change and transformation?

The notion of the *ekklēsia* of wo/men seeks to embody the diverse feminist-democratic struggles to overcome kyriarchal oppression traversed by racism, class exploitation, hetero-sexism, and colonialist militarism, and to claim these struggles as the political ecclesial site from which to speak. Since its aim is to recover bible, history, and theology as memory and heritage, the expression "*ekklēsia* of wo/men" does not only seek to make visible the suffering and victimization of wo/men. It also seeks to repossess this heritage of struggle as the memory of all those wo/men who have shaped Christian history as religious interlocutors, agents of change, and survivors in their struggles against kyriarchal dominations.

Western society and family, I have elaborated, are not simply male-dominated. Rather they are *patriarchal* (ruled by the father), or, more accurately, *kyriarchal* (ruled by the master or lord), because elite propertied men have had and still have power and control over those subordinated to and dependent on them. With the emergence of democracy, ancient and modern political-religious philosophy was compelled to justify the relationship between rulers and ruled in household and state, and it did so by articulating a philosophy of "deficient" or "different" human natures.[51]

Consequently, the Western kyriarchal system of domination has produced not only sex-gender ideologies but also colonialist theories of inferior races and cultures. Racist kyriocentric theories have argued that peoples are at different levels of development. In the hierarchy of evolution Europeans believed themselves (and often still do) to be the better and more highly developed human beings. For instance, they considered aboriginal peoples, or "the natives," of colonialized countries to be "uncivilized" and inferior by nature. Wo/men were deemed to be at the bottom of the racial pyramid of evolution. In analogy to white wo/men, wo/men of all "colors" were deemed to be rationally and morally inferior because they were wo/men.

Although in theory Western democracy has promised freedom and equality to all its citizens, in practice it has realized equality only in kyriarchal ways, and it has, for the most part, restricted leadership to elite male citizens only. Hence I have felt it necessary to qualify and define *ekklēsia* with the genitive construct "wo/men" in order to bring to consciousness the kyriarchal overdetermination of Western forms of *ekklēsia*. The radical democratic vision of a citizenry of equals has been realized only partially. Nevertheless, throughout its history this radical democratic vision has also inspired emancipatory movements for full citizenship and justice. These movements, including feminism, have emerged again and again because of the disparity between the radical democratic vision of the *ekklēsia* of wo/men and its actual sociopolitical and cultural-religious realizations.

This radical democratic religious vision is feminist insofar as it continues to insist that equality, freedom, and democracy cannot be realized if wo/men's voices are not raised or not heard and heeded in the struggle for justice and liberation for everyone regardless of sex, class, race, nationality, or religion. If our diverse struggles for the radical democratic equality, dignity, and well-being of all in society and church continue this feminist tradition of struggle, the *ekklēsia* of wo/men will become an ever-expanding reality.

By using a reconstructive model that reads kyriocentric biblical texts in terms of the early Christian struggles and arguments about both the politics and the rhetorics of "equality in the Spirit" and "kyriarchal submission," one can identify the cultural roots and effects generated by these early Christian debates and struggles.[52] This radical egalitarian spiritual vision inscribed in Christian scriptures is at once a new articulation and a reaffirmation of the red, brown, and black roots of feminism.

In an article on the "Red Roots of White Feminism," Paula Gunn Allen, one of the foremost Native American literary critics, has argued that the roots for a radical democratic *feminist* vision cannot be derived only from the democratic traditions of Ancient Greece or modern America or France because the classic European form of democracy did not allow wo/men and subjected men to participate in decision-making government. Rather, she argues, a feminist spiritual vision of radical democracy must be derived from tribal forms of government in the Americas, such as the Iroquois Confederacy, in which the Council of Matrons was the ceremonial, executive, and judicial center. I quote Paula Gunn Allen:

> The root of oppression is loss of memory. An odd thing occurs in the minds of Americans when Indian civilization is mentioned: little or nothing. . . . How odd then must my contention seem that the gynocratic tribes of the American continent provided the basis for all the dreams of liberation that characterize the modern world. . . . The vision that impels feminists to action was the vision of the Grandmothers' society, the society that was captured in the words of the sixteenth-century explorer Peter Martyr nearly five hundred years ago. It is the same vision repeated over and over by radical thinkers of Europe and America. . . . That vision . . . is of a country where there are "no soldiers, no gendarmes or police, no nobles, kings, regents, prefects, or judges, no prisons, no lawsuits. . . . All are equal and free."[53]

I join Paula Gunn Allen in maintaining that only the "indigenization"[54] of classical notions of democracy and biblical understandings of *ekklēsia*, a merging of the "Grandmothers' society" with Western articulations of individual freedoms and equal rights, will result in a Christian vision and practice of radical egalitarianism that can fashion a global societal and religious vision of well-being for all without exception. A feminist theological revisioning of the biblical past for creating a just society and future for the "global village" must consequently locate itself in such a radical oppositional democratic imagination. If it does so, I have argued, it can engender biblical interpretations and discourses of possibility and vision for a different church and society.

Consequently, positioned in the space of the *ekklēsia* of wo/men, a critical feminist biblical interpretation must attempt to reconceptualize the traditional practice of "discerning the spirits" as an attentive critical practice. As religious subjects, Christian feminists must claim their spiritual authority to assess both the oppressive as well as the liberating imagination of particular biblical texts and their interpretations. The *ekklēsia* of wo/men must be put into practice as a form of "deliberative democracy,"[55] one which, however, does not have to strive for consensus.[56] Rather it must present interpretive "cases," strategies, and their ramifications as well as evaluative principles and theoretical models for public discussion, deliberation, and debate.[57] The *ekklēsia* of wo/men can thus enact a feminist public space, a space that attempts to keep communication between its various "denominations" (womanist, mujerista, Asian, Africana, lesbian, differently abled, gender-feminist, liberationist feminist, etc.) and its various religious audiences (Jewish, Muslim, Christian, Goddess, atheist, agnostic) "open."[58] By deconstructing the kyriarchal rhetorics and politics of prejudice which is inscribed both in biblical texts and our own consciousness, we will be able to generate new possibilities for the ever-new articulations of religious and cultural identities and emancipatory practices.

As my cursory discussion of the different meanings of the Syrophoenician's story has indicated,[59] biblical texts and their interpretations continue to reinscribe, in the name of G*d, religious prejudice and relations of oppression if their kyriarchal rhetoric and religious identity formations are not only accepted without question but also legitimated in the process of interpretation. Therefore the primary theological task of a critical liberationist hermeneutics consists in scrutinizing and marking biblical texts and interpretations as to how much they promote a kyriarchal ethos and a dehumanizing religious vision that legitimates injustice and oppression.

As a root metaphor, the bible informs, I want to underscore again, but does not specify the theological criteria for a critical feminist reading of particular biblical texts in the interest of liberation. This, however, does not mean that feminist interpretation is not always already inspired and informed by scripture. It only means that such evaluative criteria with which to assess the kyriocentric character of biblical texts must be articulated again and again in contemporary struggles for justice and liberation. Liberation movements, I continue to argue, cannot afford to relinquish religious truth claims in their struggles for human dignity, equal rights, emancipation, equality, self-determination, and well-being for everyone. Hence they must interrogate biblical texts, Christian traditions, and institutional practices as to how much they foster equality, justice, and the logic of the *ekklēsia* rather than that of kyriarchal domination.

When trying to assess whether the story of the Syrophoenician advocates kyriarchal values and visions, participants in my classes and workshops usually disagree. Those arguing that the narrative is not kyriarchal point to the fact that the wo/man is the major protagonist in this story, that her argument convinces Jesus, and that her daughter was healed. But at what cost? other students ask. The wo/man does not challenge the ethnic-religious prejudice of Jesus but confirms it with "Yes, Lord." She does not argue for equal access; she begs for crumbs. Thus she accepts the second-class citizenship that she herself has internalized. She acts like a dog who is grateful even when kicked. Hence it is not surprising that commentators praise her for her humble submission. This is indeed a sacred text that advocates and reinscribes kyriarchal power-relations, anti-Jewish prejudices, and wo/men's feminine identity and submissive behavior.

In one of these debates, when we came to this impasse in the discussion, Renee, an African-American Baptist student, chided us for not taking seriously the wo/man's situation of powerlessness and the ironic cast of her words. Maria, a Hispanic student, countered that according to Theissen the woman was upper-class, urban, and well-educated. Nevertheless, the first student persisted. Even as a privileged, educated wo/man, she argued, the wo/man of the story remains a religious outsider, a despised foreigner, and a female who dares to disrupt the discourse of men. If she wants to achieve what she has come for, she needs to "play the game." Readers miss the irony of the story, Renee countered, if they do not see that the wo/man humors the great religious man in order to get what she wants. The wo/man from Syro-Phoenicia wins the argument, her daughter is liberated.

In a socioeconomic and cultural-political situation of increasing exploitation and repression that provokes insecurities and engenders the languages of hate, I have argued that feminist biblical interpretation must continue to cultivate a hermeneutics of desire for articulating emancipatory biblical visions and liberatory politics of meaning that do not vilify and block access to the table. Biblical interpretation can do so, however, only if it utilizes a hermeneutics of indeterminacy to overcome its exclusivist unitary kyriarchal formations and absolute truth claims. The deliberations, debates, strategies of the *ekklēsia* of wo/men must again and again articulate a radical and plural democratic vision of biblical faith and hope in a liberating Wisdom G*d who is "justified (*edikaiothē*) by all Her children" (QLk 7:35). Once again, the Syrophoenician challenges us to set liberating readings and arguments against the word that dehumanizes and excludes.

Then the righteous will stand with great confidence
in the presence of those who have oppressed them
and those who make light of their labors.
When the unrighteous see them, they will be shaken
with dreadful fear,
and they will be amazed at the
unexpected salvation of the righteous.
They will speak to one another in repentance,
and in anguish of spirit they will groan, and say,
"These are persons whom we once held in derision
and made a byword of reproach—fools that we were!
We thought that their lives were madness
and that their end was without honor.
Why have they been numbered among the children of God?
And why is their lot among the saints?"

WISDOM 5:1–5 (NRSV)

The Justice of Wisdom-Sophia:
Love Endures Everything—Or Does It?

CHAPTER 6

IN THE RECENT PAST the importance of context has been dis-
covered again in biblical scholarship. Not only have the "studies
of the social world" of Israel and early Christianity enriched
our knowledge about the social, historical, and political context
of biblical writings, the elaboration of "reader-response criticism"
in biblical studies has also rediscovered the actual reader as distinguished from the one inscribed in the text.[1] Moreover, because of
the insistence of feminist and liberation theologies, biblical studies
have begun to focus on the positionality and social location of
historical biblical interpreters. However, less attention has been paid

to the social-political location of those who read or hear biblical texts and interpretations today. A hermeneutics of proclamation would require that biblical scholars, teachers, and preachers learn how to explore not only their own but also the cultural-religious locations of their audiences and adjudicate the impact or effects that their biblical interpretations have on such audiences, especially on those who credit the scriptures with divine authority.

In the following I would like to demonstrate how such a hermeneutics of proclamation works, and I will do so with reference to a specific biblical text, 1 Corinthians 13:4–8, which I will read in the context of violence against wo/men. In their review of scholarship on family violence, Wini Breines and Linda Gordon have observed that only a few decades ago the terms "family violence" and especially "wife battering" had no meaning because child abuse, wife beating, and incest were understood as "personal" or "private" family problems and not recognized as serious social issues.[2] This does not mean, however, that such family violence did not exist. It only means, according to Teresa de Lauretis, that most work in the area failed to analyze the terms of its

> own inquiry, especially terms such as family, power, and gender. For, Breines and Gordon maintain, violence between intimates must be seen in the wider context of social power relations; and gender is absolutely central to the family. In fact, we may add, it is as necessary to the constitution of the family as it is itself, in turn, forcefully constructed and inevitably reproduced by the family.[3]

In short, feminist discourses have not only introduced a new concept of "family violence," they have also brought about a change in its understanding: they have replaced the notion of family violence as "a breakdown of social order" with one that sees it as a sign of the "power struggle for the maintenance of a certain kind of social order."[4] This example shows how important it is to recognize that cultural shifts in the understanding of commonsense notions such as family, violence, or love change and determine the capacity of the audience to read or hear certain biblical texts. A hermeneutics of proclamation therefore must not only explore and adjudicate the possible meanings of biblical texts but also inquire as to the conditions of their reception today.

The subtitle for this chapter is derived from the first letter of Paul to the Corinthians. Paul's hymn to love contrasts love with other spiritual gifts and asserts:

> Love is patient; love is kind; love is not envious or boastful or arrogant or rude. It does not insist on its own way; it is not irritable or resentful; it does not rejoice in wrongdoing, but rejoices in the truth. It bears all things, believes all things, hopes all things, endures all things. Love never ends. (1 Cor 13: 4–8, NRSV)

I am not so much interested here in investigating the original meaning of this Pauline text or that of any other Christian Testament text which extols love. Nor will I discuss the authorial intentions of this text or explore their function in their original historical contexts, although one could show that Paul has already used this rhetoric in order to counter the liberatory rhetoric of the Corinthian wo/men.[5] Instead, I want to explore the oppressive impact of such scriptural texts on Christian self-understanding and identity formation today, in a sociopolitical, cultural, and religious situation of violence against wo/men. In so doing I want to focus attention on how ostensibly non-kyriarchal scriptural texts such as 1 Corinthians 13 and their central message of love function within contemporary cultural exchanges. In short, in this chapter I hope to demonstrate how the central Christian principle of love can serve to sustain wo/men's internalized oppression today although the text in its original context may not have done so at all.

In modernity the word "love" has been not only privatized and individualized but also deeply genderized. A whole relationships industry—with know-how seminars, videos on the techniques of "making love," courses in romance, and mountains of self-help books and TV soap operas—promotes heterosexual love relationships. "Love," according to these cultural standards, is woman's and not man's natural calling and G*d-given vocation. Fully actualized femininity supposedly expresses itself in romantic love and self-sacrificing motherhood, whereas true masculinity actualizes itself in the exercise of freedom, autonomy, and equality. The cultural ethos of femininity relentlessly proclaimed in print and on the air inculcates in all of us the notion that true wo/men find their fulfillment in heterosexual love, marriage, and children.

Traditional Christian preaching on love tends to reinforce this cultural ethos of romantic love, feminine calling, and sacrificial service. However, it does so not by stressing sexual gratification and egalitarian relationship but by teaching a pre-modern view of heterosexual marriage that promotes the headship of men and the submission of wo/men. This conflation of traditional notions of submission and headship with modern notions of romantic heterosexual love is at the heart of patriarchal-kyriarchal relations of oppression today. Domestic violence against wo/men and their children is the logical outcome.[6] Violence against wo/men knows no cultural boundaries. It is not limited to one specific class, geographical area, or type of person. Rather it cuts across social differences and status lines: wo/men in all categories of difference—be they white or black, indigenous or immigrant, rich or poor, Asian or European, Latina or Anglo-Saxon, Aotearoan or Korean, urban or rural, religious or secular, professional or illiterate, heterosexual or lesbian, able-bodied or differently abled, young or old—all face daily violence because they are wo/men.

Feminist work has documented and analyzed the multifarious forms of violent attack against wo/men just because of the mere fact that they are wo/men.[7] Such violence can take many forms, and the list of abuse is endless: sexual and domestic abuse,[8] child pornography, sexual harassment in schools or at work, lesbian-bashing, prison rape, sex shops and tourism, prostitution, forced sterilization, psychiatric hospitalization, battering, incest, rape in all its forms, homelessness, poverty, right-wing neo-Nazi terror,[9] intellectual colonization, spiritual exploitation, impoverishment of widows and older wo/men, sexual abuse of the mentally ill, emotional violence in all forms, cosmetic surgery, welfare harassment, surrogacy, incarceration of pregnant wo/men with substance abuse, witch-burning, food deprivation, serial murder, sadomasochism, and femicide. Moreover, such violence is not always forced upon wo/men but can also be self-inflicted in the interest of feminine identity, love, and marriage. For instance, in the

United States more than two million wo/men have supposedly "freely elected" breast implants. The number of wo/men who have allegedly freely chosen cosmetic surgery has increased more than sixty percent in the past decade.[10]

Femicide, the murder of wo/men, is the deadly outcome of domestic violence.[11] Statistically, a wo/man is more likely to be raped, battered, or killed at night in her own house than on the most crime-infested streets. Across the United States at least one third— and, since many incidents go unreported, probably more like one half—of all femicide victims are murdered by husbands or lovers, most of whom have no criminal records or known psychiatric histories; nevertheless, the public perception still prevails that such murders are rare and are committed by hardened criminals or psychiatric patients. Headlines such as "Woman Shot By Jealous Lover" or "Woman Stabbed By Betrayed Husband" make femicide not only anecdotal but also (subtly) "deserved." If a batterer says, "I hit her and then she deliberately defied me until I had to hit her again," this is excused because she allegedly provoked him into losing his self-control. If he says that he battered or killed his wife or girlfriend because he loved her so much, all too often the media report it as an understandable "crime of passion."

Although men usually wage assaults on wo/men, wo/men are all too often portrayed as deliberately trying to provoke male jealousy or anger. In many cases the battered wo/man is held responsible for the problem: her uppity demeanor, her sloppy dressing, her withholding sex or other marital services, her nagging and accusations, her low self-esteem, her indirect expression of needs, her love for her children, her whining, or, worst of all, her sexual promiscuity—all these and more are construed as provocative and valid excuses for battering or murder. Journalistic accounts, psychological discourses, courtroom hearings, religious moral prescriptions, and biblical laws have all tended to blame the wo/men who are victimized rather than hold perpetrators responsible for practices of victimization. Worse, wo/men victims have often internalized such guilt themselves.

Very vocal and well financed political "New Right" organizations, which are often championed by conservative wo/men, do not condemn this increased violence against wo/men but blame feminists for turning wo/men into whining victims. While the New Right overtly advocates "traditional family values," its real interest is in upholding the Christian patriarchal form of the middle-class nuclear heterosexual family. This kyriarchal Christian family ethos is proclaimed as "true love." It legitimates the chastising and battering of wo/men and children in the home, the silence about incest and child abuse, and the attack on shared parenting, child care programs, and reproductive rights, as well as the rejection of affirmative action programs that would guarantee economic justice for wo/men. Since feminist movements around the world have challenged patri-kyriarchal regimes that sustain physical, sexual, cultural, and religious violence against wo/men, they have become primary targets for the political and religious right.[12]

Like their conservative counterparts, political liberals also view the family as the basis of social cohesion and societal order that transmits accepted values, shapes national identities, and engenders basic loyalties. Although wo/men's political and economic roles have changed, the ethos of the kyriarchal family has been maintained throughout the ages. Wo/men are to be supported by and subordinated to their husbands. Their love has to maintain the well-being of the family by socializing children into their proper adult roles, caring for the sick and aged, and overseeing the household. Although this family ethos was only practical and possible for middle-class wo/men throughout history, it is no longer livable today even for middle-class wo/men. Nevertheless, it still undergirds the treatment of wo/men in the welfare system and in the marketplace.[13] Although today most wives and mothers have to work outside the home in order to either make ends meet or sustain middle-class living standards, they still have primary responsibility for homemaking and child care. Despite two decades of equal rights struggles, the number of female heads of families living in poverty has sharply increased. Older wo/men are twice as likely to live in poverty than male senior citizens.

In short, violence against wo/men must not be thought to be the result of random acts by criminal or deranged, isolated men. Rather such violence is best understood in systemic terms and seen as falling on a continuum of elite male power and control over wo/men and children, a continuum that encompasses not only incidents of physical violence but also dehumanizing impoverishment. Such violence against wo/men and children is motivated by proprietary control and jealous love, which in turn are engendered by kyriarchal notions of family. Violence against wo/men constitutes the heart of kyriarchal oppression.

The Kyriarchal Love Ethic and Its Disciplining Practices

Since in modern times in the West wo/men are no longer forced to marry and are (theoretically, at least) free to choose their husbands and to determine the number of children they will bear, one might object that wo/men freely choose to enter into or remain in violent family situations. Educated and privileged wo/men, for example, often stay married or remain in abusive relationships although they have achieved success in their own right, gained economic independence, and enjoy sexual and reproductive freedoms. In response to this objection, feminist studies have pointed out that wo/men of all classes continue to "put themselves in harm's way" because cultural and religious socialization has instilled in them the conviction that without a man they are nothing and without children they cannot be happy. Wo/men's self-worth and self-esteem continue to be defined by their attachment to a man and/or by their success as mothers.

Yet, rather than speaking of a persistent "false consciousness" that keeps wo/men in violent family situations, feminist theologians point to the cultural and religious disciplining or socializing practices that play a decisive role in securing wo/men's continuing collaboration in and their acquiescence to domestic and sexual violence. The Western kyriarchal family ethos and its educational practices continue to socialize girls into self-effacing love and feminine subservience. This Western romantic ethos produces the cultural-religious understanding that a wo/man is nothing without a man. In order to be respectable she has to do everything in her power to attain or to keep "wedded status."

Feminist analyses have amply documented how the disciplining practices of culture and religion enact and reenact received gender norms. Such cultural socializing practices on the one hand produce the genderization of people and on the other hand secure the cultural production of the "feminine" body.[14] These practices fashion the docile, subjected, and made-up body as the ideal body of "femininity."[15] They also serve to reinforce, sustain, and legitimate domestic and sexual violence. Such bodily discipline in the interest of a kyriarchal family ethic, however, is not "forced" upon wo/men. Rather it is perceived to be "freely chosen" for the sake of beauty and love, or to be endured because of fate and family honor.

A four-fold strategy of bodily disciplining in the name of love can be detected. This strategy seeks to produce as the ideal "feminine woman" the White Lady, firstly by prescribing the perfect shape of the body, secondly by controlling bodily movement, thirdly by refashioning bodily appearance, and fourthly by eroticizing submission and domination.

The *first* type of disciplining practice seeks to produce the ideal feminine body as a body of a certain size and general configuration. Its regimes are obsessive dieting, in order to produce the slender boyish body, as well as forms of exercise that shape the "ideal" feminine body form. Ninety percent of all persons with eating disorders are wo/men. Only one in 40,000 wo/men meets the requirements of a model's size and shape, who today weighs twenty-three percent less than the average wo/man. Fifty-three percent of high school girls are found to be unhappy with their bodies by age thirteen and seventy-eight percent by age eighteen. Negative body images lead to the erosion of self-affirmation and self-confidence in girls, as well as to tendencies in wo/men to renounce and devalue their own perceptions, beliefs, thoughts and feelings.[16] Even highly accomplished professional wo/men exhibit such negative self-appraisal and self-worth; they tend to feel "illegitimate, apologetic, undeserving, anxious, tenuous, out-of-place, misread, phony, uncomfortable, incompetent, dishonest, and guilty."[17]

The *second* type of disciplining practice seeks to produce the "docile" female body by enforcing a specific repertoire of gestures, postures, and mannerisms as well as by constricting wo/men's spatiality and movement. Wo/men are taught that when sitting, walking, and speaking they must constrict their gestures.

Such a restriction of movement in the name of "graceful" behavior is reinforced through clothing designs such as very short skirts or high-heeled shoes, which are again in fashion, and certain forms of "feminine" etiquette. At all cost, wo/men must communicate that they are "nice," unthreatening, and subservient, in short, that they are "feminine." Wo/men who are perceived as loud, uppity, or nagging, or who wear comfortable shoes or pants, encounter derision, rejection, and discrimination of all sorts. By stressing subordination, refinement, and helplessness, such feminine bodily socializations aim to produce the cultural characteristics of the White Lady.

The *third* type of disciplining practice is directed toward the display of the feminine body as an ornamental surface. Wo/men's faces and bodies must be made up and made over according to normative standards of beauty. No wonder that the manufacture of cosmetics is a twenty-billion-dollar-a-year industry worldwide. Early on wo/men are expected to become skilled in numerous techniques of camouflage. Girls learn to practice the narrowly circumscribed "art" of cosmetics and even to suffer corrective surgery so that the "properly" made-up Lady can appear in public. Conformity to the prevalent standards of feminine dress and make-up is a prerequisite for well-paying jobs and social mobility. Such inscriptions of the body seek to produce the submissive feminine by inculcating the desirability of the hegemonic feminine—the White Lady.[18]

Hence normative standards of beauty remain Eurocentric and racially biased. The blond, blue-eyed, white Barbie doll—even if her skin is brown—communicates such a racist standard of "femininity." This racist "politics of beauty" not only undermines the self-esteem of wo/men of all colors, it also compensates white wo/men who do not measure up to the ideal standard of beauty by telling them that they are "better wo/men" by the mere fact of being white. Wo/men of all colors who are not "ladylike" are stereotyped as "dirty, ugly, stupid, lazy, uppity, devious, and promiscuous" in such colonialist racist discourses. These racist stereotypes of femininity serve to label all wo/men who are assertive, uppity, pushy, overbearing, or promiscuous as really being "nonwhite" or "unfeminine." Because they have failed to achieve the feminine standards that characterize the White Lady, they "deserve," according to this racist stereotype, to be victimized, like black wo/men or lesbians.[19]

A *fourth* kind of disciplining practice presupposes and articulates, in conjunction with the first three types, the White Lady as the sexualized ideal of cultural-religious submission. It seeks to produce kyriarchal heterosexual gender relations of control and submission not only in terms of "natural" physical sex but also in terms of personal desire, pleasure, and love. To that end it organizes the social relations between the sexes in such a way that domination and submission become naturalized. Eroticized submission defines femininity whereas eroticized dominance constitutes masculinity. Not only gender but also sexuality and desire are socially constructed.

In her article "Your Comfort vs. My Death," Chung Hyun Kyung observes how Asian wo/men are desired because they allegedly still conform to the stereotype of the White Lady:

> One of the main reasons Western men come to Asia for prostitution or mail-order brides from Asia is: they want a "real woman," a real feminine woman. . . . They say there are no more woman-like women in the West because of the feminist movement. Women have become man-like, no more softness, no more vulnerability, no more obedience! So they come to Asia to find small, brown (more natural), soft, vulnerable, obedient, real women. . . . They say they are willing to *sacrifice* a little bit of status because they feel happier (feel more like a normal man) being with Asian women because of their femininity, a trait which white women do not have any longer.[20]

To sum up my argument: in order to earn the love of a man and to fulfill their supposedly natural drive to motherhood, wo/men must not only make themselves available to serve the sexual or emotional needs of men, they must also define their identity in terms of romantic love. Their goal in life must be to fulfill men's erotic and emotional desires and sexual needs. To question these disciplining practices of "femininity" or the White Lady threatens wo/men not only with the loss of jobs, family, and liveli-hood but also with a loss of self-identity, status, and self-esteem. Not only is this heterosexist kyriarchal regime sanctioned by the loss of patriarchal "patronage" for those wo/men, especially femi-nists, who fail to comply, it is also maintained through wo/men's own self-surveillance and collusion in the disciplining of other wo/men. Finally, it is inculcated in and through a Christian spiri-tuality of love and service that seeks to maintain the traditional patriarchal family.

The Religious Politics of Meaning

Christian and other right-wing religious fundamentalisms seek to recreate the traditional family and its world that supposedly ex-isted before the changes brought about by the civil rights, wo/men's liberation, and gay and lesbian rights movements.[21] Christian TV preachers and popular authors encourage wo/men to display their "femininity" and to dedicate their lives to the cul-tivation of loving family relationships. They no longer preach as-ceticism but tell wo/men to utilize make-up, cosmetic surgery, diets, and fashion for "keeping" their husbands and maintaining their marriages. At the same time, groups like the "Promise Keep-ers" insist on the headship of men in the Christian family. In de-fense of the traditional "Christian" family they support public policies that penalize pregnant teenagers and unwed mothers on welfare.

It is true that Christian theology *overtly* condemns oppressive forms of the exploitation and victimization of wo/men, such as in-cest, sexual abuse, femicide, or rape. Nevertheless, the Christian proclamation of the kyriarchal politics of submission and its at-tendant virtues of self-sacrifice, docility, subservience, obedience, suffering, unconditional forgiveness, male authority, and unques-tioning surrender to "G*d's will" *covertly* promotes, in the name of G*d and love, such patriarchal-kyriarchal practices of victim-ization as Christian virtues. However, not only the religious right but also liberal theological and religious discourses that do not question but instead reproduce the sociocultural ideals of "femi-ninity" promote the inferior or marginal status of wo/men and reinforce rather than challenge the victimization of wo/men and children.

In short, both types of malestream religious regimes, the conservative and the liberal ones, tend to buttress theologically the sociocultural kyriarchal construction of feminine submission and to maintain heterosexist kyriarchal structures of subordination in the name of "love." As long as they do not publicly renounce these institutionalized structures of violence, Christian theology and Christian churches continue to support and legitimate the sociocultural and religious discourses of domination, economic exploitation, and political objectification that produce violence against wo/men. Yet public rejection of these structures of violence is only a first step. Christians must also develop a theoretical vision and institutional practice of radical democratic family relations. Christian churches and theologies that promote heterosexist kyriarchal "Christian" family values continue to jeopardize the survival of all those wo/men who struggle at the bottom of the sociocultural and economic-political pyramid of domination. As long as structural ecclesial change does not take place, Christian theologies will continue to collude in and support practices of physical and spiritual violence against wo/men.

Feminist theological work on violence against wo/men and on child abuse[22] has pointed to four traditional theological key discourses of "love" that are major roadblocks in the way of abused wo/men and children who seek to change their violent family situations. These are: *first*, love as enacting a pattern of domination/subordination; *second*, the traditional association of wo/men with evil and sin; *third*, the christological valorization of suffering; and *fourth*, the preaching of forgiveness without redress.

First: The Western sociocultural politics of love enacted as domination and submission has its roots in Greek political philosophy, Roman law, and Near Eastern religions. This classical model of family based on inequality is theologized and mediated through Christian scriptures which intertwine it with an ethos of "selfless" love. The so-called household code texts trajectory of the Pauline tradition in particular has reformulated the ancient discourses of subordination in Christian terms. The ethos of the household in antiquity becomes an authoritative scriptural revelation which demands submission and obedience as an expression of Christian love not only from freeborn wives and children, but also from servant, slave, and barbarian wo/men. This scripturalized ethos of a kyriocentric (master/lord/father/husband–centered) politics of self-sacrificing subordination is compounded if it provides the lens for all biblical readings. If it functions as an interpretive framework for reading originally anti-kyriarchal biblical texts, such as, for instance, 1 Corinthians 13, it proclaims kyriarchal relationships and values as central to Christian revelation. It also has disastrous effects when, for instance, it contextualizes theological and liturgical language about G*d and G*d's relation to the world within such a kyriarchal framework of meaning. A Christian symbolic universe that proclaims an Almighty Father-King-God[23] whose will and command is revealed in the texts of scripture religiously legitimates and reinforces not only misogyny, but also racism, status inferiority, homophobia, and xenophobia.[24]

It is not only scriptural inscriptions that reproduce this patriarchal-kyriarchal politics of meaning but also theological teachings on headship, which maintain kyriarchal family relations and church structures. The christological doctrine of male headship and kyriarchal authority both legitimates the exclusion of wo/men from ordained ministries and makes it impossible for Christian children and wo/men to resist sexual abuse by marital and ecclesial "heads of household"—by natural and spiritual "fathers." How can battered wo/men or abused children turn to and trust "priestly authority" for help if it is the same kind of authority that maims and kills them daily?

Second: This ethos of the so-called household code texts is soon theologized and its politics of kyriarchal submission linked with the teaching of wo/men's wickedness. Already in Paul's second letter to the Corinthians he not only refers to the image of marriage between Christ and the church, which is patterned after that of G*d and Israel,[25] he also associates this metaphor with the deception of Eve (2 Cor 11, 2–3). The pseudo-Pauline Pastoral Epistles explicitly link the kyriarchal theology of submission with the teaching on wo/man's sinfulness. They prescribe the silence of wo/men and prohibit wo/men's authority over men by claiming that not Adam but "the woman" was deceived and became a transgressor (1 Tim 2:11–15).

Hence the cultural pattern of making the victims of rape, incest, or battering feel guilty and responsible for their victimization has its religious roots in the scriptural teaching that sin came into the world through Eve and that wo/men gain salvation primarily through bearing children and by continuing in "faith and love and holiness with modesty." This religious reinscription of the cultural politics of femininity and patriarchal-kyriarchal submission has been amplified by theologians throughout the centuries. Such theological discourses of victimization have stressed either wo/men's sinfulness and culpability or their failure to measure up to the feminine ideal of "faith, love, and holiness with modesty." In either case, it is the victims rather than the victimizers that are held responsible.

Third: Both Christian scriptural texts and traditional christological discourses theologize kyriarchal suffering and victimization.[26] For instance, Hebrews 12:1–11 admonishes Christians to resist sin to the point of shedding their blood. The text points to the example of Jesus, "who for the joy that was set before him endured the cross, despising the shame." Because they are "sons," they have to expect suffering as disciplining chastisements from G*d. Just as they respect their earthly fathers for having punished them at their pleasure, so they should subject themselves to "the Father of spirits and life" who "disciplines us for our good, that we may share his holiness"(Heb 12:1–11). The First Epistle of Peter, which stands in this Pauline tradition, explicitly enjoins slave wo/men, in 2:18–23, to practice the kyriarchal politics of submission, by pointing to the example of Christ. They are admonished to subordinate themselves not only to kind and gentle but also to unjust and overbearing masters: "For to this you have been called, because Christ also suffered for you, leaving you an example, that you should follow in his steps . . . for he trusted him who judges justly" (1 Peter 2:21, 23).

Such admonitions are not isolated aberrations but go to the heart of Christian faith: trust in G*d the Father and belief in redemption through the suffering and death of Christ. Feminist theology has underscored the pernicious impact of such theological and christological discourses which stress that G*d sacrificed his son for our sins. If one extols the silent and freely chosen suffering of Christ who was "obedient to the point of death" (Phil 2:8) as an example to be imitated by those suffering from domestic and sexual abuse, one does not simply legitimate but one also facilitates violence against wo/men and children. The work of Rita Nakashima Brock has shown that christological discourses which are articulated within the paradigm of kyriarchal submission, as she puts it, "reflect views of divine power that sanction child abuse on a cosmic scale."27

By ritualizing the suffering and death of Jesus and by calling the powerless in society and church to imitate his perfect obedience and self-sacrifice, Christian ministry and theology do not interrupt but continue to foster the cycle of violence which is engendered by kyriarchal social and ecclesial structures as well as by cultural and political disciplining practices. Moreover, as Christine Gudorf has pointed out in response to René Girard, the sacrifice of surrogate victims does not contain or interrupt the cycle of violence.28 Rather, by rechanneling violence, it serves to protect those in power from the violent protest of those whom they oppress. A theology that is silent about the sociopolitical causes of Jesus' execution and stylizes him as the paradigmatic sacrificial victim whose death was either willed by G*d or was necessary to propitiate G*d continues the kyriarchal cycle of violence and victimization instead of empowering believers to resist and transform the system.

Fourth: When preached to wo/men and subordinated men, central Christian values such as love and forgiveness help to sustain relations of domination and to foster the acceptance of domestic and sexual violence. Hence scriptural texts and Christian ethics often continue the cycle of violence by preventing resistance to it. For instance, rape victims who believe obedience to G*d's will requires that they preserve their virginity and sexual purity at any cost may not only endanger their own lives but may also suffer from guilt for their victimization and from the loss of self-esteem. For that reason, rape survivors often feel not only that they are "used goods" but also that they are sinners responsible for their own rape. Battered wives, in turn, many of whom believe that divorce is against G*d's will, often remain in violent marriage relationships "for better and for worse." Children who are taught to trust and obey adults as the representatives of G*d, particularly parents and ministers, are especially prone to being victimized. If such victims are taught that it is essential for a Christian to suffer for love's sake, to trust and to love unconditionally, to remain sexually inexperienced, to be obedient to and to forgive beloved authority figures,[29] it becomes nearly impossible for them, particularly for little girls, either to recover their damaged self-image and self-worth or to speak about sexual abuse by a beloved father, priest, relative, or teacher.

Although their original intention might have been quite different, scriptural texts such as "blessed are the peacemakers and those who suffer for righteousness sake," "but I say to you that everybody who is angry with his brother is liable to judgment," "it is better that you lose one of your members than that your whole body goes to hell," "love your enemies, and pray for those who persecute you," or "do not resist evil" construct a sacred canopy that compels victims to accept their sufferings without resistance. Injunctions of Jesus, such as to forgive the one "who sins against you not seven times, but . . . seventy times seven"(Mt 18:21–22)—or Paul's praise of love as not insisting on its own way, "not irritable or resentful," bearing and enduring all things and never ending (1 Cor 13:4–8)—provoke guilt feelings in those wo/men and children who do not patiently and lovingly submit to domestic violence, sexual abuse, or ecclesiastical control. They rob wo/men who are victims of such violence of the spiritual power to resist and convince them that they fail their Christian calling if they do not submit unconditionally to abusive love. Not surprisingly, those wo/men and children who take their faith seriously are often convinced that resistance against violence is unchristian and that their suffering is willed by G*d.

A Hermeneutics of Proclamation: Empowering Justice

A hermeneutics of proclamation therefore challenges Christian theology and pastoral practice to publicly repent their preaching of unconditional love, which has colluded in sexual, domestic, and political violence against wo/men and children. If they do not take the conditions of their audience into account, then the victims of such violence will continue to be forced to choose between remaining victims or rejecting their Christian birthright. However, such an either/or alternative deprives religious wo/men who refuse to be victimized any longer not just of communal support but also of the belief systems that give meaning to their lives.

In consequence, a critical feminist spirituality of liberation continues to foster resistance and change by exploring the contradictions between the religious-cultural kyriarchal politics of "femininity," on the one hand, and the radical democratic politics of meaning and self-worth that is also inscribed in Christian texts and traditions, on the other. Such a sophialogical strategy seeks to change the cultural and spiritual discourses that sustain violence against wo/men and children by focusing on the meanings that hinder or negate such agency for survival. It also does so by focusing on contradictions and alternative traditions inscribed in biblical texts. I want to focus attention here on the story of the persistent widow in Luke 18, as an example of such a different tradition which could generate and sustain an alternative discourse of justice on biblical grounds:

> Then Jesus told them a parable about their need to pray always and not to lose heart. He said, "In a certain city there was a judge who neither feared God nor had respect for people. In that city there was a widow who kept coming to him and saying, 'Grant me justice against my opponent.' For a while he refused; but later he said to himself, 'Though I have no fear of God and no respect for anyone, yet because this widow keeps bothering me, I will grant her justice, so that she may not wear me out by continually coming.'" And the Lord said, "Listen to what the unjust judge says. And will not God grant justice to his chosen ones who cry to him day and night? Will he delay long in helping them? I tell you, he will quickly grant justice to them. And yet, when the Son of Man comes, will he find faith on earth?" (Luke 18:1–8, NRSV)

Scholars are debating as to whether this story is a Lukan com-positional creation or whether it is a Lukan redaction of an older story which might go back to Jesus.[30] The meaning of the story in the Gospel of Luke is quite clear: it is a parable about the practice of persistent prayer, similar to Luke's stories of the importunate neighbor in Luke 11:5–8 and of the Pharisee and the toll collector in Luke 18:9–14. In its Lukan form, the judge becomes a G*d fig-ure and the parable reasons from the lesser (the judge) to the greater (G*d): if the judge reacts to the pestering of the widow, how much more will G*d respond to the prayers and outcries of G*d's people? In Luke's understanding, the widow exemplifies persistent prayer in a situation where the Christian movement is suffering oppression and persecution and G*d has delayed the vindication of the elect.[31] *The Study Bible for Women* sums up the meaning of the story in Luke as follows: "This parable was told to encourage those who do not receive immediately an an-swer to their prayers. God is by no means indifferent, but there are often obstacles that must be overcome by persistent believing prayer."[32]

It is obvious that the Lukan text draws a very problematic image of G*d by likening G*d to the unjust judge who only gives in because he is pestered. Scholars sense this problem when they try to explain why the parable speaks in such a negative fashion about G*d. Most importantly, when read in a situation of vio-lence against wo/men, the Lukan version does not empower wo/men to resist such violence but encourages them to pray harder so that G*d will come to their rescue. It fosters a spiritual-ity of quietism that accepts violence and in "typically feminine" fashion waits for the "all-powerful man" to come to one's rescue. A hermeneutics of proclamation, therefore, must deconstruct his-torically and theologically the Lukan version of the story.

Yet this parable has a contrary meaning and functions quite differently if it is read against the grain of the Lukan meaning. If in a form critical analysis one pares away the layers of Lukan in-terpretation in verse 1 and verses 6–8, the following story emerges:

> He [Jesus] said: "In a certain city there was a judge who neither feared God nor had respect for people. In

that city there was a widow who kept coming to him and saying, 'Grant me justice against my opponent.' For a while he refused; but later he said to himself, 'Though I have no fear of God and no respect for anyone, yet because this widow keeps bothering me, I will grant her justice, so that she may not wear me out [*hypopiazein*, "batter down"] by continually coming.'" (Luke 18:2–5)

In this story the two characters, the judge and the widow, are drawn as opposites. The judge is clearly marked as unjust because he is said to neither fear G*d nor respect people. The widow is not characterized as just, but by her actions she is defined as tirelessly insisting on justice: she kept coming to him and asking for justice against her adversary. Nothing is said about why she had to approach the judge over and over again. No reasons are given as to why he refused her demand. The story climaxes in the judge saying to himself, "I will grant her justice so that she may not give me a black eye (bruise, batter down, or wear me out) by her nonstop coming." The soliloquy of the judge expresses a typical sentiment of those who act violently; the judge blames the wo/man victim for "battering" him although she only seeks her rights and vindication whereas he acts violently by denying justice to her.

Most scholars agree that the judicial case at hand is probably an inheritance dispute. They try to make sense out of the story by assuming that the widow was poor, helpless, without any male support and hence in danger of becoming destitute. They claim that she had only two choices left: either to stay in her former husband's house and do menial work or to return to her father's house.[33] Moreover, they argue that wo/men could not appear in court by themselves. That she herself appears before the judge, therefore, indicates that she has no male guardian or relatives left.

However, the text does not portray the widow either as poor or as lacking male protection.[34] Rather she is characterized as independent, resourceful, and assertive. As Jewish feminist scholars such as Tal Ilan and Judith Wegner have pointed out, although Jewish wo/men's participation in public life was heavily circumscribed, three types of wo/men, the emancipated daughter, the divorcée, and the normal widow, were considered legally to be autonomous persons.[35] In other words, when "no man has a legal claim on a woman's sexuality, the system always treats her as a person, both in sex-related and other matters."[36] Or, as the rabbis put it, "A woman acquires her freedom [lit. acquires herself] in two ways . . . by a bill of divorce and by the death of her husband" (mQidd.1.1).[37]

By arguing against the standard interpretation of the widow as poor and destitute, I do not mean to deny that in the first century C.E. many widows lived in poverty and dire straits, as they do in our own day. Rather I want to point to the pitfalls of this interpretation. Not all Jewish widows were poverty-stricken and in need of male support since a widow could own property, live independently, and inherit her husband's estate if she was designated as his heir in his will. The Book of Judith portrays such a wealthy and independent widow. To see the widow of the parable first of all as a victim of the social system overlooks the fact that she acts as an autonomous member of the community. Such a reading disempowers wo/men in violent home situations to recognize and identify the "powers" and resources for resistance and survival that are still available to them.

Scholars also debate as to whether the story situates the action in a Roman or a Jewish court.[38] However, the judge seems to be characterized in Jewish terms since it is said that he neither fears G*d (not the Gods)[39] nor respects humans. It is most likely, moreover, that the story mentions only one judge (and not three or seven as was customary) not because of historical reasons but because of the literary contrast judge/widow. It has also been suggested that the judge delays because he expects more bribes and sides with the widow's opponent. However, no indications of this are found in the story. Rather, the story "works" because of its stark opposition and sparse characterization.

It is the widow who is at the center of the action. The widow is characterized as bold, assertive, and persistent. She has suffered injustice and will not rest until she gets her rights. Justice must be done. She will not be silent and tolerate injustice. Susan Praeder writes, "She is trying to insure that justice prevails, but in her view the cause of justice and her side of the case are identical. If the judge supports her and favors her side in the case, then justice will prevail."40 The narrator's interest is clearly focused on the character of the widow, who takes her fate into her own hands by attempting to right the wrong and by doing everything in her power to ensure that justice prevails. She is the advocate of justice.

In contrast, the judge, who as official of the court should represent justice, is pictured as representing *adikia* (injustice). In the end, the judge does not give the widow her due because he is convinced of her rights but because he wants to get rid of her. He is the representative of a corrupt justice system that claims to defend rights and laws but in actuality undermines and perverts them.

The plight and courage of the assertive widow comes best to the fore in an intertextual reading of this story with the following passage from " A Letter from a Battered Wife." The letter writer introduces herself as being in her thirties, a mother of four children, and married to a college graduate who is a professional in his field. She has been battered for most of her married life and seeks to stick it out until she gets her college degree and a good job.

> Now the first response to this story, which I myself think of, will be "Why didn't you seek help?"
>
> I did early in our marriage. I went to a clergyman who, after a few visits, told me that my husband meant no real harm. . . . Most important I was told to forgive him the beatings just as Christ had forgiven me from the cross. I did that too.
>
> Things continued. Next time I turned to a doctor. I was given little pills to relax me and told to take things a little easier. . . .
>
> I turned to a professional family guidance agency. I was told there that my husband needed help and that I should find a way to control the incidents. . . .
>
> I did go to two more doctors. One asked me what I had done to provoke my husband. The other asked if we had made up yet.
>
> I called the police one time. They not only did not respond to the call, they called several hours later to ask if things had "settled down." . . .
>
> Everyone I have gone to for help has somehow

wanted to blame me and vindicate my husband. . . . The clergyman, the doctor, the counselor, my friend's husband, the police—all of them have found a way to vindicate my husband.

I know that I have to get out. But when you have nowhere to go, you know that you must go on your own and expect no support. I have to be ready for that. I have to be ready to support myself and the children completely, and still provide a decent environment for them. I pray that I can do that before I am murdered in my own home.[41]

Like the social system represented by the unjust judge, contemporary social systems do not want to render justice on behalf of battered wo/men but rather choose to vindicate their male adversaries. Like the courageous and persistent widow of the parable, the letter writer who suffers from domestic violence reaches out again and again to demand justice and help. Yet, unlike the parable of Jesus, her story may not have a "happy ending." On the one hand, to tell this woman that she has to love her husband unconditionally, to forgive him as Christ did, and to suffer everything in order not to provoke him, means to act like the unjust judge of the parable. On the other hand, to hold up the relentlessness of the widow in demanding "her justice" means to strengthen battered women in their struggle and resistance to violence. Hence a hermeneutics of proclamation must identify biblical stories and traditions that empower wo/men to stand up and to demand their rights and human dignity.

In conclusion, I have argued in this chapter that a critical feminist sophialogy of liberation must develop a hermeneutics of proclamation that is able to contest the authority of the practices and discourses which advocate the politics of unconditional love, sacrifice, and subordination and thereby justify violence on theological grounds. Such a hermeneutics brings to light the contradiction between the overt and covert aims of cultural and religious practices that inculcate love as the criterion of what it means to be "feminine" and Christian. It also seeks to articulate contesting alternative religious discourses as resources of meaning and power for overcoming abusive violence, thereby aiming to empower both those victimized by kyriarchal oppressions and the whole Christian community to believe in a G*d who is with us in our struggles to eradicate violence and to foster self-determination, dignity, and well-being for all.

Contrary to Paul's hymn to love and Luke's admonition to steadfast prayer, love does not patiently wait and endure everything. It does not accept and tolerate inequality, injustice, rejection, violence, abuse, and dehumanization. Love and prayer are dangerous if they are not expressions of self-esteem, respect, dignity, independence, and self-determination. Love and prayer are nothing without engaging G*d's power to bring about the *ekklēsia* of wo/men as the harbinger of a more just world. Love and prayer are nothing without the engagement for justice that upholds us in the political struggle for the well-being of everyone. Love is nothing without the imagination to create a sustaining spiritual vision for new forms of familial relationships and world communities with equal resources. Love is nothing without justice. Indeed, love must not endure everything.

Say to Wisdom, "You are my sister,"
and call insight your intimate friend.

PROVERBS 7:4 (NRSV)

And again Jesus said,
"To what should I compare the basileia of God?
It is like yeast that a wo/man took and mixed in with
three measures of flour until all of it was leavened."

LUKE 13:20-21

Jesus [said], the Father's basileia is like a wo/man.
She took a small amount of leaven; she [hid] it into flour.
She made it into big loaves.

GOSPEL OF THOMAS 96

The Sisters of Wisdom-Sophia:
Justified by All Her Children

CHAPTER 7

FEMINIST BIBLICAL INTERPRETATION, I have argued throughout this work, must position itself within wo/men's struggles for survival and against structures of injustice and exploitation.[1] Hence it must critically question those biblical texts and hermeneutical frameworks that marginalize and dehumanize wo/men. The critical feminist interpretation for liberation which I have sought to develop further here therefore understands scripture and its interpretation as a site of struggle over religious meaning and/or theological authority.

By the use of the title "Sharing Her Word," by quoting Wis-

dom sayings at the beginning of each chapter, and indeed by referring to Her throughout the whole book, I have invoked the words
and image of Divine Chokmah-Sophia-Sapientia-Wisdom,[2] the
teacher of justice, in order to argue that she, like Diotima,[3] must
become the host of feminist interpretation and debate. Jewish as
well as Christian texts and traditions about Divine Wisdom, I
have maintained, not only represent a controverted site of struggle over meaning but also offer possibilities for a new Christian
biblical self-understanding and for a spirituality of solidarity
across the feminist either/or divide.

Although the feminist scholarly search for the footprints of
Wisdom-Sophia in biblical writings encounters a host of historical-
theological problems, it is nevertheless commonly accepted that the
biblical image of Sophia has integrated G*ddess language and traditions.[4] Hence the divide between feminist biblical theologians and
G*ddess thealogians,[5] I suggest, can be bridged by a hermeneutics
of desire that searches for female images of the Divine.

Whereas the biblical Wisdom literature has generally been seen
as kyriocentric literature,[6] written by and for elite educated men,[7]
more recent feminist studies have argued[8] that post-exilic wo/men
in Israel and Hellenistic Jewish wo/men in Egypt conceived of Divine Wisdom as prefigured in the language and images of God-
desses such as Isis,[9] Athena, or Dike.[10] Like the Goddess Isis, so
Divine Wisdom is represented as using the proclamatory "I am"
style for announcing her universal message of salvation. According to a very well known prayer, all the different nations and people use divine titles derived from their own local mythologies
when they call on the G*ddess, who is Isis. They do so in the full
knowledge that Isis is one but encompasses all. Similarly, like the
widespread Isis cult and mythology, the variegated Sophia-Wisdom discourses of post-exilic Palestinian wo/men elaborate the
image and figure of Divine Chokmah as the "other name" of
G*d. In the image of Sophia, Hellenistic Jewish wo/men hold together belief in the "one" G*d of Israel with a cosmopolitan ethos
that can respect local particularities without giving up claims to
universality.

One of the foremost titles of Isis is "savior" (*pansōteira, sōteira,
sōter*), and countless texts and inscriptions praise her as such:

Holy and eternal savior of the human race,
ever beneficent in cherishing mortals
You indeed bestow the sweet affection of a mother
upon the tribulations of the unfortunate.[11]

Like Isis, Sophia is pictured, in the Book of Wisdom, as a Divine Savior figure who promises universal salvation. The encomium of her in Wisdom 9:18–10:21 begins with the statement in verse 9:18 that people were saved by Sophia and summarizes her saving activity in 10:9: "Sophia rescued from troubles those who served her."

In line with Hans Conzelmann's pathbreaking proposal,[12] I suggested more than twenty years ago that the biblical discourses which, in the figure of Divine Wisdom, integrate aspects of Isis religion with biblical faith are best understood as engaging in "reflective mythology." This is a type of theological reflection that borrows from and reconfigures elements from G*ddess language and cult in order to speak about the loving care of G*d for Her people, Israel, as well as for all of creation. Chokmah-Sophia-Wisdom is the personification of G*d's saving activity in the world, in Israel's election, and in the salvation of all peoples.

Wisdom-Sophia's traces are found not only in post-exilic Jewish Wisdom circles, especially in Egypt, but also in apocalyptic literature and in the Qumran writings. Hence the assumption that apocalyptic and sapiential traditions are exclusive of each other—which has dominated and still dominates contemporary exegetical discussions—must be seen as a product of modern methodological conjectures. When one moves, however, from this explicit and broad-based Sophia-reflection in Jewish Wisdom literature to early Christian writings, the figure of Divine Wisdom seems to disappear. Whereas early Jewish literature struggles to integrate Sophia-G*ddess language into its monotheistic frame, early Christian literature seems to marginalize and submerge the figure and teaching of Divine Wisdom almost completely. Yet a symptomatic reading, that is, a careful attention to traces and tensions inscribed in the text, can show that a submerged theology of Wisdom, or sophialogy, permeates all Christian scripture.

Only a very few direct references to Divine Wisdom are found in Christian canonical writings;[13] Sophia emerges solely in the margins of early Christian scripture. Grammatical masculine language for "Christ-Logos" seems to have absorbed nearly wholly those "female" divine elements which were derived from reflective Wisdom mythology and which brought elements of G*ddess symbolism and cult into a new configuration. This explains why the early Christian imagination that spoke of Israel's G*d as Divine Sophia, appearing in the gestalt of the G*ddess, has become almost totally lost and forgotten in the self-understanding of the Western churches, except where it has been transferred to Mary, the mother of Jesus.

In recent years scholarship and texts about Divine Wisdom have received intensive feminist attention because of the female gender of Chokmah-Sophia-Wisdom. Feminists in the churches have translated the results of biblical scholarship on early Jewish and Christian Wisdom discourses into the idiom of song, poem, and liturgy.[14] This practical and creative feminist attention to the divine female figure of Wisdom has brought the results of scholarship on biblical Wisdom literature to public attention.

For instance, in 1993, Protestant feminists sponsored a conference in Minneapolis that not only featured lectures on Divine Sophia but also invoked and celebrated Her in prayer and liturgy. This "Re-Imagining" Conference was allegedly the most controversial ecumenical event in decades. Conservatives claimed that it challenged the very foundations of mainline Protestantism in the United States. The reaction of the Christian right to this conference was so violent that one high-ranking woman lost her church job and others have run into grave difficulties maintaining their own positions in the church.[15] This struggle indicates the significance of Divine Sophia-Wisdom for contemporary Christian self-understanding.

How can one recover the traces of this submerged sophialogical tradition in such a way that the rich table of Divine Wisdom once again provides spiritual food and drink, nourishment and strength in the struggles to transform kyriarchal relations of exploitation and marginalization? Or should one as a feminist even try to do so? Since both Jewish and Christian texts present and simultaneously obfuscate Divine Wisdom with kyriocentric theological language, some feminist scholars have asked whether it is at all possible for feminist interpretation to transform the obscured female figure of Wisdom-Sophia in such a way that she can once again develop her imaginative power. Others have argued that one must reject the traditions of Divine Wisdom altogether, as kyriarchal male traditions that are misogynist and elitist.

In the present chapter I intend to participate in this feminist debate by *first* utilizing a hermeneutics of reconstruction for examining some of the discursive fragments and traces of Divine Wisdom which, like the tip of an iceberg, still emerge in the margins of early Christian writings. In a *second* step I will then explore the issues that are at stake in the debates on whether or not the figure and traditions of Sophia can and should be reappropriated by contemporary feminists. In a *third*, concluding section I will again attempt to underscore the hermeneutical significance of the Sophia texts and traditions.

I will pay particular attention here to whether and how exclusivist arguments and kyriarchal gender constructs are reinscribed in such discourses about Divine Wisdom. My intent throughout is to critically present both biblical and contemporary scholarly discourses on Divine Wisdom as sites of struggle over religious and theological meaning. I am interested here not so much in the issue of feminine identification with the female figure of Divine Wisdom but in the gendered language and symbolism of the Wisdom traditions. Consequently, I will focus on their significance for the articulation of a critical Christian self-understanding and inclusive identity formation.

In my view, Jewish and Christian discourses on Divine Wisdom are still important today not only because they are a rich resource for female language for G*d but also because they provide a framework for developing a feminist ecological theology of creation. Moreover, they embody a religious ethos that is not exclusive of other religious visions but can be understood as a part of them. The earliest Sophia traditions that can still be traced in the margins of early Christian works intimate a perspective that combines Jewish prophetic and sophialogical traditions into a political, open-ended, and cosmopolitan religious *basileia* vision of struggle for the well-being of all people.

The Earliest Sophialogical Jesus Traditions

Martin Hengel, who certainly cannot be suspected of feminist leanings, has argued that a broad-based Wisdom theology, or sophialogy, can be traced in early Christian discourses. According to him, Isaiah 11:2 was the generative scriptural text which gave rise to those Jewish messianic expectations that were embedded in Wisdom theology.[16] Underscoring the interrelationship between Divine Wisdom and Spirit, Hengel traces the messianic traditions about the Wisdom teacher endowed with the Holy Spirit through the Hebrew Bible and other Jewish texts. Hengel points particularly to Wisdom Salomonis as expressing the complete unity between Sophia and Spirit.[17] Since Sophia has here assumed the functions of the Spirit, it can be said that she, like the Spirit, can be sent by G*d. Hence the "fictional" Solomon calls unto G*d to send Her down to earth.[18]

> If we search for a pre-Christian Jewish key in order to understand the post-Easter Christology, we will find this key in the Sapientia Salomonis, in which Palestinian traditions of apocalyptic and sapiential background are combined with Hellenistic vocabulary in a unique way.[19]

In Hengel's view, such sophialogical christological reflection was not created by the primitive post-Easter community with its exaltation christology. Rather, Hengel argues, such sophialogical reflection can be traced back to the historical Jesus, who understood himself as a messianic teacher and Spirit-endowed charismatic. Early Jewish discourses on Divine Wisdom thus provided a theological linguistic framework and tradition for Jesus that was then taken up by the myth-making of early Christian groups in order to elaborate Jesus' theological significance for their own communities.

That such variegated christological discourses developed in as brief a time span as twenty years after Jesus' death can be plausibly explained, in Hengel's view, only when one assumes Jewish Wisdom theology as the generative matrix.[20] Hence, according to him, the traditions of Jesus, the Galilean preacher and representative of Divine Wisdom, can bridge the chasm between the actual person Jesus of Nazareth who was executed by the Romans and

Jesus the Christ, who was proclaimed as powerful Lord, preexistent son of G*d and mediator of creation. If one assumes that early Jewish Sophia theology provided the language and mythological frame of reference, one is able to explain the earliest Christian attempts to make meaning out of the ministry and execution of Jesus.

Even if one does not share the confidence with which Hengel ascribes such a prophetic Wisdom discourse to the historical Jesus himself, one can nevertheless agree that the Sophia tradition is the most likely generative theological center for the earliest articulations of the Jesus traditions. It cannot be stressed enough, however, that these submerged Jesus traditions connecting Jesus' ministry with the figure of Divine Wisdom were formulated by Jewish wo/men and that they have their roots in Jewish reflective mythology.[21]

Some of the earliest traditions of the Wisdom-Jesus groups understand the ministry and mission of Jesus as that of a prophet of Sophia who was sent to proclaim that the Sophia-G*d of Jesus is the G*d of the poor, the outcasts, and all those suffering from injustice. The G*d of Jesus is Israel's G*d in the gestalt and the figure of Divine Wisdom.

As Sophia's messenger and prophet, Jesus not only proclaimed the *basileia* of G*d to the poor, the hungry, and the excluded in Israel, he also made it experientially available to everyone through his miracles and healing activities. One of the oldest sayings ascribed to Jesus stresses that "Sophia is justified or proven just by all her children" (QLk 7:35).[22] This saying most likely has its "setting in life" in the inclusive table-community of Jesus with sinners, tax collectors, and prostitutes.[23] The Sophia G*d of Jesus recognizes all Israelites as Her children. She is justified, that is, "made just," in and by all of them. However, this earliest tradition ascribes to Jesus and John an eminence and excess of meaning that heightens the significance of their work and fate. It emphasizes that the most prominent among the children of Sophia are John the Baptist and, especially, Jesus, whose work continues in the Jesus communities. This theological "more" is also expressed in the following Jesus saying regarding the Queen of Sheba:

The queen of the South will arise at the judgment with those of this generation and condemn them; for she came from the ends of the earth to hear the wisdom of Solomon, and behold, something greater than Solomon is here. (QLk 11:31)

Jesus' ministry and teaching are here seen as greater than that of the great Wisdom teacher Solomon and as excelling that of the prophet Jonah. Such a sophialogical context also makes comprehensible the very difficult saying of Matthew 12:32, paralleled in Luke 12:10, which states that blasphemy against Jesus, "the Human One" (son of man), will be forgiven whereas blasphemy against Spirit-Sophia is unforgivable.

Contrary to the majority consensus of exegetes, I have insisted that this sophialogical "more" should not be misread in an exclusivist sense as a superlative, as is often the case. Even Richard Horsley, who is very concerned to avoid biased ideological assumptions undergirding the reconstruction of the earliest sayings traditions, feels compelled to stress that Jesus is the one of utmost historical significance: "That Jesus, while obviously a prophet, far transcends the significance of any ordinary prophet for the Q people, can be seen most directly in the next set of sayings regarding John's significance (QLk 7:24–28)."[24]

Although Horsley recognizes that the least in the kingdom of G*d—and not Jesus—is compared with John, he nevertheless asserts and concludes, "Implicit, of course, is that if John was more than a prophet, how much more extraordinary is Jesus. . . . Q apparently understands Jesus as the climactic figure in the long line of Israelite prophets. *That is never articulated directly* [my emphasis] but it is implied in the insertion of 11:49–51 into the woes against the Pharisees."[25]

I want to argue, to the contrary, that Jesus does not transcend this prophetic tradition, which is an open-ended, ongoing tradition, but that he is a part of it. Jesus of Nazareth, who was understood as an eminent prophet of Sophia, does not close this tradition but activates it. As the child of Sophia-G*d, Jesus stands in a long succession or unending line of prophets who seek to gather together the children of Israel to their gracious Sophia-

G*d; just as some of the other prophets had been, so also John the Baptizer and Jesus were persecuted and killed as the emissaries of Divine Wisdom.

These earliest Jesus traditions contain four oracles in which Sophia is said to be speaking directly. The first is found only in Matthew and there placed in the mouth of Jesus. It originally represented an invitation by Sophia herself:

> Come to me, all who labor and are heavy laden, and I will give you rest. Take my yoke upon you, and learn from me; for I am gentle and lowly in heart, and you will find rest for your souls. For my yoke is easy, and my burden is light. (Mt 11:28–30, RSV)

As Sophia's messenger, Jesus calls all the nobodies who are heavy laden and promises them rest and *shalom*. The yoke of Sophia is not heavy but light.

In the "lament over Jerusalem," again placed in the mouth of Jesus, Sophia mourns the murder of her messengers:

> O Jerusalem, Jerusalem, killing the prophets and stoning those who are sent to you! How often would I have gathered your children together as a hen gathers her brood under her wings, and you would not! (QLk 13:34, RSV)

This lament compares the work of Divine Sophia with the care of a mother bird for her young. If this statement expressing Sophia's gracious care and invitation is taken out of its original Galilean historical-rhetorical context and universalized in a Christian reading, it becomes a saying rife with anti-Jewish meaning. Hence Richard Horsley has correctly warned Christian readers not to misread this lament in a Christian fashion as an anti-Jewish statement. Rather, in his view, this lament expresses the sentiment of Galilean "folks" against the governing authorities whose center is Jerusalem.[26] This Sophia lament is not directed against all of Israel or against Judaism as a whole, but only against the governing authorities in the capital. However, even such an emphasis can be read in an anti-Jewish way if Galilee is understood as "Galilee of the gentiles." Susannah Heschel has rightly pointed out[27] that during the Nazi period German exegetes argued that Jesus was not a racial Jew but a member of the foreign peoples, among them Aryans, who lived in Galilee.[28] While in its original Jewish context the saying is a prophetic lament, in a Christian contextualization it becomes an anti-Jewish threat.

A prophetic sophialogical understanding of the death of Jesus is also expressed in the following, very difficult and ambiguous Jesus saying: "Since the days of John the Baptist until today the *basileia* of G*d suffers violence and is hindered by those who are violent" (QMt 11:12). This saying brings the Sophia and *basileia* traditions together. It also speaks of the violence encountered by those who struggle for the *basileia* of the Sophia-G*d of Jesus.

Finally, the following Sophia saying, attributed to Jesus, indicates clearly that theological reflection on the fate of Jesus who was executed as an insurrectionist by the Romans resulted in an understanding of him as a prophetic messenger of Sophia who, like John the Baptist and other prophets before him, was persecuted and killed. It indicates how it was possible theologically to shift the blame for Jesus' execution from the Romans to the Jews.

> Therefore also the Wisdom of God said, "I will send them prophets and apostles, some of whom they will kill and persecute," that the blood of all the prophets, shed from the foundation of the world, may be required of this generation, from the blood of Abel to the blood of Zechariah, who perished between the altar and the sanctuary. Yes, I tell you, it shall be required of this generation. (QLk 11:49–51, RSV)

Angelika Strotmann[29] has pointed out that feminist interpretation has tended to neglect the severe second part of this Sophia saying and therefore has not sufficiently addressed the problem that it is a harsh pronouncement of judgment against Israel. She is correct in emphasizing that this prophetic judgment oracle[30] has been articulated by Jews and should not be interpreted in an anti-Jewish fashion. However, it is not clear why this observation should vitiate the reconstruction of the Jesuanic *basileia* movement as an inclusive movement that is open to everyone. Judgment sayings are warnings that do not have the function of excluding but rather that of challenging their addressees not to behave in a certain way.[31]

While it is conceivable that QLuke 7:35 could go back to Jesus himself, this last saying is clearly a later interpretation because it unwittingly shifts the blame for Jesus' execution from the Romans to the Jews. The question therefore is not so much whether this theological threat of judgment can be understood in a fashion that is not anti-Jewish but whether this saying already contains the seeds of anti-Judaism.

In short, the earliest sophialogical traditions speak of Jesus as standing in a succession of Sophia's prophets and messengers, who proclaim the oracles of Sophia. Jesus—who opens up a future for the poor and oppressed in Israel and promises salvation and well-being without exception to all the children of Israel— was one of Sophia's children who has vindicated Her. This prophetic line of succession is continued in the Jesus movements. However, insofar as early sophialogical reflection understands the execution of Jesus as it does that of John and other prophets, as the outcome of his mission as messenger and prophet of Divine Sophia, it opens the door to an anti-Jewish reading.

By stressing that Jesus' execution has not been intended or willed by Sophia-G*d, but is rather the outcome of his prophetic ministry and mission, this sophialogical reflection on Jesus' death soon ascribes the responsibility for the execution of Jesus to Israel.

These earliest discourses of the Jesus movement, which understand Jesus as a sage and prophet of Sophia, provide us with two images of Jesus which are not separate but interactive. One presents Jesus as a powerful teacher of Wisdom who addresses the ongoing quest for a gracious G*d; the Sophia-G*d of Jesus loves all of humanity irrespective of their ethnic and social standing and shows concern for liberation and empowerment of the underprivileged. The other image pictures Jesus as a powerful prophet of Divine Sophia, challenging readers not only to hear but also to act upon Jesus' proclamation of the *basileia*, Sophia-G*d's alternative society and world. This sophialogical discourse opens up a way to respond to religious pluralism and to the greater problem of suffering and injustice in the world.[32]

Such a positive reading of the earliest Wisdom discourses does not mean, however, that feminist scholars should not challenge the kyriocentric frameworks of the Wisdom tradition, just as they must scrutinize all other biblical traditions. When attempting to reconstruct scriptural discourses, feminist theologians must be particularly careful not to reinscribe the elite male, kyriarchal prejudicial frames of meaning that are inscribed in such discourses.[33]

Whereas these prophetic Sophia oracles understand Jesus as part of an open-ended, ongoing movement, the so-called Johannine "father-son" saying, representing another early tradition, advocates an exclusivist stance. The so-called Johannine saying of Jesus (QMt 11:25–27) not only seems to understand Jesus in terms of Divine Sophia but also emphatically identifies him as *the son of the father* who mediates exclusive revelation.

At that time Jesus declared, "I thank thee, Father, Lord of heaven and earth, that thou hast hidden these things from the wise and understanding and revealed them to babes; yea, Father, for such was thy gracious will. All things have been delivered to me by my Father; and no one knows the Son except the Father, and no one knows the Father except the Son and any one to whom the Son chooses to reveal him." (QMt 11:25–27, RSV).

It is debated whether QMatthew 11:25 was originally an independent saying or whether it was from the beginning a part of the present thanksgiving prayer. In any case, in its present context verse 25 shares in the exclusionary meaning frame of verse 27. Every feature of this exclusivist father-son saying (QMt 11:27) can be traced back to Wisdom tradition. Just as Wisdom has received everything from G*d, so Jesus has received everything from G*d (v. 27a). Just as Wisdom is only known by G*d and is the only one who knows G*d, so Jesus has all Wisdom; he is even Wisdom herself (v. 27b, c). Just as Divine Sophia gives her wisdom as a gift, so also Jesus reveals Wisdom to all those to whom he wants to reveal her (v. 27d).[34] Hence it could be concluded that here Jesus replaces Sophia. However, John Kloppenborg has

drawn attention to the fact that "nowhere in the Wisdom tradition is it stated that Sophia has *received* either knowledge or
power from God. Sophia indeed has knowledge of all things (Wis
7:18–21; 8:8) and *exousia* in Jerusalem (Sir. 24:11b) but these derive from the fact that She was present with God at the creation
and is the instrument of creation."[35]

The shift from the linguistic chain *Sophia-prophets-Jesus-fol-
lowers* to that of *Father-Son-Logos* indicates that in this tradition
the father/son relationship, of both the patriarchal household and the
Wisdom school, is operative. Thus this second early Sophia tradition suggests a shift in social location as well as a linguistic shift.

In my view, the Logos tradition, which understands the Logos
to be the firstborn son not only of Sophia but also of G*d, has determined the theological reflection of QMatthew 11:25–27. It has
affinities with the sophialogical tradition which was developed by
the Jewish theologian Philo of Alexandria, who lived in the first
century C.E. in Alexandria (ca. 25 B.C.E. to 40 C.E.). According to
the gender understanding of Philo, "femaleness" is "weak, easily
deceived, the cause of sin, lifeless, diseased, enslaved, unmanly,
nerveless, mean, slavish, sluggish."[36] With Aristotle, Philo holds
that the human male is perfect and that the human female is nothing but an imperfect male. Hence masculinity and maleness but
not femininity and femaleness are qualities that can express the
Divine. In his work *De Fuga*, Philo speaks of Wisdom as the
daughter of G*d. He explains that she is only imaged as a female
figure in order to give first place to the Creator G*d, who must be
understood as masculine because masculinity has priority over
femininity and femininity is always lesser than masculinity. Since
in reality Wisdom is masculine (arsen), Philo argues, one should
not attribute any significance to the grammatical gender of Sophia.

Within Philo's philosophical framework, only maleness and
masculinity can signify preeminence, whereas femaleness and femininity are always secondary and defective. Consequently, Philo is
forced to stress that Divine Wisdom, whom he calls the daughter
of G*d, is not only masculine but also must be called "father."
She is a father who sows and begets learning, education, knowledge, and insight as well as good and laudable deeds in human
souls.[37] This text documents that the ancients were well aware

that so-called grammatical gender is not identical with so-called natural gender.

Philo expands his theological system of asymmetric gender dualism into a system of cosmological dualism. This theoretical move enables him to transfer the attributes of Woman-Wisdom onto the Logos who, in Wisdom 18:14–19, is still a subordinate figure to Sophia. According to Philo, two worlds exist: Sophia's heavenly world of life and salvation and our earthly world of mortality and struggle. Whereas Divine Sophia (Wisdom) is in the heavenly world of G*d, her son, the Logos (the Word), lives in the historical world in order to clear a path for the soul to return to heaven. Insofar as Philo restricts the sphere of Divine Wisdom to the heavenly world, he vacates her place as mediator of creation and salvation on the one hand and as people's advocate in a historical world on the other, so that her son, the Logos, can take over her functions and titles. This grammatical and theological replacement of the feminine-typed figure of Sophia with the masculine-typed figure of the Logos has produced the masculine-typed linguistic chain Father–Son of G*d–Sons of the Son of G*d.

Christian Testament scholars largely agree that, just as in the work of Philo, in early Christian writings two levels of reflection on Divine Sophia can be distinguished. The first level, which may or may not go back to the historical Jesus himself, is barely traceable any longer. On this level, Jesus is understood as a messenger and prophet of Divine Sophia. The second level of theological reflection identifies Jesus with Divine Wisdom. Jesus is not called Sophia but receives grammatically masculine christological titles such as *kyrios* and *sōtēr*, which also were titles of Isis-Sophia. Just as in Philo, so also in early Christian discourses one finds a middle stage where the attributes and discourses of Divine Wisdom are applied to the Logos. Early Christian sophialogical reflection also knows such a transitional stage in which attributes and features of Divine Sophia were given to Jesus. This transitional state comes to the fore in the debates on whether the pre-Pauline hymns and the gospels of Matthew and John already *identify* Jesus with Sophia or whether they see Jesus and his work only in analogy with Divine Wisdom. With this summary sketch of a reconstruction of the Jesus movements' reflective sophialogical discourses, I will leave the historical discussion and turn to feminist objections against the revalorization of the Sophia-traditions.

The Gospel of Sophia and the Gospel of the Poor

Luise Schottroff has raised serious historical and theological objections against feminist attempts at re-covering the earliest Sophia discourses in order to valorize Lady Wisdom.[38] She maintains that the fascination of feminist theologians with Sophia christology is misplaced. Wisdom speculation is at home in Israel's elite male circles and bespeaks their interests, and Wisdom literature is addressed to and seeks to give instruction to the pater familias of upper-class standing. Therefore, to privilege the early Christian Sophia traditions in feminist theology would mean to eclipse the "gospel of the poor" (*Armenevangelium*) that is at the heart of Jesus' preaching. This *Armenevangelium* is completely determined and shaped by the prophetic tradition. Hence, she argues, texts such as Matthew 11:25 and 11:28–30 are not to be considered as Wisdom texts but rather represent sapiential elements that have been integrated into the *Armenevangelium*. Moreover, she argues that the rejection of the messengers of Sophia is not comparable to the rejection of Sophia since she is not killed but withdraws unharmed to heaven.

Hence, Schottroff argues, the traces of Sophia ought not to be the starting point of feminist liberation theology. Rather, such a theology must begin with the fact that the *Armenevangelium*, the revelation of G*d to the *nēpioi*—the babes, the uneducated, or nobodies—is a wo/men's gospel (*Frauenevangelium*) since more wo/men than men are to be counted among the nobodies. Schottroff concludes, therefore, that the feminist emphasis on a Sophia theology is misplaced. It must be rejected on historical and theological grounds. The *historical* reason is given with Schottroff's negative evaluation of the Wisdom tradition, which in her estimation is not at all oriented toward the G*d of all-encompassing justice but instead preserves the interests of elite males. The *theological* reason consists of the very important connection that Schottroff makes between the *Armenevangelium* that spells justice for wo/men and the feminist vision of wo/men's liberation.

Yet Schottroff seems to assume that we are able to single out and definitely identify the *Armenevangelium* as *the* liberating early Christian tradition for wo/men that can be separated from the Wisdom tradition. She can make such an assumption only because she conjectures that prophetic-apocalyptic and Wisdom traditions were clearly separated in first-century theological discourses. However, the *Armenevangelium* seems to me closely related if not totally integrated with the open-ended Q tradition that understands Jesus and John as the messengers of Sophia who continue but do not close off a long line of prophets. Moreover, recent scholarship has convincingly shown that Wisdom and apocalyptic traditions are intertwined in Jewish and early Christian literature. Hence it is no longer feasible to sharply divide sapiential and apocalyptic discourses from each other and to brand the Wisdom traditions as discourses of male elites that supposedly were articulated over against the apocalyptic gospel of poor and oppressed people (*Armenevangelium*).

I agree with Schottroff, however, that the reflective sophialogy of the earliest Jesus groups did not emerge from the rarefied atmosphere of elite Wisdom schools. I suggest, moreover, that such sophialogical reflection was forged in a deliberative communal process by which wo/men sought to make sense out of the execution of Jesus within a sapiential-apocalyptic framework. In the everyday life of Galilean villagers and townspeople, "folk wisdom" was widespread and treasured. Moreover, divine female figures were in all likelihood well known. Hence it is quite plausible to argue that Jesus could have been remembered as one of the prophets whom Divine Sophia had sent, who was executed, and who was experienced by Galilean wo/men as the Living One. Finally, in this reflective meaning making of the Jesus movements, a creative interaction between Wisdom theology and *basileia* proclamation which had the power to transform both of these traditions could have taken place.

Rather than exploring the possibility of an integration of Wisdom and *basileia* discourses, Schottroff insists to the contrary that the Sophia tradition is permanently suspect not only as an elite male, kyriocentric tradition but also as one that, in a dualistic fashion, plays the "good" woman against the "evil" woman.[39]

Such a misogynist tradition cannot be concerned with justice at all. Yet Silvia Schroer has rightly objected to such a negative evaluation of the Wisdom traditions.[40] She has not only pointed out that Wisdom discourses are permeated with the teachings of "Wo/man Justice" but also agrees with me that in the first century, prophetic-apocalyptic and sapiential traditions were intertwined, integrated, and changed. In addition, Schroer argues that the Wisdom traditions had been democratized in the first century and that much of the sapiential tradition in the Gospels reflects folk wisdom which very well could have been articulated by and for wo/men. Finally, Schroer points out that Schottroff's exegetical-historical objection against the feminist regeneration of Divine *Chokmah-Sophia*-Wisdom may also be due to her different confessional location[41] and her indebtedness to neo-orthodox theology.[42]

To sum up my argument, recent studies have shown that one is no longer justified in seeing the Wisdom tradition purely as a male tradition that not only reveals little about actual wo/men but also functioned to oppress them. The positive feminist valence of the female figure of Wisdom comes to the fore not only in the grammatical feminine gender of the Hebrew (*Chokmah*) and Greek (*Sophia*) terms for Wisdom but also in the sociological changes which engendered Wisdom discourses and their theological consequences.[43] Dieter Georgi has argued, for instance, that wo/men belonged to the communities in which the Wisdom of Solomon was at home. He suggests that the book served dramatic-liturgical purposes and was composed by a group of male and female worshippers.[44] For support of his thesis, Georgi points to Philo's portrayal of the Therapeutae as an example of such a Wisdom community of wo/men. In *De Vita Contemplativa*, Philo describes an ascetic group of wo/men and men who weekly gather around the table of Divine Wisdom to feast on her teaching as a kind of heavenly food.[45] Moreover, feminist research on Egypt has pointed out that wo/men were independent and powerful in Egyptian culture.[46] The same is also probably true for Jewish wo/men in Egypt. Philo's polemical arguments and negative portrayal of the feminine can be seen in a new light when they are perceived as directed against the actual power of influential wo/men in the Jewish community,[47] and in all likelihood they have their rhetorical roots in such polemics.[48]

A Sophialogical Hermeneutic

My own work has introduced and elaborated the Sophia tradition as one *but not the sole* early Christian discourse that might open up unfulfilled possibilities for feminist liberation theological reflection. As I have argued above, I find the traces of the "Jesus, prophet of Sophia" traditions theologically significant because they maintain the unique historical particularity of Jesus without having to resort to assertions of exclusivity and superiority. More importantly, Jewish sophialogy that is funded by the interactive meaning making of apocalyptic, prophetic, and Wisdom traditions valorizes life, creativity, and well-being in the midst of injustice and struggle. These elements—open-endedness, inclusivity, justice, and a cosmopolitan emphasis on creation spirituality as well as on practical insight—have been especially attractive not only to feminists but also to Asian liberation theologians.

Yet it must also be pointed out that feminist interpretations of Divine Wisdom are sometimes in danger of succumbing to a "romanticized" notion of femininity and to reinscribing Western kyriocentric gender dualism, which either devalues wo/men and femininity or idealizes them as representing superior transcendent and salvific qualities. Extolling the femininity of Sophia, I argue, cannot but reinscribe the Western cultural sex/gender system in theological terms, insofar as it divinizes the sociopolitical patriarchal gender notion of cultural femininity modeled after the image and likeness of the White Lady. Whenever theology in general and Wisdom christology in particular are positioned within a framework of essentialist gender dualism, they cannot but reproduce this ideological frame.[49]

In a fascinating article on "The God of Jesus in the Gospel Sayings Source," Antoinette Clark Wire has argued that the Jewish Jesus traditions did not use the images of the "generous father" and the "abused woman Wisdom" to confirm kyriocentric gender stereotypes but rather to counteract them. In her view, the Q sayings' source does not conceive of the "Divine Father" in patri-kyriarchal terms but understands G*d as the one "who cannot resist the weak and becomes their sure resource; the abused Woman who is the Wisdom of God outlasts the powerful until all the abused in the world are vindicated. . . . [This discourse] disorients our gender stereotypes to see God's caring face as male and God's demanding face as female."[50]

Although this attempt to subvert kyriarchal gender inscriptions by reversing them opens up new possibilities for Christian theological reflection, it nevertheless at the same time tends to reinscribe into G*d language the same cultural-theological sex-gender system that it seeks to overcome.

In order to avoid this pitfall, I have argued, in my book *Jesus: Miriam's Child, Sophia's Prophet*, that one must explicitly read against the grain of the cultural feminine framework and shift the discussion of the female figure of Divine Wisdom from the ontological level to a linguistic, symbolic, hermeneutical level of reflection. Such a shift is justified insofar as Wisdom theology and Divine Father language are best understood not as producing a unified theological discourse about the essence and true being of G*d but rather as a discourse embodying a variegated "reflective mythology."

As I have tried to show in my own work, the grammatically masculine language adopted by ancient Wisdom discourses and modern biblical interpretation has a difficult time speaking adequately of Divine Wisdom in the "preconstructed" kyriocentric framework of Jewish and Christian monotheism. Insofar as this language struggles to avoid turning Divine Wisdom into a second feminine deity who is subordinate to the masculine deity, it also struggles against the theological reification of monotheism in terms of Western cultural elite male hegemony.

When speaking about the biblical G*d, scriptural discourses and Christian liturgies and theologies, however, have not succeeded in avoiding this danger because they have used predominantly masculine language, metaphors, and images for speaking of the Divine. Biblical interpretation reinscribes such kyriocentric G*d language as given or revealed when it understands Divine Wo/man Wisdom in metaphorical terms but understands the kyriocentric language about G*d the Father, King, and Lord as de-

scriptive theological language that adequately expresses G*d's nature and being. Such an uncritical use of masculine G*d language
neglects the fact that human language about G*d is always to be
understood as metaphorical language. G*d language is symbolic,
metaphoric, and analogous because human language can never
comprehend and speak adequately about Divine reality.

Critical theological reflection on the biblical traditions of
Sophia must therefore adopt a theory of language, I have argued
in the preceding chapters, that does not subscribe to linguistic determinism. Grammatically kyriocentric language is often understood as "natural gender" language that describes and reflects
reality rather than as a grammatical classification system that
constructs reality in androcentric and kyriarchal terms. Conventional androcentric language is produced, regulated, and perpetu-
ated in the interest of patri-kyriarchal society, culture, and
religion. If language is not a reflection of reality but rather a so-
cial-cultural linguistic system, then the relationship between language and reality is not an essential given but is constructed in
discourse. This is especially true when language speaks about
spiritual reality since the Divine cannot be comprehended in
human language.

In short, I have argued here and elsewhere that the rediscovery
of Divine Wisdom's traces inscribed in biblical writings requires
that theology reflect on the inadequacy of kyriocentric language
and problematize it. Rediscovery of the ancient Wisdom traditions does not invite us to simply repeat the language of early
Jewish and Christian reflective mythology about Divine Wisdom.
Rather it compels us to continue to struggle not only with conventional masculine language for G*d but also with the exclusivist authoritarian functions and implications of such language.
Theology must rearticulate the biblical symbols, images, and titles
of Divine Wisdom-Chokmah-Sophia in a way that not only radically questions and undermines ossified masculine and absolu-
tized language about G*d and Christ but also deconstructs the
Western cultural sex/gender system. I have therefore argued for a
reconceptualization of biblical interpretation as reflective mythology in rhetorical terms. Such a rhetoric mobilizes cultural, sociopolitical, and religious imagination in the struggle over

meaning. It is able to lift up and valorize those traces of Divine
Wisdom that open up possibilities of liberation and visions of
well-being which have not yet been realized in history.[51]

Such a feminist sophialogical hermeneutics—one that understands itself as exploring and elaborating the words of Wisdom—
argues that Wisdom-Sophia, the divine power of liberation,
reveals Her presence in the emancipatory theologizing and struggles within the horizon of the *basileia*. Hence one cannot speak of
G*d either as utterly transcendent or as totally immanent. Although G*d is "beyond" oppression, G*d's revelatory presence
can be experienced *within* the struggles against dehumanization
and injustice. The Divine must be renamed again and again in the
experiences of wo/men struggling for change and the transformation of oppressive structures and dehumanizing ideologies. G*d is
to be named as active power of well-being in our midst. Thus
feminist theology becomes sophialogy, a speaking of and about
Divine Wisdom, whose name oscillates between divine transcen-
dence and human immanence. It is S/he who accompanies us in
our struggles against injustice and for liberation, just as S/he accompanied the Israelites on their desert journey from slavery to
freedom.[52]

Divine Wisdom-Sophia, as G*d the Creator and Liberator, is
not exclusive of other religious traditions but is at work among
all peoples, cultures, and religions. She teaches justice, prudence,
and well-being. She is present as the crafty trickster, the guide of
the people, and the wise wo/man of the ancients and indigenous
peoples. She embraces creation in its living beauty and manifold
variety and delights in its wonders. Divine Wisdom encompasses
and sustains everything and everyone. While the Eastern Orthodox tradition has always retained the memory of Her as *Hagia
Sophia* in its worship, She has been virtually forgotten in Western
christocentric theology. In Catholicism, traces of Her splendor
have been reflected in the image of Mary, but in the process She
has suffered from the same bias that affects all wo/men. She has
been relegated to second-class citizenship or completely erased
from the religious consciousness of the dominant culture.

Yet Her hour has finally come. In the past two decades or so,

Christian feminist theology has rediscovered Sophia and made Her voice heard among Her people. It has pointed out that Jesus was a prophet of Divine Wisdom-Sophia who used the idiom of folk wisdom and spoke in parables that sought to puzzle and startle hearers into recognition. Such sapiential or Wisdom stories reveal Divine Wisdom at work in everyday life and its struggles.

Four stories or parables in the Gospels which are ascribed to Jesus have wo/men as their central agents and characters. They tell of Divine Wisdom at work in our midst. I would like to use these parables here in order to characterize the practices of feminist biblical interpretation as a boundary-breaking activity of Divine Wisdom and for concluding my explorations of a critical feminist interpretation for liberation.

First: The parable of the leaven (Mt 13:33; Lk 13:20–21) sees Divine Wisdom as a baker wo/man, likening the *basileia*—G*d's world of well-being—to a wo/man mixing leaven into a large amount of meal. Jesus' hearers must have been startled by this story, because in the Hebrew Bible and in early Christian discourses leaven is seen as corrupting, something that foments ungodly behavior. This parable of the baker wo/man (Sophia) preparing leavened bread probably affronted the sensibilities of the pious in Jesus' audience because it images the *basileia*—that is, G*d's alternative world of well-being, or the alternative commonweal of G*d—as being brought about by the "fomenting" and "corrupting" activity of Divine Sophia who is at work still today in and through feminist theologies.

The *second* parable tells the story of the wo/man who lost a coin and diligently sweeps the house in search for it (Lk 15:8–10). This parable likens the activity of the wo/man and her joy over her success to the search of Divine Wisdom for the lost and hidden, for those who have fallen through the cracks. The party of celebration that takes place after the coin is found not only calls to mind the stories about the messianic banquet and its joy, it also alludes to the joy of recovering lost emancipatory Christian traditions of wo/men's agency and struggle—a heritage that can be experienced by reclaiming wo/men's theologies and histories as their own heritage.

The *third* parable, which I have already discussed in the previous chapter, is the story of the assertive widow who insistently demands justice (Lk 18:1–8). This story pictures Divine Wisdom as a strong wo/man who insistently works for justice. The unfair and sinister judge of the town, who finally gives in to her demand, does not therefore represent G*d (as is often assumed) but rather embodies a corrupt justice system that does not care about people's rights or G*d's law but only about its own prospering. Such a situation of blatant inequity will change only when threatened by those daughters of Sophia who forcefully and insistently struggle for their rights. The point of the story is that the widow does not give up her demand for justice. She represents Divine Wisdom and her followers as forcefully fighting for justice and as righting wrongs.

The *fourth* parable does not represent Divine Wisdom, but it carries a warning for her daughters and messengers. It is the story of the wise and foolish young wo/men who are participants in a wedding party (Mt 25:1–13). As was custom in the ancient Near East, they wait for the bridegroom to appear, but he is very much delayed. Whereas the wise ones have prepared for such an occasion, the foolish ones run out of oil for their lamps. This story cautions those who engage in movements and struggles against injustice to plan for the long haul: burnout is no excuse for giving up the struggle. A biblical hermeneutic and spirituality that does not sustain our commitment to struggle for justice is not of Spirit-Sophia.

I have introduced these stories as wo/men parables[53] or Wisdom stories "through which to construct an elsewhere of vision that will lead us into a truly liberating future."[54] I hope that they will help us to construct such "an elsewhere of vision" that enables us to see the work of feminist interpretation and feminist movements for justice as continuing the work of Divine Wisdom in the world—bringing about and fomenting radical change, searching for lost and buried emancipatory traditions, and insistently struggling for justice without ever giving up the fight or exhausting our resources.

The table of Divine Wisdom provides spiritual food and drink in our struggles to transform the oppressive structures of religion and society, structures that shackle our spirits and stay our hands.

This spiritual struggle for a different religion and world of justice, equality, and well-being does not turn us into idealistic dreamers but gathers the *ekklēsia* of wo/men as a movement of those who, in the power of Wisdom, seek to realize the dream and vision of G*d-Sophia's alternative community, society, and world of justice and well-being for everyone. A Christian feminist theology is inspired and compelled by Her gospel of liberation.

NOTES

PREFACE

1. I owe this expression to Christine Schaumberger. See Christine Schaumberger, "Subversive Bekehrung," in *Schuld und Macht, Studien zu einer feministischen Befreiungstheologie*, ed. C. Schaumberger and Luise Schottroff (München: Kaiser Verlag, 1988), 153–82.

CHAPTER 1: *The Invitation of Wisdom-Sophia*

1. The first such conference took place in 1971 at Alverno College (see Rita M. Gross, *Feminism and Religion: An Introduction* [Boston: Beacon Press, 1996]). The following books were important for the development of feminist theology: *Sexist Religion and Women in the Church*, ed. Alice Hageman in collaboration with the Women's Caucus of Harvard Divinity School (New York: Association Press, 1974); Mary Daly, *The Church and the Second Sex* (New York: Harper and Row, 1968), and her classic *Beyond God the Father* (Boston: Beacon Press, 1973). Rosemary Radford Ruether's *Religion and Sexism: Images of Women in the Jewish and Christian Traditions* (New York: Simon & Schuster, 1974) came out of the Grailville conference. Other important milestone publications which are often overlooked are Sheila Collins, *A Different Heaven and Earth* (Valley Forge, Pa.: Judson Press, 1974); the issue of *Theological Studies* on women, edited by W. Burkhardt, S.J. (vol. 36 [1975]); and an issue of *Concilium* edited by Gregory Baum (vol. 7 [1975]).

2. See Janet Kalven's article on the Grail movement, "Women Breaking Boundaries: The Grail and Feminism," *Journal of Feminist Studies in Religion* 5, no. 1 (1989): 119–42. For the Seminary Quarter at Grailville, see her article "Grailville in the Seventies and Eighties: Structural Changes and Feminist Consciousness," *U.S. Catholic Historian* 11, no. 4 (1993): 45–58. Ten years later, in June 1982, another landmark feminist conference took place at Grailville; see Janet Kalven and Mary I. Buckley, eds., *Women's Spirit Bonding* (New York: The Pilgrim Press, 1984).

3. See Carol P. Christ's works *Diving Deep and Surfacing: Women Writers on Spiritual Quest* (Boston: Beacon Press, 1980), *The Laughter of Aphrodite: Reflections on a Journey to the Goddess* (San Francisco: Harper

and Row, 1987), and *Rebirth of the Goddess: Finding Meaning in Feminist Spirituality* (Reading, Mass.: Addison-Wesley, 1997). See also the two path-breaking collections edited by Carol P. Christ and Judith Plaskow, *Womanspirit Rising: A Feminist Reader in Religion* (San Francisco: Harper and Row, 1979) and *Weaving the Visions: New Patterns in Feminist Spirituality* (San Francisco: Harper and Row, 1989).

4. The section on "Women and Religion" was initiated in 1972 and has been crucial for the development of the field. See Judith Plaskow Goldenberg, ed., *Women and Religion: 1972 Proceedings* (Waterloo, Ontario: CSR Executive Office, 1973), Joan Arnold Romero, ed., *Women and Religion: 1973 Proceedings* (Waterloo, Ontario: CSR Executive Office, 1973), and Judith Plaskow and Joan Arnold Romero, eds., *Women and Religion: Papers of the Working Group on Women and Religion, 1972–73* (Chambersburg, Pa.: American Academy of Religion, Scholars Press, 1974).

5. I write wo/men in this fashion in order to indicate that I do not understand wo/men in either essentialist or naturalized terms. In this way I seek to bring to consciousness that "woman/women" is not a unified concept but an ambiguous one. This way of writing seeks to point out that there are many differences among wo/men and within wo/man.

This spelling also seeks to signal that I use the expression "wo/men" as inclusive of disenfranchised men and "s/he" as inclusive of he. It seeks to avoid expressions such as "women and minority men" or "women and other oppressed groups," which continue to reinscribe "woman" as "other." Such phrases communicate that women are a unitary group which does not need to be qualified or that wo/men do not belong to the other oppressed groups mentioned.

Writing "wo/men" in this way invites male readers always to "think twice" and to adjudicate whether they are meant or not. This experience is an important intellectual and spiritual exercise because it forces men to engage in a similar thought process to that in which wo/men always have to engage in a kyriocentric language system. Such a writing of "wo/men" is not anachronistic because biblical languages also are grammatically male-defined languages which subsume wo/men under the generic masculine and thereby "naturalize" cultural-religious gender ideologies. It also seeks to avoid the kind of overspecialized academic postmodern language that is necessary to alert readers to the instability of the term when written in the conventional way.

6. Whereas the work of Hedwig Meyer-Wilmes, in *Rebellion on the Borders*, trans. Irene Smith-Bowman (Kampen: Kok Pharos, 1995), provides a substantive intellectual historiography of the development of feminist theology in German-speaking countries, such a work is lacking for North America, although American feminist theology has greatly influenced Germany and Europe.   •

7. See Joyce Gelb and Marian L. Palley, *Women and Public Policies* (Princeton, N. J.: Princeton University Press, 1982), Ethel Klein, *Gender Politics* (Cambridge, Mass.: Harvard University Press, 1984), and Mary Feinsod

Katzenstein and Carol McClurg Mueller, eds., *Women's Movements of the United States and Europe* (Philadelphia: Temple University Press, 1987).

8. See, for example, the report by Laura Flanders, "'Stolen Feminism' Hoax: Anti-Feminist Attack Based on Error-Filled Anecdotes," *Extra*, September/October 1994.

9. See Vévé Clark et al., *Antifeminism in the Academy* (New York: Routledge, 1996), xii, for a definition of antifeminist intellectual harassment: "Antifeminist intellectual harassment, a serious threat to academic freedom, occurs when 1. Any policy, action, statement, and/or behavior has the effect of discouraging or preventing women's freedom of lawful action, freedom of thought, and freedom of expression; 2. Or when any policy, action, statement, and/or behavior creates an environment in which the appropriate application of feminist theories or methodologies to research, scholarship, and teaching is devalued, discouraged, or altogether thwarted; 3. Or when any policy, action, statement, and/or behavior creates an environment in which research, scholarship, and teaching pertaining to women, gender, or gender inequities [I would add here race, class, religious, ethnic inequities] are devalued, discouraged or altogether thwarted."

10. In order to indicate the brokenness and inadequacy of human language to name the Divine, I have switched in my book *Jesus: Miriam's Child, Sophia's Prophet: Critical Issues in Feminist Christology* (New York: Continuum, 1994) from the orthodox Jewish way of writing G-d, which I had adopted in *But She Said: Feminist Practices of Biblical Interpretation* (Boston: Beacon Press, 1992) and *Discipleship of Equals: A Critical Feminist Ekklesialogy of Liberation* (New York: Crossroad, 1993), to this way of spelling G*d, which seeks to avoid the conservative malestream association that the writing of G-d has for Jewish feminists but still communicates the inadequacy of our G*d language.

11. I have taken over this expression from the feminist sociologist Dorothy Smith. I use it as a descriptive term indicating that throughout the centuries and still today biblical interpretation and scholarship is defined by elite, mostly European and American men.

12. Jean L. Cohen, "Critical Social Theory and Feminist Critiques: The Debate with Jürgen Habermas," in *Feminists Read Habermas: Gendering the Subject of Discourse*, ed. Johanna Meehan (New York: Routlege, 1995), 76.

13. Ibid., 77.

14. Elisabeth Schüssler, *Der vergessene Partner* (Düsseldorf: Patmos Verlag, 1964). For a sample English translation, see also my book *Discipleship of Equals*.

15. See Gertrud von Le Fort, *Die ewige Frau*, 19th ed. (München: Kösel, 1960); see also Alfred Rosenberg, *Die Erhebung des Weiblichen* (Freiburg: Herder, 1959).

16. See Elisabeth Schüssler Fiorenza, "Women Studies and the Teaching of Religion," in *Occasional Papers on Catholic Higher Education* 1 (1975): 26–30.

17. Elisabeth Schüssler Fiorenza, "Feminist Theology as a Critical Theology of Liberation," *Theological Studies* 36 (1975): 606–26 (reprinted in *Woman: New Dimensions*, ed. W. Burghardt [New York: Paulist Press, 1977], 19–50).

18. See the remarks in my introduction to this article in my book *Discipleship of Equals*.

19. Elisabeth Schüssler Fiorenza, "Die Rolle der Frau in der urchristlichen Bewegung," *Konzilium* 7 (1976): 3–9.

20. See Elisabeth Schüssler Fiorenza, "Interpreting Patriarchal Traditions of the Bible," in *The Liberating Word*, ed. L. Russell (Philadelphia: Westminster, 1976), 39–61. As far as I remember, my use of the term "feminist" and my hermeneutical proposal were edited out. I had a similar experience when publishing my article "Word, Spirit, and Power: Women in Early Christian Communities" in *Women of the Spirit*, ed. R. Radford Ruether and E. McLaughlin (New York: Simon & Schuster, 1979), 29–70; because one of the editors objected to my hermeneutical proposal my ending was rewritten for "stylistic reasons."

21. Elisabeth Schüssler Fiorenza, "Feminist Spirituality, Christian Identity, and the Catholic Vision," *NICM Journal* 1 (1976): 29–34 (reprinted in Christ and Plaskow, *Womanspirit Rising*).

22. For literature, see my books *In Memory of Her: A Feminist Reconstruction of Christian Origins* (New York: Crossroad, 1983) and *Bread Not Stone: The Challenge of Feminist Biblical Interpretation* (Boston: Beacon Press, 1984).

23. For a review of the terminology, see V. Beechey, "On Patriarchy," *Feminist Review* 3 (1979): 66–82; Gerda Lerner, *The Creation of Patriarchy* (New York: Oxford University Press, 1986), 231–41; and Christine Schaumberger, "Patriarchat als feministischer Begriff," in *Wörterbuch der feministischen Theologie* (Gütersloh: Mohn, 1991), 321–23, with literature. Since, however, my use of "patriarchy" continues to be understood in terms of gender dualism, I have proposed a new term, "kyriarchy" (see note 51, below).

24. bell hooks, in *Feminist Theory: From Margin to Center* (Boston: South End Press, 1984), 63, points out that "woman-to-woman negative, aggressive behavior is not unlearned when all critical judgment is suspended"; only when wo/men accept that we "are different, that we will necessarily disagree, but that we can disagree and argue with one another without feeling that we are fighting for our lives" will such behavior cease. With Jane Rule, hooks points out that women can disagree without "trashing" each other only if and when their self-esteem is sound: "No one can discredit my life if it is in my own hands, and therefore I do not have to make anyone carry the false burden of my frightened hostility" (hooks, 63).

25. See my discussion in *But She Said*, 106–08.

26. Pamela Milne, "What Shall We Do with Judith? A Feminist Reassessment of a Biblical 'Heroine,'" in *Textual Determinacy*, part 1, *Semeia* 62 (1993): 39.

27. Phyllis Trible, "Depatriarchalizing Biblical Interpretation," *Journal of the American Academy of Religion* 41 (1973): 30–48; Phyllis Trible, *God and the Rhetoric of Sexuality* (Philadelphia: Fortress, 1978).

28. Phyllis Trible, *Texts of Terror* (Philadelphia: Fortress, 1984).

29. Esther Fuchs, "For I Have the Way of Women: Deception, Gender, and Ideology in Biblical Narrative," *Semeia* 42 (1988): 68–83; Esther Fuchs, "Marginalization, Ambiguity, Silencing: The Story of Jephta's Daughter," *Journal of Feminist Studies in Religion* 5 (1989): 35–45.

30. Milne, "What Shall We Do with Judith?", 39.

31. Mieke Bal, "Introduction," in Anti-Covenant: *Counter-Reading Women's Lives in the Hebrew Bible*, ed. Mieke Bal (Sheffield, England: Almond Press, 1989), 11–24.

32. Milne, "What Shall We Do with Judith?", 40.

33. Leonard J. Swidler, *Biblical Affirmations of Women* (Philadelphia: Westminster Press, 1979).

34. Milne cites my book *In Memory of Her* and George Nickelsburg, *Jewish Literature Between the Bible and the Mishnah* (Philadelphia: Fortress, 1980); Carey Moore, "Judith," in *Anchor Bible* 40 (Garden City, NY: Doubleday, 1985); Toni Craven, "Artistry and Faith in the Book of Judith," in *SBLDS* 70 (Chicago: Scholars Press, 1983); John Craghan, "Esther, Judith, and Ruth: Paradigms for Human Liberation," *Biblical Theology Bulletin* 12 (1982): 11–19, and "Judith Revisited," Biblical Theology Bulletin 12 (1982): 50–53; and Amy-Jill Levine, "Sacrifice and Salvation: Otherness and Domestication in the Book of Judith," in *No One Spoke Ill of Her: Essays on Judith*, ed. James C. VanderKam (Atlanta: Scholars Press, 1992), 17–30.

35. Milne, "What Shall We Do with Judith?", 46; she quotes from Betsy Merideth, "Desire and Danger: The Drama of Betrayal in Judges and Judith," in Bal, *Anti-Covenant*.

36. Milne, "What Shall We Do with Judith?", 54.

37. Burke O'Long, "Textual Determinacy: A Response," in Bal, *Anti-Covenant*, 158.

38. Schüssler Fiorenza, *In Memory of Her*, 115.

39. On the problem of periodization, see the by now classic article by Joan Kelly, "Did Women Have a Renaissance?" in her book *Women, History, and Theory* (Chicago: University of Chicago Press, 1984), 19–50.

40. Sarah Blustain, "Constructing (Not Deconstructing) the Jewish Feminist Pantheon: What's Going on Behind the Pillars of Academia?" *Lilith* 21 (1996): 28–31.

41. See Ann Ferguson, "Feminist Community and Moral Revolution," in *Feminism and Community*, ed. Penny A. Weiss and Marilyn Friedman (Philadelphia: Temple University Press, 1995), in which she argues that the "argument *ad feminam*" has been devastating for feminist debates (381). The "no-trashing rule" invites us instead to discuss the issue at hand and therefore is a primary cornerstone of an "ethics of disagreement." The Bible and Culture Collective, in *The Postmodern Bible* (New Haven: Yale University

Press, 1995), 263, and the review of my work in *Religious Studies Review* by Elizabeth Castelli also seem to resort to such an "argument *ad feminam.*"

42. For a similar debate going on in other fields, see E. Ann Kaplan, ed., *Generations: Academic Feminists in Dialogue* (Minneapolis: University of Minnesota Press, 1997).

43. Blustain, "Constructing," 28.

44. Ibid., quoting Judith Plaskow, *Standing Again at Sinai: Judaism from a Feminist Perspective* (San Francisco: Harper and Row, 1990).

45. Interestingly enough, Blustain refers here to a recent book by Rita M. Gross (*Feminism and Religion: An Introduction* [Boston: Beacon Press, 1996]), but according to her own account, Gross belongs to the "first generation" of academic feminists.

46. For the cultural-academic context of this discussion, see Leslie Heywood and Jennifer Drake, eds., *Third Wave Agenda: Being Feminist, Doing Feminism* (Minneapolis: University of Minnesota Press, 1997).

47. Blustain, "Constructing," 29.

48. Ibid., 31.

49. See also the diverse contributions in Miriam Peskowitz and Laura Levitt, eds., *Judaism Since Gender* (New York: Routledge, 1997), especially Rebecca Alpert's open letter "On Seams and Seamlessness" (109–13).

50. See Elisabeth Schüssler Fiorenza, "Der 'Athenakomplex' in der theologischen Frauenforschung," in *Für Gerechtigkeit streiten: Theologie im Alltag einer bedrohten Welt,* ed. Dorothee Sölle (Gütersloh: Christoph Kaiser, 1994), 103–12.

51. Rosemary Henessy, *Materialist Feminism and the Politics of Discourse* (New York: Routledge, 1993), 94. See also Teresa L. Ebert, *Ludic Feminism and After: Postmodernism, Desire, and Labor in Late Capitalism* (Ann Arbor: University of Michigan Press, 1996).

52. I have coined the neologism *kyriarchy* in analogy to the German term "Herrschaft" and have used it since 1990 in my work. This neologism, I submit, is historically more adequate and theologically more appropriate than the word "hierarchy," which is commonly used in English to designate a pyramidal system of power relations. *Kyriarchy* connotes a social-political system of domination and subordination that is based on the power and rule of the lord/master/father. Such a sociohistorical analytic model allows one to relate the cultural-religious discourses of kyriocentrism and kyriarchy differently. Whereas much of white feminist thought still locates the roots of misogyny and patriarchal oppression in gender dualism, I continue to argue that it is kyriocentric symbolic gender constructions that shape and legitimate the sociopolitical kyriarchal system of oppression that *in turn* produces such ideological constructions.

53. See Barbara Caine, "Women's Studies, Feminist Traditions, and the Problem of History," in *Transitions: New Australian Feminisms,* ed. Barbara Caine and Rosemary Pringle (Sydney: Allen & Unwin, 1995). "At the same time historians have to recognize that the frequent rejection of the term 'fem-

inism'—and of any sense of connection with earlier feminists—by women who have embraced the notion of female emancipation indicates that women find it hard to establish trans-generational links or to set themselves up as legitimating or authoritative figures for each other or for future generations" (3).

54. This has been pointed out and documented by the classic work of Dale Spender, *Women of Ideas (And What Men Have Done to Them)* (Boston: ARK Paperbacks, 1983). One of the effects of historical forgetfulness is that women have to "reinvent the wheel" again and again in their knowledge production.

55. The Bible and Culture Collective, *The Postmodern Bible* (New Heaven: Yale University Press, 1995). One wonders whether it is an accident that the title *The Postmodern Bible* alludes to that of *The Woman's Bible*.

56. Although such collective authorship is touted as a countercultural academic practice associated with many risks, it also documents how the erasure of the authorial voice does not demystify the power relations of authority but only elides accountability. For instance, the chapter on "Feminist and Womanist Criticism" enacts a quite different politics if written by a nonfeminist author than it does if written by a feminist one. (The chapter claims to be written by feminists but seems to be much more concerned with classifying and evaluating feminist/womanist interpretation from the perspective of and in the interest of postmodernism than with evaluating postmodernism from a feminist perspective.)

57. *The Postmodern Bible,* 233.

58. Ibid., 235.

59. For the continuing use of androcentrism as an analytic category, see, for instance, Barbara F. McManus, *Classics and Feminism: Gendering the Classics* (New York: Twayne Publishers, 1997), 77,78: "Part of any feminist enterprise involves making androcentric bias visible and revealing the partiality and inequity it fosters. In feminist classical scholarship this process has required a double critique: of the pervasive ancient conceptualization of the male as the universal human norm and of the patriarchal contents and methods of classical scholarship. . . . The purpose of deconstructing ancient androcentrism is not merely to provide a more comprehensive view of the past, however; it is also to gain a greater understanding of the present."

60. In its review of *The Postmodern Bible,* the editorial board of *biblicon* observes approvingly, "It [*The Postmodern Bible*] includes a thoughtful analysis of Elizabeth [*sic*] Schussler [*sic*] Fiorenza's dismissal of postmodern feminism and of the dichotomy she creates between a good feminist whose work is informed by theology, and a bad feminist, who turns to gender studies for her/his intellectual agenda" (*biblicon: Bible, Media, Culture* 1, no. 1 [1997]: 73). Since *The Postmodern Bible* Collective's misreading of my work is characterized as "thoughtful," the reader must assume that the reviewers agree on this point. However, no mention is made of the fact that I critique only a certain kind of postmodern feminism (not feminists!) and that my major difference with postmodern readings stems from the fact that I assert

the necessity for feminist emancipatory interpretations to keep the tension and dialectic between both a "deconstructive" and a "reconstructive" or "transformative" reading. In the face of such willful misreadings, I challenge anyone to point to a sentence in my work that would even come close to maintaining such a distinction between a "good" and "bad" feminist as *The Postmodern Bible* Collective and the *biblicon* editorial board's review allege. If I critically assess different feminist frameworks or approaches, *I do not evaluate feminists!* Rather I seek to assess feminist frames of meaning on feminist emancipatory and not on theological-normative grounds. The "reconstructive" or "transformative" moment (not of the bible but of wo/men's agency and subjectivity) in our work is necessary—I continue to argue—if feminist scholarship wants to bring about change.

A similar but even more egregious misreading of my text is found in Irena Makarushka's (one of the editors) article "Elizabeth Cady Stanton and *The Woman's Bible*: Dissent and Marginalization," in the same issue of *biblicon*. (Parenthetically she thanks her colleague Burke O'Long for his "thoughtful" feedback especially on "the sections that pertain to contemporary feminist biblical scholarship" [59, n. 7]. Was he the "thoughtful" reader the Collective had in mind? What makes him an expert to evaluate contemporary feminist scholarship? As much as I respect Burke O'Long, he has hardly distinguished himself as a feminist.) Makarushka quotes a dialectical statement on the ambivalent relationship of wo/men to scriptures, canon, and authority culled from the introduction to *Searching the Scriptures* (x) and then goes on to berate me for not seeing the contradictions in my account. Worse, by skipping the critical part and misreading as well as personalizing the "constructive" intention of my statement, she turns me into a bigot. Whereas I speak about the task of a feminist introduction and commentary—and not about persons—she claims that I want to delimit "who" is in and "who" is out. Why do feminists who celebrate "difference" react personally when one points out theoretical-epistemological differences? Moreover, when I speak of "claiming the power of the 'Word'" she misreads this as saying "that feminist biblical scholarship must *begin with a belief in the Word*" (57, emphasis added). This misreading of my text serves to focus her whole argument against my position. One wonders whose interests are served by this forced feminist reinscription of the old malestream feud between theological and academic studies. It seems clear that Makarushka misreads the capitalized "Word" in my text to mean "the Word of G*d." However, my text intends the opposite by attempting to signal a wordplay and to speak of claiming the "power of the Word" ("Word" in quotation marks). Only by claiming the "power of the 'Word,'" I argue, will wo/men be able to decenter and deconstruct the hegemonic dogmatic claims to the bible as the "Word of G*d" or divine revelation. Yet my point is and has been the opposite: rather than to reject all logocentrism (culture, history, religion, language), I argue, feminist work needs to both decenter kyriarchal logocentrism and at the same time reclaim the power of "logos" in a different way and to feminist ends.

61. *The Postmodern Bible*, 262.

62. See Francis Schüssler Fiorenza, "Theological and Religious Studies: The Contest of the Faculties," in *Shifting Boundaries* (Louisville, Ky: Westminster/John Knox Press, 1991).

63. E. Schüssler Fiorenza, *But She Said*, 41.

64. Jane Braaten, "From Communicative Rationality to Communicative Thinking: A Basis for Feminist Theory and Practice," in *Feminists Read Habermas: Gendering the Subject of Discourse*, ed. Johanna Meehan (New York: Routledge, 1995).

65. *The Postmodern Bible*, 263.

66. Ibid., 262.

67. Teresa L. Ebert, *Ludic Feminism and After: Postmodernism, Desire, and Labor in Late Capitalism* (Ann Arbor: University of Michigan Press, 1996); see also Helene Moglen, "Losing Their Edge: Radical Studies from the Seventies to the Nineties," in *The Politics of Research*, ed. E. Ann Kaplan and George Levine (New Brunswick, N.J.: Rutgers University Press, 1997), 181–92.

68. *The Postmodern Bible*, 265.

69. See the review articles of Janice Capel Anderson, "Mapping Feminist Biblical Criticism," *Critical Review of Books in Religion* (1991): 21–49, and Elizabeth Castelli: "Heteroglossia, Hermeneutics, and History: A Review Essay of Recent Feminist Studies of Early Christianity," in *Journal of Feminist Studies in Religion* 2, no. 2 (1994): 73–98.

70. *The Postmodern Bible*, 255.

71. Ibid., 9.

72. Ibid., 234.

73. Joan Hoff, "Gender as a Postmodern Category of Paralysis," *Women's History Review* 3, no. 2 (1994): 149–68, citing Carroll Smith-Rosenberg, *Disorderly Conduct: Visions of Gender in Victorian America* (New York: Oxford University Press, 1985), 245–96.

74. Laura E. Donaldson, *Decolonizing Feminisms: Race, Gender, and Empire Building* (Chapel Hill: University of North Carolina Press, 1992), 135.

75. Ibid.

CHAPTER 2: *The Call of Wisdom-Sophia*

The first draft of this chapter was prepared for lectures in South Africa. Part of it has appeared in a different form as "Feminist Studies in Religion and a Radical Democratic Ethos," *Religion & Theology* 2, no. 2 (1995): 122–44.

1. For the distinction between method and methodology, see Annette Noler, *Feministische Hermeneutik: Wege einer neuen Schriftauslegung* (Neukirchen-Vluyn: Neukirchener Verlag, 1995).

2. Judith Plaskow, "We Are Also Your Sisters: The Development of Women's Studies in Religion," *Women's Studies Quarterly* 20, no. 1 (1993): 9–21.

3. Denise Ackermann, "Faith and Feminism: Women Doing Theology," in J. de Gruchy and C. Villa-Vicencio, eds., *Doing Theology in Context: South African Contributions* (Maryknoll: Orbis, 1994), 197–212.

4. Ibid., 207.

5. Anna Julia Cooper, *A Voice from the South* (1892), republished in the Schomburg Library of Nineteenth-Century Black Women Writers (New York: Oxford University Press, 1988), 122–23.

6. Francis Martin, in *The Feminist Question: Feminist Theology in the Light of Christian Tradition* (Grand Rapids: Eerdmans, 1994), mistakes this assertion as modernist individualism and charges that the "feminist question" is not properly theological because its starting point is feminist consciousness and "does not have as its basis the teaching of revelation and expects to be modified by it." However, he overlooks that a Christian feminist consciousness is always already shaped and informed by biblical faith. Moreover, he argues that feminist theology is methodologically deficient because it is not "*from* Revelation." Since it allegedly "does not have a biblical view of God," it is, in his view, also deficient in its content (408ff). However, this criticism begs the question because the issue is not revelation but the androcentric and kyriocentric language and conceptualization of revelation and its interpretation in malestream tradition and theology. Thus Martin overlooks the paradigm shift in the central question of theology. At stake in feminist theology is not the modern question of whether G*d exists but the liberation theological question as to *who is responsible* for the dehumanizing and oppressive historical effects of Christian Scriptures, traditions, theologies and church practices—elite clergy*men* or G*d. Because Martin overlooks this shift from the modern question of *whether* G*d exists, raised by secularization, to the liberation theological question as to "how" to speak of G*d without legitimizing dehumanizing oppression, he condemns feminist theology as being indebted to the modern rationalism of the European Enlightenment However, one has the suspicion that such a misapprehension is dictated by his desire to trivialize and marginalize feminist theology as not being "theo-logical" in the proper sense.

7. For this argument, see Caroline Ramazanoglu, *Feminism and the Contradictions of Oppression* (London: Routledge, 1989), 149–54; she is one of the few feminist theorists who take religion into account.

8. Cf. Shirley Rogers Radl, *The Invisible Woman: Rage of the Religious New Right* (New York: Dell, 1981); Sara Diamond, *Spiritual Warfare: The Politics of the Christian Right* (Boston: South End Press, 1989); Hans Küng and Jürgen Moltmann, *Fundamentalism as an Ecumenical Challenge* (Concilium; London: SCM Press, 1992); and the issue on "Fundamentalism" of *Beiträge zur feministischen Theorie und Praxis* 32 (1992).

9. Iris Marion Young, "Five Faces of Oppression," in *Justice and the Politics of Difference* (Princeton: Princeton University Press, 1990), 38–65. For a critical discussion of Young's theoretical proposal, see Nancy Fraser, *Justice Interruptus: Critical Reflections on the "Postsocialist" Condition* (New York: Routledge, 1997) 189–206.

10. Peggy L. Day, ed. *Gender and Difference in Ancient Israel* (Minneapolis: Augsburg/Fortress, 1989), 1–2.

11. Cooper, *A Voice from the South*, 134.

12. See also Linda M. Perkins, "The Impact of the 'Call of True Womanhood' on the Education of Black Women," *Journal of Social Issues* 39, no. 3 (1983): 17–28, and Evelyn Brooks Higginbotham, *Righteous Discontent* (Cambridge: Harvard University Press, 1994).

13. Mary Helen Washington, "Introduction," to Cooper, *A Voice from the South*, xlvii.

14. For the term "whitemale," see Houston A. Baker, Jr., "Caliban's Triple Play," in *Race, Writing, Difference*, ed. Henry Louis Gates, Jr. (Chicago: University of Chicago Press, 1985), 381–95, 382.

15. See the excellent article of Maria Pilar Aquino, "The Collective 'Discovery' of Our Own Power: Latina American Feminist Theology," in Ada Maria Isasi-Diaz and Fernando F. Segovia, eds., *Hispanic/Latino Theology: Challenge and Promise* (Minneapolis: Augsburg Fortress, 1996), 240–60.

16. See Barbara Smith, ed., *Home Girls: A Black Feminist Anthology* (New York: Kitchen Table: Women of Color Press, 1983) and bell hooks, *Feminist Theory: From Margin to Center* (Boston: South End Press, 1984).

17. Cheryl Johnson-Odim, "Common Themes, Different Contexts: Third World Women and Feminism," in *Third World Women and the Politics of Feminism*, ed. Chandra Talpade Mohanti, Ann Russo, and Lourdes Torres (Bloomington: Indiana University Press, 1991), 314–27, 316.

18. For a comparative study of the ordination question see Jacqueline Field-Bibb, *Women Towards Priesthood: Ministerial Politics and Feminist Praxis* (Cambridge: University Press, 1991).

19. For pre-1980 statistics, see the Cornwall Collective, *Your Daughters Shall Prophesy: Feminist Alternatives in Religious Studies* (New York: Pilgrim Press, 1980), 49–53. In the past decade the number of wo/men in liberal theological schools has far surpassed the fifty percent mark.

20. See Genevive Lloyd, *The Man of Reason: "Male" and "Female" in Western Philosophy* (Minneapolis: University of Minnesota Press, 1984), 108: "Philosophers have at different periods been church men, men of letters, university professors. But there is one thing they have had in common throughout the history of the activity. They have been predominantly male; and the absence of women from the philosophical tradition has meant that the conceptualization of Reason has been done exclusively by men."

21. See Stanley Fish, *Is There a Text in This Class?: The Authority of Interpretive Communities* (Cambridge, Mass.: Harvard University Press, 1980).

22. See Florence Howe, *The Myth of Coeducation: Selected Essays 1964–1983* (Bloomington: University of Indiana Press, 1984), 221–30.

23. See the critical reflections on the Arizona project for curriculum integration, S. Hardy Aiken, K. Anderson, M. Dinnerstein, J. Nolte Lensinck, and P. MacCorquodale, eds., *Changing Our Minds: Feminist Transformations of Knowledge* (Albany: State University of New York, 1988), 134–63.

24. Adrienne Rich, "Toward a Woman-Centered University," in *On Lies, Secrets, and Silence: Selected Prose, 1966–1978* (New York: Norton, 1979), 134.

25. Thomas Kuhn, *The Structure of Scientific Revolutions*, 2d. ed. (Chicago: University of Chicago Press, 1962). For a recent detailed study of how this process works in academia, see Lani Guinier, Michelle Fine, and Jane Balin, *Becoming Gentlemen* (Boston: Beacon Press, 1997).

26. See especially the reflections of bell hooks on revolutionary feminist pedagogy, graduate school, being black at Yale, and class and education, in her book *Talking Back* (Boston: South End Press, 1989), 49–84.

27. Jo Anne Pagano, *Exiles and Communities: Teaching in the Patriarchal Wilderness* (Albany: State University of New York Press, 1990), 135f.

28. See Hazel Carby, "On the Threshold of Woman's Era: Lynching, Empire and Sexuality," in Gates, *Race, Writing, and Difference*, 301–28.

29. See Max Weber, "Wissenschaft als Beruf," in M. Weber, *Gesammelte Aufsätze zur Wissenschaftslehre* (Tübingen, 1922). See also Ija Lazari-Pawloska, "Das Problem der Wertfreiheit im Universitätsunterricht," in Halina Bendowski and Brigitte Weisshaupt eds., *Was Philosophinnen denken* (Zürich: Amman Verlag, 1983), 30–36.

30. See M. L. Andersen, "Changing the Curriculum in Higher Education," *Signs* 12, no. 2 (1987): 222–54.

31. On the process of an experientially based education, see John H. Fish, "Liberating Education," in *Liberation and Ethics*, ed. C. Amjad-Ali and W. Alwin Pitcher (Chicago: Center for the Scientific Study of Religion, 1985), 15–29, especially the chart on p. 27.

32. For further elaboration, see my books *But She Said: Feminist Practices of Biblical Interpretation* (Boston: Beacon Press, 1992) and *Discipleship of Equals: A Critical Feminist Ekklesialogy of Liberation* (New York: Crossroad Press, 1993).

33. Chandra Talpade Mohanti, "Introduction: Cartographies of Struggle," in Mohanti, Russo, and Torres, *Third World Women and the Politics of Feminism*, 1–47: p. 4.

34. Nancy Fraser, *Unruly Practices: Power, Discourse and Gender in Contemporary Social Theory* (Minneapolis: University of Minnesota Press, 1989), 165.

35. E. Frances White, "Africa on My Mind: Gender, Counter Discourse and African-American Nationalism," *Journal of Women's History* 2, no. 1 (1990): 87.

36. See Vèvè Clark et al., eds., *Antifeminism in the Academy* (New York: Routledge, 1996).

37. Throughout its twenty-year history, the Women's Ordination Conference in the United States has insisted on the ordination of wo/men to a new priesthood in a renewed church. It therefore has denounced the exclusion of wo/men from ordination as a structural sin and explored the meaning of ordination in the church as a discipleship community of equals. To construe

this creative—albeit conflictive—tension as opposition or a dualistic either/or choice, as recent press reports on the 1995 WOC anniversary celebration have done, is to misunderstand the theological stance of WOC.

CHAPTER 3: *The Works of Wisdom-Sophia*

This chapter was prepared for a conference organized by the National Park Service in celebration of the centennial of *The Woman's Bible* at Seneca Falls in November 1995. It draws on my article "Das zwiespältige Erbe der *Woman's Bible*," which was published in German, and on my introductions to *Searching the Scriptures*.

1. Adrienne Rich, *On Lies, Secrets, and Silence: Selected Prose 1966–1978* (New York: Norton, 1979), 11.

2. Mary D. Pellauer, *Toward a Tradition of Feminist Theology: The Religious Social Thought of Elizabeth Cady Stanton, Susan B. Anthony, and Anna Howard Shaw* (Brooklyn, N. Y.: Carlson, 1991).

3. Anna Howard Shaw, as quoted in Pellauer, *Toward a Tradition*, 260.

4. See Elisabeth Gössman, "History of Biblical Interpretation by European Women," in *Searching the Scriptures*, ed. Elisabeth Schüssler Fiorenza, vol. 1 (New York: Crossroad, 1993), 27–41. See also Gerda Lerner, *The Creation of Feminist Consciousness: From the Middle Ages to the Eighteenth Century* (New York: Oxford University Press, 1993), and Marla J. Selvidge, *Notorious Voices: Feminist Biblical Interpretation 1500–1920* (New York: Continuum, 1996).

5. Elizabeth Cady Stanton, *The Woman's Bible* (Seattle: Coalition on Women and Religion, 1986).

6. See Cynthia Scheinberg, "Measure Yourself a Prophet's Place: Biblical Heroines, Jewish Difference, and Victorian Women's Poetry," in *Women's Poetry: Late Romantic to Late Victorian Gender and Genre, 1830–1900*, ed. Isabel Armstrong and Virginia Blain (London: McMillan Press, forthcoming, 1997).

7. ". . . und sie legte ihnen die Schrift aus: Internationales Symposium Bibel und feministische Theologie anlässlich 100 Jahre Woman's Bible," 15–17 June 1995.

8. Marie-Theres Wacker, "100 Jahre Frauen und Bibel im deutschsprachigen Raum," *Bibel und Kirche* 50, no. 4 (1995): 203–10. See also her chapter in Marie-Theres Wacker, Silvia Schroer, and Luise Schottroff, eds., *Feministische Exegese: Forschungserträge zur Bibel aus der Perspektive von Frauen* (Darmstadt: Wissenschaftliche Buchgesellschaft, 1995).

9. Carol A. Newsome and Sharon H. Ringe, eds., *The Women's Bible* (Philadelphia: Westminster Press, 1992).

10. Elisabeth Schüssler Fiorenza, ed., *Searching the Scriptures*, 2 vols., A Feminist Introduction and A Feminist Commentary (New York: Crossroad, 1993).

11. Anna Julia Cooper, *A Voice From the South*, 1892, republished in the Schomburg Library of Nineteenth-Century Black Women Writers (New York: Oxford University Press, 1988), 122–23.

12. See Clarice Martin, "Biblical Theodicy and Black Women's Spiritual Autobiography," in *A Troubling in My Soul: Womanist Perspectives on Evil and Suffering*, ed. Emilie M. Townes (Maryknoll, N. Y.: Orbis Books, 1993) 13–36.

13. Quoted in Gerda Lerner, *Black Women in America* (New York: Pantheon Books, 1972), 610.

14. Quoted in Karlyn Kohrs Cambell, *Man Cannot Speak for Her*, vol. 1 (New York: Greenwood Press, 1989), 19.

15. Katie G. Cannon, "Slave Ideology and Biblical Interpretation," *Semeia* 47 (1989): 9–24. See also her book *Katie's Canon: Womanism and the Soul of the Black Community* (New York: Continuum, 1995).

16. Bert Lowenberg and Ruth Bogin, eds., *Black Women in Nineteenth-Century American Life: Their Words, Their Thoughts, Their Feelings* (University Park, Md.: University of Maryland, 1977), 229.

17. See Vincent L. Wimbush, "The Bible and African Americans: An Outline of an Interpretative History," in *Stony the Road We Trod: African American Biblical Interpretation*, ed. Cain H. Felder (Minneapolis: Augsburg Fortress, 1991), 88.

18. Emilie Townsend Gilkes, "Mother to the Motherless," *Semeia* 47 (1989): 65.

19. Jacquelyn Grant, *White Women's Christ and Black Women's Jesus* (Atlanta: Scholars Press, 1989).

20. Howard Thurman, *Jesus and the Disinherited* (Nashville, Tenn.: Abingdon, 1949), 31f.

21. Schüssler Fiorenza, *Searching the Scriptures*, vol. 2, *A Feminist Commentary*.

22. Elizabeth Cady Stanton, "The Degradation of Disenfranchisement," *The Woman's Tribune*, 7 February 1891, quoted in Pellauer, *Toward a Tradition*, 23.

23. See Elizabeth Cady Stanton, *The Original Feminist Attack on the Bible: The Woman's Bible*, ed. and introduced by Barbara Welter (New York: Arno Press, 1974). See also *Searching the Scriptures*, vol. 1, *A Feminist Introduction*.

24. See especially *The Journal of Feminist Studies in Religion*, which is distributed by Scholars Press of Atlanta, Ga.

25. Matilda Joslyn Gage, *Women, Church and State* (1893; reprint Watertown, Mass.: Persephone Press, 1980), xxix.

26. For this interpretation, see Kathi L. Kern, "Rereading Eve: Elizabeth Cady Stanton and *The Woman's Bible*, 1885–1896," in *Women's Studies* 19 (1991): 371–83.

27. Stanton, *The Woman's Bible*.

28. Toni Morrison, *Playing in the Dark: Whiteness and the Literary Imagination* (Cambridge, Mass.: Harvard University Press, 1992), 12.

29. Stanton as quoted by Barbara Hilkert Andolsen, *"Daughters of Jefferson, Daughters of Bootblacks": Racism and American Feminism* (Macon, Ga.: Mercer University Press, 1986), 31.

30. Stanton, *The Woman's Bible*, vol. 1, 126.

31. Ibid., 117.

32. To point out these limitations does not diminish or marginalize Cady Stanton's accomplishment but situates it historically. If I disagree with Cady Stanton, I do not do so because she was "a secularist, anticlerical, radical feminist," as Ilena Makarushka alleges, but rather on methodological grounds (see Makarushka, "Elizabeth Cady Stanton and *The Woman's Bible*," *biblicon* 1, no. 1 [1997]: 57ff). Makarushka is bent on reading my work (which has consistently pointed to the importance of Cady Stanton) with an anti-theological lens, insisting that our differences are "at least in part determined by the fact that Cady Stanton was not a Christian theologian and Schüssler Fiorenza is" (57). This allows her to disqualify my argument without seriously engaging its theoretical and hermeneutical proposal. Moreover, she claims that "Schüssler Fiorenza privileges the logocentric theological perspective as normal. As a theologian she stands firmly in a community of believers and interprets that stance as authoritative. As a consequence, she marginalizes Cady Stanton and *The Woman's Bible* as well as those contemporary secularist feminists who like me, do not stand within a community of faith" (59). By resorting to caricaturizing my theological position as authoritarian, exclusivist, and narrow-minded—a familiar anti-Catholic argument—she does not need to acknowledge that I have consistently sought to problematize and to deconstruct all dogmatic claims to biblical-theological authority and normativity.

33. Stanton, *The Woman's Bible*, vol. 1, 70: "If we begin by taking some parts of the Scriptures figuratively we shall soon figure it all away."

34. For criticism of Bruce Malina's work, which is very influential also among feminist interpreters, see, for instance, Mary Ann Tolbert, "Social, Sociological, and Anthropological Methods," in Schüssler Fiorenza, *Searching the Scriptures*, 255–71.

35. See the dissertation of Katharina von Kellenbach, *Anti-Judaism in Feminist Religious Writings* (Atlanta, Ga.: Scholars Press, 1994); Judith Plaskow, "Anti-Judaism in Feminist Christian Interpretation," *Searching the Scriptures*, vol. 1; and my article "Die werfe den ersten Stein," *Schlangenbrut* 14 (1996): 23–26.

36. Cooper, *A Voice from the South*, 59.

37. Karen Baker Fletcher, *A Singing Something: Womanist Reflections on Anna Julia Cooper* (New York: Crossroad, 1994).

38. Anna Julia Cooper, "Equality of Races and the Democratic Movement," privately printed pamphlet, Washington, DC., 1945, 5, as quoted by Baker Fletcher, ibid.

39. Fletcher, *A Singing Something*, 192–93.

40. For discussion of this theoretical context see, for instance, Anne Phillips, *Engendering Democracy* (Cambridge, Mass.: Polity Press, 1991); Judith Butler and Joan W. Scott, eds., *Feminists Theorize the Political* (New York: Routledge, 1992); Joan Cocks, *The Oppositional Imagination: Femi-*

nism, Critique, and Political Theory (New York: Routledge, 1989); Mary Lyndon Shanley and Carole Pateman, eds., *Feminist Interpretations and Political Theory* (University Park, Pa.: Pennsylvania State University Press, 1991).

41. See, for instance, Erin White, "Figuring and Refiguring the Female Self: Towards a Feminist Hermeneutics," in *Claiming Our Rites: Studies in Religion by Australian Women Scholars*, ed. Morny Joy and Penelope Magee (Adelaide: Australian Association for the Study of Religion, 1994), 135–56. White has attempted to locate my work within the hermeneutical framework of Ricoeur, although she concedes that it does not quite "fit" (154, n. 120); she seems not to recognize fully that the introduction of gender or of women as subjects explodes the hermeneutical framework of Ricoeur insofar as it makes a "second naiveté" impossible.

42. See Marsha Hewitt, "The Redemptive Power of Memory: Walter Benjamin and Elisabeth Schüssler Fiorenza," *The Journal of Feminist Studies in Religion* 10, no. 1 (1994): 73–90.

43. For such an attempt, see Linnell E. Cady, "Hermeneutics and Tradition: The Role of the Past in Jurisprudence and Theology," *Harvard Theological Review* 79 (1986): 439–63.

44. See, for example, Rebecca S. Chopp, "Feminism's Theological Pragmatics: A Social Naturalism of Women's Experience," *Journal of Religion* 67 (1987): 239–56. Chopp has perceptively situated my proposal of a critical feminist interpretation for liberation within the North American pragmatic tradition, but tends to overlook its indebtedness to critical theory.

45. For instance, I am not aware of any review of *Bread Not Stone* or *But She Said* that seeks to assess how much my theoretical framework is influenced by the work of feminist critical theory and liberationist epistemological discourses.

46. An excellent example of a careful, appreciative, and critical reading of my work in the interest of critiquing her own "sociological fathers" can be found in the contribution of Kath McPhillips, "Reconstructing Women's Religious Agency: Critical Feminist Perspectives and the Ekklesia of Women," in Joy and Magee, *Claiming Our Rites*, 247–63.

CHAPTER 4: *The Love of Wisdom-Sophia*

1. Since in *Bread Not Stone* and *But She Said* I enumerated only four such strategies, critics have often overlooked the fact that my hermeneutical model is located within a liberation theological approach (see Luise Schottroff, *Lydia's Impatient Sisters: A Feminist Social History of Early Christianity* [Louisville, Ky.: Westminster Press, 1995], 63). Such an approach engages in a process of "conscientization," which insists on an analysis of one's positionality—what we see depends on where we stand—and on systemic analysis with the goal of change and transformation.

2. For a more extensive discussion and use of this hermeneutical model in general and for interpreting a text, see my books *But She Said: Feminist*

Practices of Biblical Interpretation (Boston, Beacon Press, 1992), 51–76, and *Bread Not Stone: The Challenge of Feminist Biblical Interpretation* (Boston: Beacon Press, 1984), 1–21.

3. Catherine Belsey, in *Critical Practice* (New York: Routledge, 1980), proposes a Post-Saussurian hermeneutical model which has as its three meaning poles reader, text, ideology.

4. Agent (reader/writer), text (context/intertext), world (sociopolitical formations and institutions), and ideology (inscribed in language and signifying practices).

5. Although Anthony C. Thiselton, in *New Horizons in Hermeneutics: The Theory and Practice of Transforming Biblical Reading* (London: Harper Collins, 1992), in his discussion of my work (449f.) claims that "what is at stake is hermeneutical theory," he does not bother to discuss *Bread Not Stone* but rather focuses on a particular exegetical topic regarding wo/men's witness to the resurrection discussed in *In Memory of Her*. In so doing he seeks to show that I did not take all possible interpretations into account. Yet such a criticism overlooks the limits set by my choice of genre for this work and mistakes a work of historical reconstruction for one of hermeneutical critical theory. The interests driving his misreadings come to the fore in his emotionally laden comparison of my own work with that of Susanne Heine; although Heine's work appeared later and is dependent on my own work, albeit without acknowledging it, she finds Thiselton's favor because she attacks the work of other feminists. It also comes to the fore in his repeated question as to how much a given tradition can undergo transformation before it ceases to be *this tradition*, as well as in the question of whether the transformation of which I speak comes "into being by imposing one's community values upon another in a hermeneutic of conflict, or by progress toward a universal commitment to a transcendental critique of justice and of the cross which speaks from beyond given context-bound communities in a hermeneutic of openness." Obviously Thiselton is not able to understand either a commitment to wo/men as a universal stance nor feminist struggle as a commitment to a "transcendental critique of justice" or to the "cross" as the symbolic expression of such struggle.

6. Again, for the distinction between method and methodology, see Annette Noller, *Feministische Hermeneutik: Wege einer neuen Schriftauslegung* (Neukirchen-Vluyn: Neukirchener Verlag, 1995), and Nancy Hartsock, *Money, Sex, and Power: Toward a Feminist Historical Materialism* (New York: Longman, 1983).

7. Dorothy Lee, "Reclaiming the Sacred Text: Christian Feminism and Spirituality," *Claiming Our Rites: Studies in Religion by Australian Women Scholars*, ed. Morny Joy and Penelope Magee (Adelaide: Australian Association for the Study of Religions, 1994), 80–84, 82.

8. Ibid.

9. Mary McClintock Fulkerson, "Contesting Feminist Canons: Discourse and the Problem of Sexist Texts," *Journal of Feminist Studies in Religion* 7, no. 2 (1991): 53–74.

10. Paolo Freire, *Pedagogy of the Oppressed* (New York: Seabury Press, 1973), 31.

11. Ibid., 33.

12. Elizabeth Cady Stanton, ed., *The Woman's Bible*, 2 vols. (1884/1888; reprint Seattle: Coalition Task Force on Women and Religion, 1984).

13. Mary Ann Tolbert, "Protestant Feminists and the Bible," in *The Pleasure of Her Text: Feminist Readings of Biblical and Historical Texts*, ed. Alice Bach (Philadelphia: Trinity Press, 1990), 11.

14. Ibid., 20.

15. For a discussion of diverse hermeneutical discourses and a critique of the method of correlation, see Francis Schüssler Fiorenza, "The Crisis of Hermeneutics and Christian Theology," in *Theology at the End of Modernity*, ed. Sheila Greeve Davaney (Philadelphia: Trinity Press, 1991), 117–40, esp. 128–30; see also his earlier article "The Crisis of Scriptural Authority: Interpretation and Reception," *Interpretation* 44, no. 4 (1990): 353–68, and his forthcoming book *Beyond Hermeneutics: Theology as Discourse* (New York: Continuum, 1998).

16. For such an approach, see especially the work of Rosemary Radford Ruether, David Tracy, and Edward Schillebeeckx.

17. Such a hermeneutical approach has been consistently developed in the work of Phyllis Trible. See her biographical statement, "The Pilgrim Bible on a Feminist Journey," reprinted in *Daughters of Sarah* 15, no. 3 (1989): 4–7.

18. W. Abbott and J. Gallagher, eds., *The Documents of Vatican II* (New York: America Press, 1966), 108. See also my article "Understanding God's Revealed Word," *Catholic Charismatic* 1 (1977): 4–10.

19. Abbott and Gallagher, *Documents*, 119.

20. See my article "The Ethics of Biblical Interpretation: Decentering Biblical Scholarship," *Journal of Biblical Literature* 107, no. 1 (1988): 3–17.

21. It is curious that Gerald West, in *Biblical Hermeneutics of Liberation: Modes of Reading the Bible in the South African Context* (Pietermaritzburg: Cluster Publications, 1991), does not discuss this process model of interpretation although (or because?) he is interested in the "interface between biblical studies and the ordinary reader." Instead he tries to limit my hermeneutical proposal to a "reading behind the text," pointing out its similarity to Itumeleng Mosala's approach in *Biblical Hermeneutics and Black Theology in South Africa* (Grand Rapids: Eerdmans, 1989), although Mosala's work not only appeared later but also uses a Marxist rather than a feminist analysis. It seems that even in a "hermeneutics of liberation" the "ordinary reader" remains male.

22. For a similar theoretical framework, see bell hooks, *Feminist Theory: From Margin to Center* (Boston: South End Press, 1984).

23. The Bible and Culture Collective, *The Postmodern Bible*, (New Haven: Yale University Press, 1995), 249.

24. Stephen Breck Reid, "Endangered Reading: The African-American Scholar between Text and People," *Cross Currents* 44, no. 4 (1995): 478–79.

25. Laura E. Donaldson, *Decolonizing Feminisms: Race, Gender, and Empire-Building* (Chapel Hill: University of North Carolina Press, 1992), 18.

26. Ibid., 19.

27. On the question of "natural" versus "grammatical" gender, see Dennis Baron, *Grammar and Gender* (New Haven: Yale University Press, 1986), 137.

28. See also R. H. Robins, *A Short History of Linguistics* (London: Longmans, 1979).

29. Baron, *Grammar and Gender*, 137.

30. See Denise Riley, *"Am I That Name?" Feminism and the Category of 'Women' in History* (Minneapolis: University of Minnesota Press, 1988).

31. The same can be said for race classifications. See Gloria A. Marshall, "Racial Classifications, Popular and Scientific," in *The "Racial" Economy of Science: Toward a Democratic Future*, ed. Sandra Harding (Bloomington: Indiana University Press, 1993), 116–27.

32. For a comparison of sexist and racist language, see Mary Vetterling-Braggin, ed., *Sexist Language: A Modern Philosophical Analysis* (Littlefield, Mass.: Adams and Co., 1981), 249–319.

33. Tina Pippin, *Death and Desire: The Rhetoric of Gender in the Apocalypse of John*, Literary Currents in Biblical Interpretation (Louisville: Westminster/John Knox Press, 1992), 55.

34. Tina Pippin, "The Revelation to John," in *Searching the Scriptures*, ed. Elisabeth Schüssler Fiorenza (New York: Crossroad, 1993), vol. 2, 119.

35. From Julia Esquivel, *Threatened With Resurrection: Prayers and Poems from an Exiled Guatemalan* (Elgin, Ill.: The Brethren Press, 1982), 79–91. See also my books *Revelation: Vision of a Just World* (Minneapolis: Fortress Press, 1991), and *The Book of Revelation: Judgment and Justice* (Minneapolis: Fortress Press, 1985).

36. Brice R. Wacherhauser, ed., *Hermeneutics and Modern Philosophy* (Albany: State University of New York Press, 1986), 30.

37. *The Postmodern Bible*, 262.

38. Lone Fatum, "1 Thessalonians," in Schüssler Fiorenza, *Searching the Scriptures*, vol. 2, 251.

39. Ibid., 261.

40. Catherine Belsey, *Critical Practice* (New York: Metheuen, 1980), 128.

41. For a trenchant feminist critique of Carl Gustav Jung's theory of archetypes, see Naomi Goldenberg, *Important Directions for a Feminist Critique of Religion in the Works of Sigmund Freud and Carl Jung* (Ann Arbor, Mich.: University Microfilms International, 1977).

42. Pippin, *Death and Desire*, 47.

43. Andrea Nye, "The Hidden Host: Irigaray and Diotima at Plato's Symposium," *Hypatia* 3, no. 3 (1989): 45–61.

44. Ibid., 47.

45. Ibid., 46.

46. Ibid., 52.

CHAPTER 5: *The Public of Wisdom-Sophia*

1. Alicia Suskin Ostriker, *Feminist Revision and the Bible* (Cambridge, Mass.: Blackwell, 1993), 30.
2. Ibid., 57.
3. Ibid., 122–23.
4. Robert Reich, *The Wealth of Nations* (New York: Vintage Books, 1992).
5. See Charles B. Strozier, *Apocalypse: On the Psychology of Fundamentalism in America* (Boston: Beacon Press, 1994).
6. John Colemann, "Global Fundamentalism: Sociological Perspectives," *Fundamentalism as an Ecumenical Challenge*, ed. Hans Küng and Jürgen Moltmann (*Concilium* 1992/3; London: SCM Press, 1992), 43.
7. For a discussion of different religious fundamentalisms, see the contributions in John Stratton Hawley, ed., *Fundamentalism and Gender* (New York: Oxford University Press, 1994).
8. For these characterizations of bourgeois biblical readings, see Johannes Thiele, "Bibelauslegung im gesellschaftlich-politischen Kontext," in *Handbuch der Bibelarbeit*, ed. W. Langer (München: Kösel Verlag, 1987), 106–14.
9. Ostriker, *Feminist Revision*, 86.
10. For the struggle between dominant kyriarchal structures and the vision and practice of the *ekklēsia* as a discipleship of equals in early Christianity, see my article "A Discipleship of Equals: Ekklesial Democracy and Patriarchy in Biblical Perspective," in *A Democratic Catholic Church*, ed. Eugene C. Bianchi and R. Radford Ruether (New York: Crossroad, 1992), 17–33. For a similar but quite different discussion of such a radical democratic vision, see the discussion in Chantal Mouffé, ed., *Dimensions of Radical Democracy: Pluralism, Citizenship, and Community* (London: Verso, 1992).
11. As I have pointed out, I coined this term because it describes more accurately the patriarchal constitution of ancient and modern societies. In classical Greece wo/men were life-long statutory minors and in the legal custody of a male citizen, be he their father or husband, whom they called *kyrios*.
12. For a similar theorization of feminist politics see Mary Dietz, "Context Is All: Feminism and Theories of Citizenship," in Mouffé, *Dimensions of Radical Democracy*, 75. Over and against a liberal and a maternalist feminist understanding, Dietz defines democracy in such a way.
13. For example, Mark 3:31–35 contrasts Jesus' natural family, who are "outside," with his new family sitting around him "inside" the house. In Mark 10:28–30, Jesus assures Peter, the spokesperson of the disciples in Mark, that all who have left their households and severed their kinship ties will instead receive a much greater family, although only under persecutions. (According to Mark 13:12, such persecutions, sufferings, and executions will be instigated by their own families and households.)
14. Richard Horsley and John S. Hanson, *Bandits, Prophets, and Messiahs: Popular Movements at the Time of Jesus* (Minneapolis: Winston, 1985).

15. Ellis Rivkin, "What Crucified Jesus," in *Jesus' Jewishness: Exploring the Place of Jesus within Early Judaism*, ed. James H. Charlesworth (New York: Crossroad, 1991), 242, 257.

16. For this understanding, see Norman Perrin, *Jesus and the Language of the Kingdom* (Philadelphia: Fortress Press, 1976), 15–88.

17. See my book *Priester für Gott: Studien zum Herrschafts- und Priestermotiv in der Apokalypse* (Münster: Aschendorff, 1972).

18. For a discussion of these traditions, see ibid., 90–160.

19. For a more recent review of the vast literature, see H. Merkel, "Die Gottesherrschaft in der Verkündigung Jesu," in *Königsherrschaft Gottes und himmlischer Kult im Judentum, Urchristentum, und in der hellenistischen Welt*, ed. Martin Hengel and Anna Maria Schwemer (Tübingen: J.C.B. Mohr, 1991), 119–62.

20. See Marcus J. Borg, "Portraits of Jesus in Contemporary North American Scholarship," *Harvard Theological Review* 84 (1991): 1–22.

21. However, both terms do not totally overlap; cf. R. Banks, *Paul's Idea of Community: The Early House Churches in Their Historical Setting* (Grand Rapids: Eerdmans, 1980), 62–70.

22. See E. Käsemann, *Commentary on Romans* (Grand Rapids: Eerdmans, 1980), 139–58, 331–42. Käsemann rejects the theories of "Jewish corporate personality" and "Gnostic redeemer myth" and categorically states, "Anthropology as such is not at issue"(143).

23. For the phallic overdetermination of the "body politic" in classical Athens, see David Halperin, "The Democratic Body: Prostitution and Citizenship in Classical Athens," *Differences* 2, no. 1 (1990): 128; John Winkler, "Phallos Politikos: Representing the Body Politic in Athens," ibid., 29–45.

24. For extensive discussion of the literature, see Margaret M. Mitchell, *Paul and the Rhetoric of Reconciliation* (Tübingen: J.C.B. Mohr, 1991), 157–64.

25. Such a translation deliberately refers to the global power of multinational corporations and asks whether and what Christian theology can contribute to a "corporate" global ethos that fosters the well-being of all wo/men in the global village.

26. It seems that it was Paul who introduced, in 1 Cor 12:28–30, a ranking of spiritual gifts; his introduction of "hierarchical governance structure [is] another response to the divisions within the church" (Mitchell, *Paul*, 164]). See also J. H. Neyrey, "Body Language in 1 Corinthians: The Use of Anthropological Models for Understanding Paul and His Opponents," *Semeia* 35 (1986): 129–64. For Paul's use of the rhetorics of power, see Elizabeth Castelli, *Imitating Paul: A Discourse of Power* (Louisville, Ky.: Westminster/Knox, 1991).

27. See my article "Justified by All Her Children: Struggle, Memory, and Vision," in *On the Threshold of the Third Millennium*, ed. the Foundation of Concilium (London: SCM Press, 1990), 19–38, 32–35.

28. See also Reinhold Reck, *Kommunikation und Gemeindeaufbau Eine*

Studie zur Entstehung, Leben und Wachstum paulinischer Gemeinden in den Konmmunikationsstrukturen der Antike (Stuttgart: Katholisches Bibelwerk, 1991), 232–85.

29. For the understanding of *koinonia* as consensual *societas* and reciprocal partnership, see J. P. Sampley, *Pauline Partnership in Christ: Christian Community and Commitment in Light of Roman Law* (Philadelphia: Fortress, 1980).

30. See J. H. Elliott, A *Home for the Homeless: A Sociological Exegesis of 1 Peter, Its Situation and Strategy* (Philadelphia: Fortress, 1981).

31. 2 Corinthians 6:14–7:1; 1 Corinthians 3:16; Ephesians 2:22; 1 Peter 2:4–10.

32. See, for example, Marlies Gielen, *Tradition und Theologie neutestamentlicher Haustafelethik: Ein Beitrag zu einer christlichen Auseinandersetzung mit gesellschaftlichen Normen* (BBB 75; Frankfurt: Anton Hain, 1990), especially 24–67. However, Gielen's discussion does not explicitly refer to the extensive work of David Balch on the Greco-Roman political context of these texts nor is it aware of my own feminist theory and exegetical work.

33. See Page duBois, *Centaurs and Amazons: Women and the Pre-History of the Great Chain of Being* (Ann Arbor: University of Michigan Press, 1982), 9–16.

34. See D. L. Balch, *Let Wives Be Submissive: The Domestic Code in 1 Peter* (SBLM 26; Chico, Calif.: Scholars Press, 1981).

35. See Chapter 4 of my book *Bread Not Stone*, and Clarice J. Martin, "The Haustafeln (Household Codes) in African American Biblical Interpretation," in *Stony the Road We Trod: African American Biblical Interpretation*, ed. Cain Hope Felder (Minneapolis: Augsburg Fortress, 1991), 206–31.

36. For discussion and literature, see my article "Die Anfänge von Kirche, Amt und Priestertum in feministisch-theologischer Sicht," in P. Hoffmann, ed., *Priesterkirche*, 62–95. For a Marxist reconstruction of the early Christian developments after the first century, see Dimitris J. Kyrtatas, *The Social Structure of the Early Christian Communities* (London: Verso, 1987).

37. For this distinction, see Anne Phillips, *Engendering Democracy* (University Park, Pa.: Pennsylvania State University Press, 1991), 162.

38. See Clifford Geertz, "Religion as a Cultural System," in *Anthropological Approaches to the Study of Religion*, ed. M. Banton (London: Tavistock, 1966), 1–46.

39. Mieke Bal, *Death and Disymmetry: The Politics of Coherence in the Book of Judges* (Bloomington: Indiana University Press, 1987), 11.

40. Delores Williams, in *Sisters in the Wilderness: The Challenge of Womanist God Talk* (Maryknoll, N. Y.: Orbis, 1993), has aptly characterized what I call here kyriarchy as "demonarchy." However, such a term is limited by its belief in the demonic.

41. See, for instance, Herman C. Waetjen, *A Reordering of Power: A Socio-Political Reading of Mark's Gospel* (Minneapolis: Fortress Press, 1989), 135. Waetjen explains Jesus' ethnocentric refusal as "Jesus' passion-

ate dedication to the fulfillment of Jewish need." Although Waetjen notes the weak manuscript attestation of "yes," he bases his interpretation on it: "She affirms the validity of his proverb by acknowledging Jewish priority. She does not want to deprive the children of their bread."

42. For a feminist reading, cf. Monika Fander, *Die Stellung der Frau im Markusevangelium unter besonderer Berücksichtigung kultur und religionsgeschichtlicher Hintergründe* (MthA 8; Altenberge: Telos Verlag, 1989), 75. Fander argues that the "but" (de) in v. 28 places the response of the wo/man in the center of attention. Moreover, the doubling of the verb (*apekrithei kai legei*) places an additional emphasis on her speech act.

43. The word "yes" (*nai*) is not found anywhere else in the gospel and is missing from important manuscripts such as Papyrus 45. See T. A. Burkill, *New Light on the Earliest Gospel* (Ithaca, N. Y.: Cornell University Press, 1972), 72, n. 3.

44. For the material in this section, see U. Luz, *Das Evangelium des Matthäus (2. Teilband: Mt 8–17)* (EKK I/2; Einsiedeln: Benzinger Neukirchener Verlag, 1990), 431ff.

45. H. Koester, "Introduction to the New Testament," *The History of Literature of the New Testament* (Philadelphia: Fortress Press, 1982), vol. 2, 205f.

46. Kwok Pui-lan, *Discovering the Bible in the Non-Biblical World* (Maryknoll, N.Y.: Orbis, 1995), 71–83.

47. Hisako Kinukawa, *Women and Jesus in Mark* (Maryknoll, N.Y.: Orbis, 1994), 61.

48. Ibid., 61.

49. Sharon Ringe, "A Gentile Woman's Story," in *Feminist Interpretation of the Bible*, ed. L. Russell (Philadelphia: Westminster Press, 1985), 68.

50. See now also Irene Dannemann, *Aus dem Rahmen fallen: Frauen im Markusevangelium—Eine feministische Re-Vision* (Berlin: Alektor-Verlag, 1996), 77–124, for a review of interpretations in the twentieth century.

51. For the discussion of different interpretations of Aristotle's thought, see Richard Mulgan, "Aristotle and the Political Role of Women," *History of Political Thought* 15, no. 2 (1994), 179–202; Gareth B. Matthews, "Gender and Essence in Aristotle," *Australasian Journal of Philosophy* 64 (1986): 16–25; and the contributions on Aristotle in Julie K. Ward, ed., *Feminism and Ancient Philosophy* (New York: Routledge, 1996).

52. For a sociohistorical account along the reconstructive model of M. Weber, see Margaret Y. Macdonald, *The Pauline Churches: A Socio-historical Study of Institutionalization in the Pauline and Deutero-Pauline Writings* (Cambridge, England: University Press, 1988).

53. Paula Gunn Allen, "Who Is Your Mother?: Red Roots of White Feminism," in *Multicultural Literacy*, 18f.

54. Ibid., 219.

55. For such an understanding, see the work of Seyla Benhabib, *Situating the Self* (New York: Routledge, 1992), and "Toward a Deliberative Model of

Democratic Legitimacy," in Seyla Benhabib, ed., *Democracy and Difference: Contesting the Boundaries of the Political* (Princeton: Princeton University Press, 1996), 67–94.

56. See Chantal Mouffé, "Democracy, Power, and the Political," in Benhabib, *Democracy and Difference*, 255. Mouffé advocates "a conception of democracy that, far from aiming at consensus and transparency is suspicious of any attempt to impose a univocal model of democratic discussion."

57. See Nancy Fraser, "Gender Equity and the Welfare State," in Benhabib, *Democracy and Difference*, 218–42; and Jean Cohen, "Democracy, Difference, and the Right to Privacy," ibid., 187–217.

58. See Jane Mansbridge, "Using Power/Fighting Power: The Polity," in Benhabib, *Democracy and Difference*, 46–66.

59. In "Reading Tabitha: A Final Reception History," in *The New Literary Criticism and the New Testament*, ed. Malbon and McKnight (Sheffield, England: Sheffield Academic Press, 1994), 108–44, Janice Capel Anderson has staged a similar reading approach. However, she conceptualizes her reading in terms of "reception history" rather than in terms of a debate over meaning in the *ekklēsia* of wo/men.

CHAPTER 6: *The Justice of Wisdom-Sophia*

This chapter draws on a lecture that I prepared for the Ecumenical Association of Third World Theologians international women's dialogue, 7-12 December 1994, in San Jose, Costa Rica, part of which was published as "Ties That Bind: Domestic Violence Against Wo/men," in *Voices from the Third World* 18, no. 1 (1995): 122–67. (See also the whole issue, which contains articles on violence against wo/men in Africa, Latin America, and Asia, as well as the final statement of the "Women Against Violence" dialogue.) However, I use this material here for different purposes.

1. This change can be seen when one compares the two volumes edited by Fernando Segovia, *Discipleship in the New Testament* (Philadelphia: Fortress Press, 1985) and *Reading from This Place* (Philadelphia: Fortress Press, 1995). In my contribution to *Discipleship* I was the only one to argue that "we should not reduce 'the reader' to a timeless, ideal reader because in so doing we essentialize and dehistorize the reader. Rather than pose an abstract reader," I argued, "we must detect and articulate our own presuppositions, emotions and reactions to the work in an explicit way, as well as sort out what kind of quality of response becomes dominant in our own reading."

2. Wini Breines and Linda Gordon, "The New Scholarship on Family Violence," *Signs* 8, no. 3 (1983): 490–531.

3. Teresa de Lauretis, "The Violence of Rhetoric: Considerations on Representation and Gender," in *The Violence of Representation: Literature and the History of Violence*, ed. Nancy Armstrong and Leonhard Tennenhouse (New York: Routledge, 1989), 239–58. De Lauretis underscores the similarity and difference of her understanding to that of Michel Foucault: "To say

that (a) the concept of 'family violence' did not exist before the expression came into being, as I said earlier, is not the same as saying (b) family violence did not exist before 'family violence' became part of the discourse of social science. The enormously complex relation binding expression, content and referent (or sign, meaning, and object) is what makes (a) and (b) not the same. It seems to me that of the three—the expression, the concept, and the violence—only the first two belong to Foucault's discursive order. The third is somewhere else, like 'bodies and pleasures' outside the social" (241).

4. Beines and Gordon, "Family Violence," 511.

5. See Antoinette Clark Wire, *The Corinthian Women Prophets: A Reconstruction through Paul's Rhetoric* (Minneapolis: Augsburg Fortress, 1990), 139. See also my commentary on "1 Corinthians," in *Harper's Bible Commentary*, ed. James L. Mays (New York: Harper & Row, 1988), 1168–89.

6. See Ann Jones, *Next Time She'll Be Dead* (Boston: Beacon Press, 1993). Jones sees the expression "domestic violence" as insinuating "domesticated violence"; I would argue that the concept of "domestic violence" underscores that the patri-kyriarchal household—the paradigm of society, religion, and state—produces, sustains, and legitimates violence against wo/men.

7. See J. Hanmer and M. Maynard, eds., *Women, Violence, and Social Control* (London: Macmillan Press, 1987); Kate Young, Carol Wolkowitz, and Roslyn McGullagh, *Of Marriage and the Market: Women's Subordination in International Perspective* (London: CSE Books, 1981); Roxana Carillo, *Battered Dreams: Violence against Women as an Obstacle to Development* (New York: United Nations Development Fund for Women, 1992); Margaret Schuler, ed., *Freedom from Violence: Women's Strategies from Around the World* (New York: United Nations Development Fund for Women, 1992); Jessie Tellis Nayak, "Institutional Violence against Women in Different Cultures," *In God's Image* 8 (September 1989): 4–14.

8. See Yvonne and Chandana Yayor, eds., "Prostitution in Asia," *In God's Image* 9 (June 1990); Elizabeth Bounds, "Sexuality and Economic Reality: A First and Third World Comparison," *In God's Image* 9 (December 1990): 12–18; Mary Ann Millhone, "Prostitution in Bangkok and Chicago: A Theological Reflection on Women's Reality," *In God's Image* 9 (December 1990): 19–26.

9. See Charlotte Bunch, *Gender Violence: A Development and Human Rights Issue* (New Brunswick, N. J.: Center for Women's Global Leadership, 1991).

10. *The Women's Action Coalition Stats: The Facts About Women* (New York: The New Press, 1993), 18f.

11. See Jill Radford and Diana E. H. Russell, *Femicide: The Politics of Woman Killing* (New York: Twayne Publishers, 1992).

12. For documentation, see Robin Morgan, ed., *Sisterhood Is Global: The International Women's Movement Anthology* (Garden City, N. Y.: Anchor Books, 1984).

13. See Elisabeth Schüssler Fiorenza and Anne Carr, eds., *Women, Work, and Poverty, Concilium* 194 (Edinburgh: T. & T. Clark, 1987).

14. See, for instance, Andrea Dworkin, *Woman Hating* (New York: E. P. Dutton, 1974); Mary Daly, *Gyn/Ecology: The Metaethics of Radical Feminism* (Boston: Beacon Press, 1978); Naomi Wolf, *The Beauty Myth* (New York: William Morrow, 1991).

15. Sandra Lee Bartky, "Foucault, Femininity, and the Modernization of Patriarchal Power," in *Feminism and Foucault: Reflections on Resistance*, ed. Irene Diamond and Lee Quinby (Boston: Northeastern University Press, 1988), 61–86.

16. Lori Stern, "Disavowing the Self in Female Adolescents," in *Women, Girls, and Psychotherapy: Reframing Resistance*, ed. Carol Gilligan, Annie G. Rogers, and Deborah L. Tolman (New York: Harrington Park Press, 1992), 105–18.

17. Peggy McIntosh, "Feeling Like a Fraud," *Works in Progress*, no. 18 (Wellesley, Mass.: Stone Center Working Paper Series, 1984), 1.

18. For these terms, see Katie G. Cannon, "Womanist Perspectival Discourse and Canon Formation," *Journal of Feminist Studies in Religion* 9 (1993): 29–38, 31f. See also Katie Russel, Midge Wilson, and Ronald Hall, *The Color Complex* (New York: Harcourt, Brace, & Jovanovich, 1992); and Chandra Taylor Smith, "Wonderfully Made: Preaching Physical Self-Affirmation," in *Sermons Seldom Heard: Women Proclaim Their Lives*, ed. Annie Lally Milhaven (New York: Crossroad, 1991), 243–51.

19. See Martha Mamozai, *Herren-Menschen: Frauen im deutschen Kolonialismus* (Reinbeck: Rowohlt Taschenbuchverlag, 1982), 160; Martha Opitz, Katharina Oguntoye, and Dagmar Schultz, eds., *Showing Our Colors: Afro-German Women Speak Out* (Amherst, Mass.: University of Massachusetts Press, 1992).

20. Chung Hyun Kyung, "Your Comfort vs. My Death," in *Women Resisting Violence: Spirituality for Life*, ed. Mary John Mananzan et al. (Maryknoll, N. Y.: Orbis, 1996), 136.

21. See the analysis of Heather Rhoads, "'Racist, Sexist, Anti-Gay . . .': How the Religious Right Helped Defeat Iowa's ERA," *On the Issues*, Fall 1993, 38–42.

22. See, for instance, Regula Strobel, "Der Beihilfe beschuldigt: Christliche Theologie auf der Anklagebank," *Fama: Feministisch Theologische Zeitschrift* 9 (1993): 3–6, for a review of the discussion.

23. See Brian Wren, *What Language Shall I Borrow? God-Talk in Worship: A Male Response to Feminist Theology* (New York: Crossroad, 1989).

24. For historical documentation and theo-ethical evaluation of the politics and theology of submission see my books *Bread Not Stone: The Challenge of Feminist Biblical Interpretation* (Boston: Beacon Press, 1984), 65–92; and *In Memory of Her: A Feminist Historical Reconstruction of Christian Origins* (New York: Crossroad, 1983), 243–314.

25. See the excellent study of Renita J. Weems, *Battered Love: Marriage,*

Sex, and Violence in the Hebrew Prophets (Minneapolis: Augsburg Fortress, 1995), which unmasks the violence against wo/men operative in this image.

26. For a critical discussion of christological discourses, see my book *Jesus: Miriam's Child, Sophia's Prophet: Critical Issues in Feminist Christology* (New York: Continuum, 1994).

27. Rita Nakashima Brock, "And a Little Child Will Lead Us: Christology and Child Abuse," in *Christianity, Patriarchy, and Abuse: A Feminist Critique*, ed. Joanne Carlson Brown and Carol R. Bohn (New York: Pilgrim Press, 1989), 42–61, 43. See also Brock's book *Journeys by Heart: A Christology of Erotic Power* (New York: Crossroad, 1988).

28. Christine E. Gudorf, *Victimization: Examining Christian Complicity* (Philadelphia: Trinity Press, 1992), 14–15.

29. See Sheila Redmond, "Christian 'Virtues' and Recovery from Child Sexual Abuse," in *Christianity, Patriarchy, and Abuse: A Feminist Critique*, ed. Joanne Carlson Brown and Carol R. Bohn (New York: The Pilgrim Press, 1989), 70–88, 73f.

30. For literature and discussion of the parable, see Edwin D. Freed, "The Parable of the Judge and the Widow (Luke 18:1–8)," *New Testament Studies* 33 (1987): 38–60; Susan M. Praeder, *The Word in Women's Worlds: Four Parables* (Wilmington: Glazier, 1988); and William R. Herzog, *Parables as Subversive Speech: Jesus as Pedagogue of the Oppressed* (Louisville, Ky.: Westminster/John Knox Press, 1989), 215–32.

31. Eta Linnemann, *Jesus of the Parables: Introduction and Exposition* (New York: Harper & Row, 1966), 121.

32. Catherine Clark Kroeger, Mary Evans, and Elaine Storkey, eds., *Study Bible for Women: The New Testament* (Grand Rapids, Mich.: Baker Books, 1995), 162.

33. Herzog, *Parables*, 223.

34. See, for example, John Donahue, *The Gospel in Parable: Metaphor, Narrative, and Theology in the Synoptic Gospels* (New York: Crossroad, 1988), 182. Donahue suggests that the case may be a life and death issue for her: "She is faced with poverty and starvation if her rights are not respected."

35. Tal Ilan, *Jewish Women in Greco-Roman Palestine* (Tübingen: Mohr, 1995), 147–51. However, at the end of her section on widows Ilan repeats the malestream judgment that widowhood was "a dismal state for a woman to fall into."

36. Judith Romney Wegner, *Chattel or Person? The Status of Women in the Mishnah* (New York: Oxford University Press, 1988), 14, 19.

37. Ilan, *Jewish Women*, 147.

38. Josephus claims to have appointed local courts of seven judges (Jewish War 2.20.5 and 2.14.1), and the Mishnah speaks of local courts of three judges in noncapital cases (Sanhedrin 1.1–6).

39. See Herzog, *Parables*, 221.

40. Praeder, *The Word*, 60.

41. Del Martin, "A Letter from a Battered Wife," in *Feminism and Community*, ed. Penny A. Weiss and Marilyn Friedman (Philadelphia: Temple University Press, 1995), 46–48.

CHAPTER 7: *The Sisters of Wisdom-Sophia*

1. For a fuller development of the arguments in this chapter, see my book *Jesus: Miriam's Child, Sophia's Prophet: Critical Issues in Feminist Christology* (New York: Continuum, 1994).

2. *Chokmah* is the Hebrew, *Sophia* the Greek, and *Sapientia* the Latin expression for Wisdom.

3. For the hermeneutical importance of Diotima, see the discussion at the end of chapter 4.

4. It is interesting to note that Jewish feminists have not elaborated the figure of Chokmah-Sophia but that of the Shechinah, representing Divine Presence.

5. See Carol P. Christ, *Rebirth of the Goddess: Finding Meaning in Feminist Spirituality* (Reading, Mass.: Addison-Wesley, 1997).

6. Cf., for example, W. C. Trenchard, *Ben Sira's View of Women* (Chico, Calif.: Scholars Press, 1982); Claudia V. Camp, "Understanding a Patriarchy: Women in Second Century Jerusalem through the Eyes of Ben Sira," in *"Women Like This": New Perspectives on Jewish Women in the Greco-Roman World*, ed. Amy-Jill Levine (Atlanta: Scholars Press, 1991), 1–40. Camp suggests that Ben Sira's "shrill, sometimes virulent instructions on women" are due to stress generated by two social forces: "One is the loss of control that the sage experienced in the larger social realm, which may have translated into an obsession for control in the closer sphere, specifically his sexuality and his household. The second is the conflict of social values which stress exacerbates"(38).

7. See Carol A. Newsome, "Woman and the Discourse of Patriarchal Wisdom: A Study of Proverbs 1–9," in *Gender and Difference in Ancient Israel*, ed. Peggy L. Day (Minneapolis: Fortress Press, 1989), 142–60. Here she concludes her study with a helpful methodological insight: "Having learned from the father how to resist interpolation by hearing the internal contradictions in discourse, one is prepared to resist the patriarchal interpolation of the father as well. For the reader who does not take up the subject position offered by the text, Proverbs 1–9 ceases to be a simple text of imitation and becomes a text about the problematic nature of discourse itself" (159).

8. See especially Silvia Schroer, *Die Weisheit hat ihr Haus gebaut: Studien zur Gestalt der Sophia in den biblischen Schriften* (Mainz: Grünewald, 1996), with extensive references to the literature on Chokmah-Sophia-Wisdom.

9. See James M. Reese, *Hellenistic Influences on the Book of Wisdom and Its Consequences* (Analecta Biblica 41; Rome: Biblicum, 1970). See John S. Kloppenborg, "Isis and Sophia in the Book of Wisdom," *Harvard Theological Review* 75 (1982): 57–84, for review of the literature.

10. See Hermann von Lips, "Christus als Sophia? Weisheitliche Traditionen in der urchristlichen Christologie," in *Anfänge der Christologie: Festschrift Ferdinand Hahn*, ed. Cilliers Breytenbach and Henning Paulsen (Göttingen: Vandenhoeck & Ruprecht, 1991), 75–96.

11. Apuleius, *Metamorphoses*, 11.25.

12. Hans Conzelmann, "The Mother of Wisdom," in *The Future of Our Religious Past*, ed. James M Robinson (1964; English translation, New York: Harper & Row, 1971). In the English-speaking context, W. L. Knox, in "The Divine Wisdom," *JST* 38 (1937): 230–37, has already pointed to this connection between Isis and Sophia, before Conzelmann.

13. For the Gospels, see Leo G. Perdue, "The Wisdom Sayings of Jesus," *Foundations and Facets Forum* 2, no. 3 (1986): 3-35. Perdue has catalogued such sapiential sayings.

14. It is important to note that a similar development can be seen among Jewish feminists. However, in difference to Christian feminists, they have privileged the female figure of the Shekinah over that of Chokmah.

15. See Nancy J. Berneking and Pamela Carter Joern, eds., *Re-Membering and Re-Imaging* (Cleveland: Pilgrim Press, 1995).

16. 1 A shoot shall come out from the stump of Jesse,
and a branch shall grow out of his roots.

2 The spirit of the LORD shall rest on him,
the spirit of wisdom and understanding,
the spirit of counsel and might,
the spirit of knowledge and the fear of the LORD.

3 His delight shall be in the fear of the LORD.
He shall not judge by what his eyes see,
or decide by what his ears hear;

4 but with righteousness he shall judge the poor,
and decide with equity for the meek of the earth. (Is 11:1–4, NRSV)

17. 22 There is in her a spirit that is intelligent, holy,
unique, manifold, subtle,
mobile, clear, unpolluted,
distinct, invulnerable, loving the good, keen,
irresistible,

23 beneficent, humane,
steadfast, sure, free from anxiety,
all-powerful, overseeing all, . . .

27 Although she is but one, she can do all things,
and while remaining in herself, she renews all things;
in every generation she passes into holy souls
and makes them friends of God, and prophets. (Wis 7:22–27, NRSV)

18. ⁹ With you is Sophia, she who knows your works
and was present when you made the world;
she understands what is pleasing in your sight
and what is right according to your commandments.

¹⁰ Send her forth from the holy heavens,
and from the throne of your glory send her,
that she may labor at my side,
and that I may learn what is pleasing to you.

¹¹ For she knows and understands all things,
and she will guide me wisely in my actions
and guard me with her glory. (Wis 9:9-11, NRSV)

19. Martin Hengel, "Jesus als messianischer Lehrer der Weisheit und die Anfänge der Christologie," in *Sagesse et Religion*, ed. Edmond Jacob (Paris: Presses Universitaires de France, 1979), 147-90.

20. Ibid., 175.

21. For a general introduction (which, however, does not problematize the androcentric character of the Wisdom literature), see Diane Bregant, C.S.A., *What Are They Saying About Wisdom Literature?* (New York: Paulist Press, 1984). In a private dedication the author answers the question of the book's title: "They are saying—Search for it in experience!! Feminist experience."

22. QLuke means that this text is found in Luke's Gospel but is attributed by scholars to a hypothetical source called Q (German *Quelle*), which is reconstructed from agreements in wording and sequence between the gospels of Luke and Matthew.

23. It is a misreading of my reconstructive model of a "discipleship of equals" when it is reduced to the "proclamation of gendered hierarchies." For such an "interested" misreading, see the otherwise excellent article by Amy-Jill Levine, "Second Temple Judaism, Jesus, and Women: Yeast of Eden," *Biblical Interpretation* 2, no. 1 (1994): 33.

24. Richard A. Horsley, "Q and Jesus: Assumptions, Approaches, and Analyses," *Semeia* 55 (1991): 206.

25. Ibid., 206.

26. Richard Horsley, "Questions about Redactional Strata and the Social Relations Reflected in Q," in *SBL Seminar Papers*, ed. J. Lull (Atlanta: Scholars Press, 1989), 186-203. According to Hosley, it expresses the sentiment of Galilean men against the central might of Jerusalem.

27. Susannah Heschel, "Nazifying Christian Theology: Walter Grundmann and the Institute for the Study and Eradication of Jewish Influence on German Life," in *Church History* 63 (1994): 587-605.

28. In particular she refers to Ernst Lohmeyer, *Galiläa und Jerusalem* (Göttingen, 1936) and Walter Grundmann, *Jesus, der Galiläer, und das Judentum* (Leipzig, 1940).

29. Angelika Strotmann, "Weisheitschristologie ohne Antijudaismus," in *Von der Wurzel getragen: Christlich-feministische Exegese in Auseinandersetzung mit Antijudaismus,* ed. Luise Schottroff and Marie-Theres Wacker (Leiden: Brill, 1996), 166–72.

30. Odil Hannes Steck, *Israel und das gewaltsame Geschick der Propheten* (WMANT 23; Neukirchen-Vluyn: Neukirchenere Verlag, 1967).

31. Strotmann, "Weisheitschristologie," 164.

32. R. S. Sugirtharajah, "Wisdom, Q, and a Proposal for a Christology," *The Expository Times* 102 (1990): 42–46. This proposal comes close to my own, although the article does not refer to *In Memory of Her.*

33. For a malestream attempt to underscore the significance of Wisdom christology, see Walter Kasper, "Gottes Gegenwart in *Jesus Christus: Vorüberlegungen zu einer weisheitlichen Christologie," in Weisheit Gottes— Weisheit der Welt,* vol. 1, ed. Walter Baier (Fs. Ratzinger; St. Ottilien: EOS Verlag, 1987), 311–27.

34. See Felix Christ, *Jesus Sophia: Die Sophia-Christologie bei den Synoptikern* (ATANT 57; Zürich: Zwingli, 1970), 81–93.

35. John S. Kloppenborg, "Wisdom Christology in Q," *Laval Théol Phil* 34 (1978): 141.

36. Cf. Richard A. Baer, *Philo's Use of the Categories of Male and Female* (Leiden: Brill, 1970), 42.

37. Philo, *De Fuga et Inventione,* 51ff., with reference to Genesis 25:20.

38. Luise Schottroff, "Wanderprophetinnen: Eine feministische Analyse der Logienquelle," *Evangelische Theologie* 51 (1991): 322–34.

39. However, in fairness to the Wisdom traditions it must be pointed out that the prophetic or apocalyptic traditions are equally suspect because they are also permeated by kyriocentric bias.

40. Silvia Schroer, "Jesus Sophia: Erträge der feministischen Forschung zu einer frühchristlichen Deutung der Praxis und des Schicksals Jesu von Nazareth," in *Vom Verlangen Nach Heilwerden,* ed. Strahm and Strobel, 112–28.

41. Whereas Schroer and I are Catholic, Schottroff and Dorothee Söelle, who is equally opposed to feminist Wisdom theology, are Lutherans. Since most of the Wisdom writings are part of the Catholic canon, Schroeder conjectures that Catholics are more inclined to work with them. However, such a confessional divide has not emerged in the U.S. context.

42. See Schroer, *Die Weisheit,* 138–39.

43. See Claudia V. Camp, *Wisdom and the Feminine in the Book of Proverbs* (BLS 14; Sheffield, England: Almond, 1985).

44. Dieter Georgi, "Frau Weisheit oder das Recht auf Freiheit als schöpferische Kraft," in *Verdrängte Vergangenheit, die uns bedrängt: Feministische Theologie in der Verantwortung für die Geschichte,* ed. Leonore Siegele-Wenschkewitz (München: Kaiser, 1988), 258ff. See also his commentary *Weisheit Salomos* (Jüdische Schriften aus hellenistisch-römischer Zeit II/4; Gütersloh: Mohn, 1980).

45. See Baer, *Philo's Use*, and Ross Shepard Kraemer, "Monastic Jewish Women in Greco-Roman Egypt: Philo Judaeus on the Therapeutrides," *Signs* 14 (1989): 342–70.

46. See the work of Sarah Pomeroy, *Women in Hellenistic Egypt: From Alexander to Cleopatra* (New York: Schocken Books, 1984).

47. See Ross Kraemer, *Her Share of the Blessing: Women's Religions among Pagans, Jews, and Christians in the Greco-Roman World* (Oxford: Oxford University Press, 1992), 106–27, on Jewish women's religious lives and offices in the Greco-Roman Diaspora.

48. See, however, Judith Romney Wegner, "Philo's Portrayal of Women— Hebraic or Hellenic?," in Levine, *"Women Like This,"* 44–66. Wegner argues that Philo's views on women owe "far more to Greek ideas, mediated through Hellenistic culture, than to the Jewish Scripture he inherited from his ancestors" (65). However, the assumption of such a clear-cut opposition between Greek and Jewish literatures and ideas does not take into account that Philo's "Jewish Scriptures" were already "translated" into Greek in more than the literal sense.

49. See, for example, Christa Mulack, *Jesus der Gesalbte der Frauen* (Stuttgart: Kreuz Verlag, 1987).

50. Antoinette Clark Wire, "The God of Jesus in the Gospel Sayings Source," in *Reading from This Place*, Volume 2: *Social Location and Biblical Interpretation in the United States*, ed. Fernando F. Segovia and Mary Ann Tolbert (Minneapolis: Augsburg Fortress, 1995), 301.

51. See, for instance, the practical exercises and liturgical ritual in Susan Cady, Marian Ronan, and Hal Taussig, eds., *Wisdom's Feast: Sophia in Study and Celebration* (New York: Harper & Row, 1989).

52. See *Wisdom of Solomon* 10:1–21.

53. For exegetical-historical documentation, see Susan M. Praeder, *The Word in Women's Worlds: Four Parables* (Wilmington, Del.: Michael Glazier, 1988).

54. Laura E. Donaldson, *Decolonizing Feminisms: Race, Gender, and Empire-Building* (Chapel Hill: University of North Carolina Press, 1992), 135.

INDEX

academic, 32, 33; disciplines, 43, 44; institutions, 17–18, 49

African-American, 36, 56, 58, 69, 89; biblical interpretation, 55, 57, 59; wo/men, 8, 58, 64–65, 68. *See also* womanist

agency, 82, 103; of wo/men, 49, 73, 76, 86–87, 94, 105, 181

alien(s): immigrant, 8, 69; resident, 44, 45, 46, 73, 118

androcentric/androcentrism, 9, 15, 16, 28; language, 67, 75, 90, 92, 96, 97; in texts, 11, 21, 76, 81, 88, 95, 99–100; in tradition, 80, 98

Armenevangelium, 174–77

Asian, 48, 146, 177

Athena complex, 13, 16

authority/authoritative, 82, 138, 158; of the bible, 52–53, 61–62, 68, 83–84, 88, 111, 124, 149; of the church, 32, 84, 149, 160; claims of, 47–48, 57–58, 66, 80, 103; of religious institutions, 4, 41, 47; theological, 32, 160; of wo/men, 64, 65, 73, 76, 80, 86–87, 103–4, 119, 149, 181

backlash, 3, 63

basileia, 114–16, 119, 120, 125, 164, 169–70, 175, 180, 181

bible: male bias in, 64, 67, 75; as revelation, 61, 63, 66, 84, 85; ways of reading, 58, 67, 70, 79, 86; as word of men, 62–63, 66

biblical: hermeneutics/interpretation, 16, 54, 55, 57, 62, 65, 86, 109, 121, 138; religions, 60, 63, 68; scholarship, 9–10, 18, 110, 137; studies, 16, 21, 32, 34, 48, 110; texts, 8, 9–10, 17, 52–54, 58, 59, 61, 66, 67, 81, 82, 86, 88, 111, 139, 149; texts as liberating, 52, 68, 75–76, 88; texts as oppressive, 62, 68, 75, 88, 114; tradition, 83, 86, 120. *See also* hermeneutics

canon/canonization, 43, 55, 82–83, 84, 124, 163

capitalism/capitalistic, 4, 83, 99, 107, 110

Catholic/Catholicism, 7, 8, 64, 84–85, 125

church, 52, 59, 66, 68, 83, 112, 114, 120, 125. *See also ekklēsia*

colonial/colonialism, 35, 46, 47, 69, 92, 99, 110, 115, 131, 145; victims of, 43, 52, 126

commonsense, 4, 38, 43, 47, 66, 70, 81, 92, 96, 97, 138

community(ies), 26, 41, 58, 98, 109, 115, 159; interpretive, 42, 43; wo/men's, 24

critical feminist biblical interpretation, 55, 66, 81, 105, 134; of liberation, 68, 77, 78, 79, 81–82, 85, 87–88, 101, 104, 111; tasks of, 25, 26, 76, 86, 103, 129. *See also* deconstructive; reading

217

dangerous memory, 49, 113, 116
deconstructive, 11, 76, 80, 88–89,
97, 100, 101, 103, 105. *See also*
reading
democratic/democracy, 9, 46–48, 55,
56, 116, 118, 148; community,
98, 108, 110, 112, 117–18, 120;
discourse, 4, 42; equality, 72,
132; political aspects of, 109,
153; struggles, 26, 131; vision,
51, 71, 111, 113–15, 119,
132–33
Diotima, 101–3, 161
discipleship of equals, 41, 107,
112–16, 119–20. *See also*
ekklēsia
Divine/Divine Wisdom, 4, 21, 78,
85, 114, 165, 166, 172–73,
177–78, 180–82; feminist
interpretation of, 177; images of,
114; titles of, 116, 161–64, 168,
171, 175–76, 179. *See also*
Sophia; Wisdom
domestic abuse. *See* violence
dualism/dualistic, 7, 28, 37, 68–69,
91, 100, 173; gender, 8, 70, 79;
opposition, 16, 17

ekklēsia, 112–14, 116–19, 132, 133
ekklēsia of wo/men, 86, 104, 121,
159, 183; as democratic biblical
symbol, 51, 70–72, 107, 112,
113, 131–36
Electra complex, 13
emancipation/emancipatory, 19, 42,
61, 87, 132; practices, 129, 134;
social movements, 3, 4, 43, 52,
114, 132; struggles, 26, 27, 52,
70, 81, 114; visions, 110, 117,
130. *See also* feminist(s), move-
ment(s); wo/men('s), movement(s)
Enlightenment, 75, 80–81, 89, 111
equal/equality, 4, 5, 52, 109, 113,
114–15, 118–20, 133. *See also*
discipleship of equals

essential/essentialism, 5, 35, 43, 177
essentialist, 6, 37, 39, 47, 69

family violence. *See* violence
feminine/femininity, 5, 6, 7, 24, 26,
28, 30, 36–37, 69–70, 91–92, 99,
100, 126, 144, 145, 146, 147,
158, 172; constructions of, 5,
148, 150
feminism, 2–3, 4, 7, 17–20, 24, 38,
39; gender-based, 37, 46;
political roots of, 15, 132
feminist(s): apologetics, 53, 63, 68;
biblical interpretation, 7, 9,
10–12, 15, 16, 19, 20, 53, 55,
65, 66–67, 69, 70, 73, 76–80, 82,
87, 97, 103, 104, 110, 128, 133,
160–61, 169; biblical scholarship, 21, 33, 50, 66; biblical
studies, 7, 17–21, 22, 35, 67,
114; critical interpretation for
liberation, 25, 68, 70, 78, 84,
160; discourse, 14, 27, 36, 37,
40, 42, 60; liberation struggles,
53, 76; movement(s), 2, 4–5, 17,
26–27, 31, 35, 36, 38, 46, 65,
146; politics, 3, 15, 27; scholars,
8, 12, 14, 15, 21, 23, 24, 35, 41,
45, 48, 60, 104, 155, 171;
scholarship, 17–21, 22–24, 33,
35–36, 54, 66–67, 75, 98, 143;
struggles, 18, 27, 52, 60, 76;
studies, 2, 7, 9, 17, 21, 22–25,
28, 33, 34–36, 37, 38, 40–43,
46–48, 56, 133; theologians, 18,
26, 40, 41, 49, 143, 171; theology, 1, 2, 4, 7, 12, 15, 18, 24,
26, 32–33, 34, 35, 39, 47, 48,
68, 73, 79, 113, 153, 180, 183;
theory, 7, 9, 12, 20–22, 28, 33,
34, 37, 40, 47, 48, 55, 68. *See
also* feminist(s), movement(s);
emancipation/emancipatory;
theology/theological; wo/men('s),
movement(s)